"REMEMBER THE LADIES"

New Perspectives on Women in American History

"REMEMBER THE LADIES"
New Perspectives on

Women in American History

Essays in Honor of Nelson Manfred Blake

Edited by CAROL V. R. GEORGE

SYRACUSE UNIVERSITY PRESS 1975

Copyright © 1975 by SYRACUSE UNIVERSITY PRESS
Syracuse, New York 13210

All Rights Reserved

FIRST EDITION

Second printing 1976

Library of Congress Cataloging in Publication Data
Main entry under title:

"Remember the ladies": new perspectives on women in
   American history.

   Includes bibliographical references and index.
   CONTENTS: Billington, R. A. Nelson Manfred Blake,
pioneering historian.—The growth of American feminist
thought: George, C. V. R. Anne Hutchinson and the
"revolution which never happened."—Fisher, M. Eighteenth-century theorists of women's liberation. [etc.]
   1. Women—United States—History—Addresses, essays,
lectures.   2. Feminism—United States—History—
Addresses, essays, lectures.   3. Blake, Nelson Manfred,
1908–   I. Blake, Nelson Manfred, 1908–

II. George, Carol V. R.
HQ1410.N48   301.41'2'0973   75-12295
ISBN 0-8156-0110-7

Manufactured in the United States of America

Contents

Contributors

David H. Bennett, who received his A.B. in American Studies at Syracuse University, is currently professor of history and chairman of the Department of History at his alma mater. A student of twentieth-century American history, he obtained his Ph.D. from the University of Chicago. He is particularly interested in the history of political extremism in the United States; his study of radical activities in the thirties, *Demagogues in the Depression,* was published by Rutgers University Press in 1969.

Gerald E. Critoph, the current president of the Southeastern American Studies Association, is chairman of the American Studies Department at Stetson University. After graduating from Syracuse University, he earned A.M. and Ph.D. degrees from the University of Pennsylvania. He taught at SUNY Buffalo; Colgate; and Michigan State. He teaches courses in American traditions, American urban studies, and leadership.

Jane B. Donegan is a professor of American history at Onondaga Community College in Syracuse, New York, where she offers courses in the History of Women and Women in Medicine. She has served as Department Chairperson and as Chairperson of the Faculty. She is revising her doctoral dissertation, "Midwifery in America, 1760–1860; a Study in Medicine and Morality," for publication, and is preparing an article on Classic Blues Singers.

Marguerite Fisher, professor of political science, emeritus, Syracuse University, served as consultant to the United Nations Conference on "The Status of Women and National Development in Asia," held in Manila in 1966. As the recipient of two Fulbright grants, she taught and did research at Philippine Women's University, Manila, and Delhi University, Delhi, India. She is the author of *Communist Doctrine and the Free World* (Syracuse University Press, 1952); *Municipal and Other Local Governments* (with D. Bishop; Prentice-Hall, 1950); *Parties and Politics in the Local Community* (National Council for the Social Studies, 1945) and has articles in *Harry Elmer Barnes, Learned Crusader,* Arthur Goddard, editor (R. Myles Co., 1968); and *Proceedings of the International Congress on Rizal* (Philippine Govt., 1963). She is currently an officer in both the National Organization for Women and the Humane Association of Central New York.

Carol V. R. George, who teaches courses in American history and Third World Studies at Hobart-William Smith Colleges in Geneva, New York, received her Ph.D. from Syracuse University. Her study of the development of independent black churches in the nineteenth century, *Segregated Sabbaths,* was published by Oxford University Press in 1973. A National Endowment for the Humanities fellowship holder in 1971–72, she is currently at work on a study of Harriet Beecher Stowe.

Masako Iino is a member of the faculty at Tsuda College in Tokyo, where she teaches courses in American history. A graduate of Syracuse University, she is especially interested in Oriental immigration into the United States.

Hisako Ito, also an alumna of Syracuse, resides in Japan where she works for a Japanese manufacturer as an editor and translator of English-language magazines.

James E. Johnson, professor of history at Bethel College, St. Paul, has added a new field in social welfare history to his teaching interest in American social and intellectual history. For his dissertation, completed at Syracuse University in 1959, he wrote a study of "The Life of Charles Grandison Finney." He is the author of "Charles Grandison Finney and Oberlin Perfectionism" (*Journal of Presbyterian History*) and "Charles G. Finney and a Theology of Revivalism (*Church History*). His other publications include *The Irish in America* and *The Scots and Scotch-Irish in America* (Lerner Publications, 1966); "The Christian and the Emergence of the Welfare State," in Pierard, Clouse, and Linder, eds., *Protest and Politics* (Attic Press, 1969); and "Evangelical Christianity and Poverty," in Pierard, Clouse, and Linder, eds., *The Cross and the Flag* (Creation House, 1972).

Ralph L. Ketcham, chairman of the American Studies Program at Syracuse University, is a student of Revolutionary and Early National America. He is the author of *Benjamin Franklin* (Washington Square Press, 1965), and *James Madison, A Biography* (published by Macmillan in 1971 and nominated for a National Book Award in 1972). In 1974, his study, *From Colony to Country: American Revolutionary Thought, 1750–1820,* was also published by Macmillan. In addition, he served as Fulbright lecturer in American intellectual history at the University of Tokyo, Tsuda College, and Japan Women's University in 1965. He has been a visiting professor at the University of Texas and the University of Sheffield.

William L. O'Neill, professor of history at Rutgers University in New Brunswick, New Jersey, received his Ph.D. from the University of California at Berkeley. He is the editor of *Echoes of Revolt, The Masses, 1911–17* (Quadrangle, 1968), and *American Society Since 1945* (Quadrangle, 1969). He is the author of *Everyone Was Brave: The Rise and Fall of Feminism in America* (Quadrangle); *Coming Apart: An Informal History of America in the 1960's* (Quadrangle, 1971); *Divorce in the Progressive Era* (Yale, 1967); *The American Sexual Dilemma* (Dryden, 1972); and *Insights and Parallels: Problems and Issues in American Social History* (Burgess, 1973). In addition, he has edited *The Woman Movement: Feminism in the United States and England* (Allen & Unwin, 1969), and co-authored *Looking Backward: A Reintroduction to American History* (McGraw-Hill, 1974).

Otey M. Scruggs, professor of history at Syracuse University, specializes in Afro-American history and nineteenth-century American history. After receiving his Ph.D. from Harvard, he taught for twelve years at the University of California at Santa Barbara, his alma mater, before coming to Syracuse in 1969. His doctoral dissertation was a study of Mexican farm labor in the United States after World War II. He has written extensively in agricultural labor history and in Afro-American history. In addition, he co-edited, with George Dangerfield, Henry Adams' multi-volume history of the United States during the administrations of Jefferson and Madison.

Noriko Shimada studied American diplomatic history and twentieth-century American history while a student at Syracuse University. Following extensive traveling, she expects to reside in Japan.

Hiroko Takamura has worked for the Fulbright Commission in Japan. Her thesis at Syracuse University was a study of post–World War II relations between the United States and Japan. Her field of interest is American diplomatic relations.

Acknowledgments

This collection of original articles is dedicated by his friends, former students, and colleagues to Nelson Manfred Blake, Maxwell Distinguished Professor of History Emeritus, Syracuse University. One of Professor Blake's most notable qualities while he was at Syracuse was his eagerness to explore new areas of the discipline, and his interest in social history has always included concern for the part that women have played in it.

This volume was coordinated with a symposium held in 1973 to honor Professor Blake's retirement from Syracuse University's Maxwell School of Citizenship and Public Affairs; this was also the year in which the School celebrated its fiftieth anniversary. The timing seemed fitting. Nelson Blake had taught at Maxwell for thirty-six of those fifty years, and his personal record of scholarship, student concern, and community interest reflected Maxwell's own. The Dean of Maxwell, Alan K. Campbell, encouraged the publication not only of this work but of many others issuing from the anniversary activities, which collectively reflect the wide range of interests of the school's staff, faculty, students, and alumni. There may, in fact, be a certain discernible Maxwellian flavor about this collection since eleven of the thirteen authors are or have been associated with the school either as faculty members or as students.

The production of this book has been a cooperative affair. Dean Campbell's contribution was a decisive one. Professors Ralph Ketcham and David Bennett of the Maxwell faculty assisted with the editorial process at every stage. And obviously, without the contributions of the authors, there would have been no collection. The editor thanks all of them for their contributions, cooperation, and patience in seeing the work through.

Finally, the editor would like to acknowledge the assistance offered by Hobart and William Smith Colleges, Geneva, New York, which made a faculty research grant available to help with the costs involved in preparing the work for publication. A special word of appreciation is also due to Judy Dollenmayer, Bill George, and Jane Donegan.

Hobart and William Smith Colleges   CAROL V. R. GEORGE
Geneva, New York
Spring 1975

NELSON MANFRED BLAKE: Pioneering Historian

THE PAGES of the twenty-five cent notebook where I recorded the grades kept during my first teaching years at Clark University in the early 1930s are fading now, and the imitation calf cover is crumbling, but a surprisingly large number of the names inscribed therein are familiar—not because of any phenomenal powers of recall on my part, but because their bearers have made a mark in the world of scholarship that justifies remembrance.

I try now as I read to picture them as they were, those students with the tenacity and foolhardiness to seek advanced degrees in that era of a darkening economy and collapsing educational institutions. The list would do credit to many schools far more prestigious and far larger than the Clark of those days: Stephen T. Riley, who has directed the Massachusetts Historical Society with great distinction; Forrest C. Pogue, the well-known biographer of General George C. Marshall; L. S. Stavrianos, whose outstanding teaching career at Smith College and Northwestern University has culminated with a series of innovative works in world history; Paul A. Varg, who occupies a chair at Michigan State University and ranks among our most respected diplomatic historians; Edwin B. Coddington, long a professor at Lafayette College and the author of a study of the Battle of Gettysburg that will survive the ravages of time far longer than most books published in our generation; the late Howard Bennett, who lent distinction to the business history department of Northwestern University; Hubert H. Wilson, one of Princeton University's most acclaimed political scientists; Milton Derber, a respected economist whose career in government earned a professorship at the University of Illinois.

This was the group with which Nelson Manfred Blake began his career in history. Classes were small enough in those days (the total enrollment at Clark in 1936 was 273, with 92 graduate students) to allow every student to make an impress on his instructors, and I remember Nelson well—tall, Lincolnesque, hair close-cropped, a bit withdrawn save in intellectual exchange, his serious intensity broken now and then with a flooding smile, hunched over a classroom desk taking notes furiously, or battling other students in the seminar room where the entire "Department of History and International Relations" gathered each Tuesday night to listen to reports, discuss the latest books, exchange ideas, and savor the peer-companionship that is so essential to graduate training. Even then Nelson Blake revealed an instinct for intellectual pioneering, for exploring hidden pockets of learning, for blazing new trails toward the borders of knowledge, that explains his importance in the world of historical scholarship.

Nelson Blake was the product of New England upbringing. Born in Vermont in 1908, educated at Dartmouth College where he earned his B.A. degree in 1930 and at Brown University where he added the M.A. a year later, he began his teaching at the Gardner High School in Massachusetts in 1931. There he remained for three years, while he continued his doctoral work at nearby Clark University where he received a Ph.D. in 1936. Fortunately for Nelson he had the good sense to prepare his dissertation, on "The United States and the Irish Revolution, 1914–1922," under the direction of Professor H. Donaldson Jordan, a scholar who was wise and good; the rigorous training that he received under that expert mentor was to be revealed in his own writings from that time on. Fortunately, too, he was able to accomplish the nearly impossible. In that day of economic chaos, when the symbol of the Clark University Yearbook was an eight ball, Nelson's abilities (he passed his final oral examination for the degree "with distinction" in May 1936) won him an instructorship at Syracuse University. How proud we of the department were of his accomplishment.

Nelson was (and is) an outstanding teacher; he became assistant professor of Syracuse in 1939, associate professor in 1946, and four years later a full professor. In 1971 he was named Maxwell Distinguished Professor of History, a post that he held until his retirement in 1974. He also held visiting lectureships or summer-school assignments at Stetson University, Pennsylvania State University, North Carolina State College, the New York State Historical Association Seminar at Cooperstown, Colgate University, Bethel College, Cazenovia Junior College, and Hartwick College.

These excursions added to Nelson Blake's fame, but his principal loyalty—and service—was to Syracuse University, where he compiled a truly remarkable teaching record. In all he taught no fewer than 11,575 students during his thirty-six years on the faculty—8,258 of them undergraduates, 1,117 graduate students, 1,000 in University College, and 1,200 in summer-school sessions. Those trained in his classes hold positions today in all parts of the nation and in virtually every profession; I am sure that every one of them looks back with gratitude to the instruction received from that gifted teacher.

Undergraduate instruction required skill in a variety of subjects—ancient history, Western civilization, the history of England, Europe since 1815, recent Europe, the Second World War, a survey of American history, American social and cultural history, American constitutional history, and twentieth-century America, as well as the basic graduate course in "Methods of Historical Investigation"—but Nelson Blake revealed his versatility even more effectively in the doctoral dissertations that he suggested and directed. Simply to read the list is to appreciate the breadth of his interests and the catholicity of his knowledge. They range from theses on the Episcopacy of Bishop John Carroll to midwifery in America, from Anglo-Irish relations to the rise of independent black churches, from submarine disarmament to the Agricultural Wheel of Arkansas, from the Oneida Community to the French Revolution in contemporary American thought, from the commercialism of baseball to the study of radical assumptions concerning the nation's imperialism. In all Nelson Blake directed or helped supervise twelve dissertations in history and twenty-one in social science.

Nelson Blake also produced an imposing number of books and articles himself. These, as much as his instructional program and the theses he directed, reveal his eagerness to investigate unusual topics or pursue fresh avenues of research. He produced his share of textbooks, most of them standard works that have made their impress on a generation of students: *A Short History of American Life* (1952; revised in 1963 as *A History of American Life and Thought*), *Since 1900: A History of the United States in Our Times* (written with Professor O. T. Barck, published first in 1947 and now in 1975 in its fifth edition), and *The United States: From Wilderness to World Power* (prepared with Professor R. V. Harlow and published in 1964). Textbooks must follow the traditional patterns demanded by publishers, but Nelson Blake's monographic studies suffered no such restraints: *Water for the Cities: A History of the Urban Water Supply Problem in the United States* (1956), *The Road to Reno: A History of Divorce in the United States* (1962), *and Novelists' America: Fiction as History, 1910–1940* (1969). These subjects may seem commonplace today, but all were startlingly fresh when they were conceived and written. Urban history was in its infancy then, women's history scarcely heard of, and the relationship between history and literature a bold new area for exploration. These books underline the fact that Nelson Blake, as much as any scholar of his generation, pioneered the study of the aspects of the past that most intrigue historians at the present time. They help explain, also, why this book of essays in his honor is focused on new perspectives on the role of women in American history. No more fitting monument to his pioneering contributions could be raised.

The diversity of Nelson Blake's historical interests was similarly revealed in the dozen-odd articles from his pen that appeared in scholarly journals and compilations of essays. These range from a study of "The Olney-Pauncefote Treaty of 1897" (published in 1949 in the *American Historical Review*), to "Ambassadors at the Court of Theodore Roosevelt" (published in the *Mississippi Valley Historical Review*), "Eunice Against the Shakers" (a study of Elizabeth Cady Stanton's reaction to the divorce bill of 1861), and "How to Learn History from Sinclair Lewis and Other Uncommon Sources," an intriguing bit of advice. All were based on solid research; all explored areas of the past generally neglected by scholars. They demonstrate anew his pioneering role in the study of comparative social history.

Nelson Blake retired from his active teaching career in the spring of 1974 amidst the acclaim of his colleagues gathered at Syracuse University for a "Symposium Honoring Nelson Blake." The fact that the two former students who spoke on this occasion chose as their topics American culture of the 1960s as interpreted by historians and film directors symbolizes his influence on them and on the study of history. Those trained under his supervision or swayed by his published works will never be able to forget that the past is threshold to the present, and that the complexity of man's social behavior justifies a multiplicity of investigatory approaches. Nelson pioneered the use of many. We among his former teachers take justifiable pride in having made some slight contribution to his intellectual growth; we also join with his thousands of students and friends in wishing him many years of continued activity, all of them spent in research into the unlighted crannies of the past where he has found so much to illuminate the story of the nation.

The Huntington Library
San Marino, California
Spring 1975

RAY ALLEN BILLINGTON

"REMEMBER THE LADIES"

New Perspectives on Women in American History

Editor's Introduction

ON March 31, 1776, Abigail Smith Adams sent what she felt was an important message to her husband, who was in Philadelphia along with Franklin, Jefferson, and others to plan for the possibility of drafting a constitution. Abigail Smith Adams' advice to John Adams, subsequently noted by many feminists, was that "in the new code of laws which I suppose it will be necessary for you to make, I desire you would remember the ladies and be more generous and favorable to them than your ancestors. Do not put such unlimited power into the hands of the husbands. Remember, all men would be tyrants if they could. If particular care and attention is not paid to the ladies, we are determined to foment a rebellion, and will not hold ourselves bound by any laws in which we have no voice or representation."

That Adams ever took his wife's caution very seriously is doubtful: he responded to her warning by saying: "As to your extraordinary code of laws, I cannot but laugh." But it was hardly a joking matter for Abigail, who observed that "whilst you are proclaiming peace and good-will to men, emancipating all nations, you insist upon retaining an absolute power over wives." The seeming failure of John Adams and the others to accomplish Abigail's objective, to incorporate women within the meaning of the Declaration of Independence, prompted feminists in the nineteenth century to recommend that the document be revised to read, "all men and women are created equal."

Adams's casual, even light-hearted, response to a serious request to "remember the ladies" comes as no surprise to anyone acquainted with the record of American history. Women's efforts have routinely been dismissed as inconsequential, if not comic, not only by husbands and politicians, but by those who have compiled the record of the past. When feminists assert, "our history has been taken from us," they are describing a pattern of historical writing that has resulted in women being either ignored or caricatured in accounts of the past. As recently as 1971, when Anne Firor Scott titled her book, *The American Woman, Who Was She?,* the author posed a hard question for most Americans over the age of thirty; when they learned American history, women, like Indians, Afro-Americans, and other minorities, were inadequately represented in the standard texts.

Fortunately that parochial style of historical writing is changing gradually, as more and more historians, in the process of having their consciousnesses raised, recognize its limitations. The list of books dealing with the role of women in history, which grows longer every year, attests to the intellectual interests of many who believe that a fundamental aspect of history has been too long ignored. Yet it would be a mistake to conclude that the study of women, as an academic discipline, has met with general acceptance: many scholars in more traditional fields, noting its origins in the women's liberation movement, continue to regard women's studies with skepticism. By a kind of skewed logic, they tend to equate the ideas of organized feminism with passing tastes in automobiles and fashion—a popular fad that will spend itself in time. History should prove their prophecy to be as misinformed as their analogy.

But because the study of women in history is a relatively new field, it is faced with problems not shared by other areas of historical investigation. It enjoys the advantage of being free from some of the usual scholarly limitations: it is bound neither to particular historical interpretations nor to conventional definitions of chronological periods, social groupings, and themes. For some students, however, these advantages are rather unevenly balanced against what initially appears to be the awesome task of constructing history from very meager sources. Once one has studied the suffrage movement and its nineteenth-century antecedents, what other subjects can one turn to? Sensitive writers have already discovered that to single out a few notable individuals—who may then be appropriated by the news media and transformed into Superwomen— can perpetuate a distorted view of women.

Some of the new social historians are suggesting the direction that future research on women in history can take. Basic to the new approach is the willingness to consider data and recoverable artifacts from a different perspective, even to adopt a new view of history. One must not be put off by J. H. Hexter's observation that certain institutions, like "the

College of Cardinals, the Consistory of Geneva, the Parliament of England, the Faculty of the Sorbonne . . . [were] pretty much stag affairs."[1] To acknowledge the accuracy of Hexter's statement does not diminish the claim that the "stag affair" theory of history represents an incomplete and slanted description of the past. Clearly women did not make policy in the British Parliament any more than they did in the United States Congress, but many did press for social change as well as the vote. The exclusively male College of Cardinals had its American counterpart in the national gatherings of the various religious denominations, but it is a narrow view of history that fails to acknowledge the participation of women in religious orders and local churches, where some also preached and ministered. By extending their research into such areas as demography, child-rearing practices, and family structure, the new social historians are finally able to document the obvious: that women have been an integral part of society and therefore its history. Their most successful efforts are thus making Mary Beard's comment about social historians in 1946 less relevant. In *Woman as Force in History*, Beard said:

> Although the social historians who recognized that women had been in history brought about some shift in the emphasis on man-made history, they gave many signs that they were puzzled in trying to deal with women. Many of them worked on as before, "bringing in" women here and there as if they were not really an integral part of all history; but none of them made any serious contributions to the bibliography, documentation, theory, and practice of the subject of women in history.

This collection of original articles attempts to address Beard's concern for making women an integral part of history. And while not designed as a historiographical handbook, the work may suggest to scholars ways to reconstitute other sections of the past so that women can be incorporated into the fabric of history. The authors have considered a wide range of subjects: women in twentieth-century politics and women in the seventeenth-century church; women as the patients of male gynecologists and women as partners in divorce; Flappers and philosophers; slave-conductors and nativists; and a woman whose place in history was previously described only in terms of her marriage to a President. Some contributors have drawn their evidence from fairly familiar sources, indicating

1. Review of Mary Beard's book, *Woman as Force in History*, by J. H. Hexter, *New York Times Book Review*, March 17, 1946; quoted by Berenice A. Carroll, "Mary Beard's Woman as Force in History: A Critique."

that revealing answers can sometimes result when new questions are asked of the material. Others have pointed out neglected sources—in medical records, nativist tracts, government documents, and popular journals. While none has employed quantification, one group of contributors has used cross-cultural analysis as a method for understanding the relative status of women in America and Japan. The collection is focused on social history; it is, together with an association with Nelson Blake, a common interest of the contributors. Never intended to be comprehensive, its purpose is to suggest new areas that can be profitably explored by a fresh approach to the data.

The book is divided into three sections, organized around a general concern with women and social change, each preceded by the editor's introductory remarks.

The first section, which comprehends roughly two hundred years— from about 1600 to 1800—deals with religious and ideological influences on the growth of American feminist thought. Marguerite Fisher and Carol George consider cross-cultural exchanges between the Old World and the New which affected the status of women. Ralph Ketcham, while conceding Abigail Adams's British and European sympathies, argues that her socio-political philosophy was modified by her Puritan beliefs and Revolutionary commitment. During the Colonial period, when the trans-Atlantic interchange of ideas was frequent and regular, people like Hutchinson and Thomas Paine were alert to intellectual developments that might favorably alter the status of women. Later, as Fisher indicates, nineteenth-century feminists were able to build on the intellectual tradition their Colonial ancestors helped create.

The chronological limits of the second section are set by the birth of Harriet Tubman in 1820 and the revival of nativism in the second decade of the twentieth century. During this period women were associated with the cultural values implied in the labels Victorian or New Victorian, with the image embodied in what Barbara Welter has described as "The Cult of True Womanhood." The Victorian woman, who has had many apologists and, until recently, few critics, has rarely been considered in terms of the psychological cost required to maintain her image. David Bennett and Jane Donegan point out that the preservation of that image produced anxiety in men as well as women, if for different reasons. According to Welter's analysis, the image was based on four attributes of the "true" woman—piety, purity, domesticity, and submissiveness. In the nineteenth century, it won a strange collection of challengers and apologists. Superficially, it may seem that nativists and upper-middle-class physicians (some of whom may have been closet nativists) had little in common, but as Donegan and Bennett observe, they shared a fundamental assumption about the structure of society. While allegedly protecting women from "immodest" medical practices, male gynecologists delayed the development of more advanced clinical techniques. Also posing as woman's protector—who would save her from the lechery of Roman Catholic immigrants—the nativist justified his own fears of social change. But those who challenged the conventional image of women had a common purpose too, to resist social and institutional restraints on freedom and personal fulfillment. Two unconventional women mentioned in this section, Harriet Tubman and Elizabeth Blackwell, did just that. Otey Scruggs's assertion that Tubman's life spoke to the "praxis of freedom" could be applied equally to Blackwell's career.

The Victorian–New Victorian image of woman has been made to seem so pervasive that in retrospect it appears as a shift to the right in terms of the development of women's interests. But we know from the evidence that that is not a wholly accurate description. The very urgency of the appeal to be a "true" woman encouraged the growth of opposition. Courage and audacity were never in short supply among nineteenth-century feminists, and to cite such people as the Grimké sisters, Sojourner Truth, Elizabeth Cady Stanton, Susan B. Anthony, and Victoria Woodhull is to single out a few notable examples from an impressively long roster. Their efforts produced significant gains, although the conventional image of woman was too well preserved to respond to any fundamental challenge. It was preserved in church and state, and as the authors of this section report, in slavery, the nativist movement, and the practice of medicine. If sexism, like racism, was implicit in the maintenance of the status quo, any challenge to either would produce serious reverberations. Women who questioned the image imposed on them could anticipate having their motives ascribed to psycho-sexual abnormalities; in nineteenth-century terms, they were simply not "true" women.

The suffrage campaign of the late nineteenth and early twentieth centuries effectively released the Victorian woman from her isolated place on the pedestal, although by its singular concern for the franchise it tacitly ignored the implications of the conventional image of woman. As Aileen Kraditor has shown,[2] radical feminists who demanded basic changes in the domestic system were generally ignored by mainstream suffragists willing to compromise with more conservative allies in order to gain the ballot. For some historians and many feminists, therefore, the suffrage amendment is viewed as a Pyrrhic victory; it won the ballot but

[2] Aileen Kraditor, *Ideas of the Woman's Suffrage Movement* (New York: Columbia University Press, 1965).

lost a chance to shatter the traditional image of woman. Reduced to simple terms, this assessment of the movement suggests that women were accepted into the political system as long as their "feminine" talents—for morality, for social concern, for good housekeeping—were politically useful. Furthermore, the adoption of the Nineteenth Amendment, it has been said, conditioned women to accept a return to the kitchen on the assumption that their battle had been won.

The articles in the third section consider issues apart from the suffrage that involved women over the last sixty years. The suffrage was, of course, an important factor contributing to the development of the twentieth-century "new woman," but it was just one of many ingredients involved in producing the change. The social disruption produced by the first world war, the advent of the Flapper, the distribution of birth control information, the agitation for divorce-law reform, and the acquisition of educational and political skills all contributed to the advent of the new woman. Further, as Noriko Shimada, Hiroko Takamura, Masako Iino, and Hisako Ito imply in their chapter, there is a correlation between a country's economic interests and its perception of the role of women. In twentieth-century America, when interest in social and economic reform ran high, feminists were encouraged to believe that they had found political allies, first among Progressives and later among New Dealers.

The twentieth-century "new woman" had become acutely sensitized to the matter of the double standard. A single standard was demanded by suffragists for voting rights, by Flappers for guiding behavior and dress, and by divorce-law reformers for determining sexual relationships.

In the case of divorce-law reform, however, William O'Neill indicates that the battle was not joined on the issue of the double standard. Instead, critics described divorce as a social "problem," rather than a personal matter, and related it to the appearance of the "liberated" woman, birth control, and sexual freedom. But behind all the polished and profane rhetoric of the critics stood the reality: marriages could and often did become intolerable, and promiscuity had served as a historically constant alternative. Society's response to known promiscuity was almost invariably related to one's sex—understandable in a man, it was inexcusable in a woman. Divorce-law reform, in addition to its other aspects, was thus an attack on the double standard of morality, a reflection of women's claim that to judge them by anything other than a single standard was unjust.

Flappers were less selective in their demand for a single standard. They seemed determined to reject all social conventions that denied them the same rights of free expression as men, creating, as Gerald Critoph documents, a very vocal anti-Flapper backlash. Critics attacked the Flapper's dress, speech, eating, drinking, and dating habits, and seeming lack of interest in emulating her mother's model of the Victorian woman. Although Flappers appeared unconcerned with the kind of political activity that occupied the suffragists, they were very much concerned with expanding the social opportunities their sisters of the previous generation had left them as a legacy.

The two Japanese women discussed by Shimada, Takamura, Iino, and Ito were contemporaries of the Flapper, but their interest in cultural feminism turned in a slightly different direction. Ume Tsuda and Motoko Hani, the authors report, took for their model not the Flapper, but rather nineteenth-century women educators. Conscious of the national effort to promote industrialization and economic growth in Japan, Tsuda and Hani adapted some of the qualities of the Western "new woman" to their own cultural setting. Progress for Japan, they believed, depended on liberalizing certain traditional practices, and a first step in that direction was the education of women. Like the Flapper, they rejected straightforward political activity, in their case because it seemed impractical within their cultural context. Short skirts and Betty beads were also out of context, although Hani did suggest ways in which the kimono could be modified to be less cumbersome.

If the Japanese "new woman" represented one aspect of the liberation of women, the four women who were instrumental in the founding of the United States Children's Bureau represented yet another. These women, as James Johnson indicates, thought it was unjust for the government to ignore the needs of mothers and children, and, with an impressive record of social involvement behind them, Kelley, Lathrop, Abbott, and Wald became lobbyists for child-welfare legislation and maternal health care. Their activities drew the kind of criticism and verbal abuse reserved for those who challenged the conventional image of the submissive woman. Labeled by male antagonists as agents of a communist plot, they were called old maids and childless women who knew nothing of the needs of mothers and infants. Despite the personal attacks, the women seemed to think the time was ripe for change; the election of Jeanette Rankin to Congress, the adoption of the Nineteenth Amendment, and the marshalling of women's organizations around the issue of child welfare held out the promise of corrective legislation. The four activists were too astute politically, however, to leave anything to chance, and they quickly developed lobbying techniques and pressure tactics to rival those of the old pros.

The wide range of activities described in the final section should encourage historians to look again at issues and activities that concerned women during the first half of the twentieth century. The myopic view that sees ratification of the Nineteenth Amendment as inaugurating a mass retreat to the kitchen needs to be corrected. Not every daughter of a Flapper cast aside her mother's bid for personal independence along with her Betty beads. Twentieth-century white women may have responded to the feminine mystique just as Southern black people responded to Reconstruction: insofar as they were politically emancipated, it represented progress; but in terms of self-realization, it was clear they still had a long way to go.

Who was the American woman? Judging from the textbooks, it appears as if historians saw her as a kind of American Eve, foolish when not inconsequential, who must be kept out of their academic garden lest she come too near the tree of knowledge. In view of this record, one of the few assured claims is that the American woman was a person who, in a society which defined her role through Puritan constraints and vapid social stereotypes, attempted in varied ways to manifest her personal identity. It is our hope that this collection will urge more scholars to reject stereotypes, return to the record, and rediscover the American woman as person and citizen, in sum, to accept Abigail Adams' advice to "remember the ladies."

SECTION I

The Growth of
American Feminist Thought

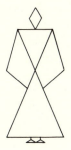

LONG FAMILIAR TERRITORY to political and intellectual historians, the Colonial period has become a rich field for new social historians who see it as a microcosm in which to explore questions related to the structure and function of social relationships in the family, community, and institutions. Their published works particularly interest students of women's role in American history, because they offer new insight into the quality of life of Colonial women, the uncommon mixture of freedom and restraint that characterized their daily existence. As valuable as these insights are, however, they fragment the Colonial woman by divorcing social realities from intellectual awareness. Especially for Colonial society, it is important to consider the relationship of social developments to intellectual issues relevant to women. The nature of the work of social historians has kept them from investigating ideology, and intellectual historians are just beginning to acknowledge the presence of women within their metaphysical framework.

The three chapters in this section, though they do not engage the methodology of the new social history, may suggest ways of bridging the gap between social and intellectual history. They discuss examples of intellectual developments that had immediate social relevance as well as subsequently broader application, once they were incorporated within the feminist intellectual tradition. Woman's right to teach, preach, vote, learn, and divorce was framed in philosophical terms by the central figures in these chapters.

The seventeenth-century Puritan dissenter, Anne Hutchinson, has been referred to as the first American feminist. The fact of her banishment from Massachusetts Bay Colony—ordinarily the only reference textbook writers make about her—provides a less substantial basis for the claim, however, than the arguments she used to justify her demand to be recognized as a teacher and preacher. Hutchinson and her associates were victimized by Bay Colony political leaders because their beliefs implied a threat to the fundamental order of their society, including its patriarchal organization. Her insistence that God had been personally revealed to her frightened her opposition because it undermined the authority of the clergy and the strength of the established church. Compounding her offense, she asserted her right to teach her nonconforming views. What were the forces that shaped her views, and how did she acquire the determination to confront the ecclesiastical and political hierarchy? These become intriguing questions for the historian. One scholar has recently answered them in terms of psychological deviance; a more convincing case can be made by examining her social relationships and her intellectual heritage. Her judges, who believed that she was patterning herself after a woman preacher in England, pointed out the close resemblance between her beliefs and those of European radical dissenters. Hutchinson may have known a great deal more than she admitted about the sexual egalitarianism that was commonly associated with the English and European radical sects. By establishing the sources of her intellectual inheritance, we may gain a better perspective not only on Hutchinson, but on the legacy she contributed to a distinctively feminist intellectual tradition in America.

Marguerite Fisher's chapter on eighteenth-century thinkers suggests that that tradition was enriched by the addition of still another source; the social and political liberalism of the Enlightenment. Citing English and Continental philosophers of the period, Fisher argues that a belief in woman's right to freedom and self-determination formed an integral part of their concept of a just society. That belief, grounded in the assumption that everyone had a "natural right" to freedom and equality, was hinged to the requirement that the social environment be adapted to accommodate woman's need to realize her "natural rights." Eighteenth-century theorists proposed sweeping social changes in laws and attitudes to improve woman's status. Along with a single standard of sexual morality, they advocated universal suffrage, educational reform, access to public office holding, divorce, and birth control. French Revolutionary ideology, they were convinced, was meant to apply as much to women as to men. And a few trans-Atlantic travelers like Thomas Paine eagerly transmitted these ideas to the colonies. But most eighteenth-century American rationalists, generally less catholic than Paine about their intellectual preferences, placed feminist interests at the bottom of their list of Revolutionary objectives.

Thomas Jefferson apparently was one who had little time for feminism, although he managed to carry on a continuing dialogue with a woman who regarded feminism as an important aspect of her total philosophy. Abigail Adams, according to Ralph Ketcham, held more enlightened views than Jefferson on such social issues as slavery, women's education, and woman suffrage, while nevertheless sharing with him a common intellectual heritage based on the Puritan ethic and Revolutionary principles. This basic intellectual compatibility enabled them to carry on a lively exchange of views, whether the subject was the function of government or the health of a child. In describing the conversations of these intellectual equals, Ketcham has offered an example of historical writing that attempts to make women "an integral part of all history."

1

Anne Hutchinson
and the "Revolution Which Never Happened"

Carol V. R. George

*A*T the conclusion of her civil trial before the General Court in New-ton, Massachusetts, in November 1637, a seemingly unrepentant Anne Hutchinson faced her judges. In what they must have regarded as another of her unladylike displays of audacity, she questioned the reason for her stern sentence.

> Mrs. H. I desire to know wherefore I am banished?
> Gov. [John Winthrop] Say no more, the court knows wherefore and is satisfied.[1]

The exchange had symbolic, if not informational, value. Hutchinson knew as well as her judges the reason that she was being banished from Massachusetts Bay Colony, and the caustic response to her question indicated that they meant to have no more dealings with her. She had been questioning their authority for the past few years, and now at the very moment of her conviction she was repeating the practice that was partly responsible for her present circumstances. She had still another trial—a religious trial—awaiting her, but for the moment, she would be out of

1. The records of Anne Hutchinson's religious and civil trials are available in C. F. Adams' documentary collection, *Antinomianism in the Colony of Massachusetts Bay, 1636–1638* (Boston: Prince Society, 1894), and David D. Hall, *The Antinomian Controversy, 1636–1638* (Middletown, Conn.: Wesleyan University Press, 1968). I have used Hall's collection here, p. 348, and elsewhere in the chapter.

their way, confined by order of the Court to the home of Joseph Weld in Roxbury.

Hutchinson had been a thorn in their collective side for nearly two years now, espousing views which threatened to undermine not only their leadership but also that of the ministers in the community, and gathering so many supporters that the colony seemed on the verge of dividing into two rival camps. The leader of the Hutchinson faction—called Antinomians by their detractors—she had to be silenced if any semblance of peace and harmony were to be restored. Her civil trial, like the religious one that followed, was a judicial charade, the outcome of which was probably no more surprising to Hutchinson than it was to her accusers. Anne was guilty of making religion too personal, of claiming that God's saving grace, personally revealed, took precedence over legal forms or acts commonly termed good works. To be an Antinomian was generally understood by the orthodox clergy as meaning one who was against or opposed to the law, and although Hutchinson protested against being defined in such terms, she was so regarded by those who found her views dangerous and heretical. She was banished from the colony in the spring of 1638, produced a grossly malformed fetus a few months later, and was eventually murdered by the Indians in 1643. For her former accusers in the Bay Colony her unhappy fate was an indication of the judgment of God.

Hutchinson's story has been examined many times before and within the context of various issues—theological, political, and economic. She has been made to appear at one time as a remnant of the old order within Puritanism,[2] and at another as the harbinger of a new age of liberalism.[3]

The trial records offer the earliest account of her views, and they have formed the basis for subsequent interpretive descriptions of her life beginning with Winthrop's[4] own assessment of her—which first appeared in 1644 and which characterizes her as the "American Jesabel"—through more recent studies, such as that by Emery Battis,[5] which was published

2. Edmund Morgan, *The Puritan Dilemma* (Boston: Little Brown, 1958), pp. 135–45. See also Morgan's "The Case Against Anne Hutchinson," *The New England Quarterly* 10(1937): 635–49.

3. See, for example, Helen Augur, *An American Jezebel* (New York: Brentano's, 1930), pp. 258ff; and Adams, *Antinomianism*, Introduction, pp. 14, 15. Adams says, however, that Hutchinson gave only "inarticulate expression" to the intellectual inquiry that was part of the movement, while Roger Williams and Henry Vane gave it "intelligent expression."

4. John Winthrop, "A Short Story of the Rise, reign, and ruine of the Antinomians, Familists & Libertines" (hereafter cited as "Short Story, etc."), in Hall, *Antinomian Controversy*, p. 310.

5. Emery Battis, *Saints and Sectaries* (Chapel Hill: University of North Carolina Press, 1962), pp. 346–48. A recent article which recognizes the feminist dimen-

in 1962 and describes her as the victim of menopausal symptoms during the crucial period of her trials. What has been overlooked in previous discussions of Hutchinson, and is therefore the purpose in this chapter, is the extent to which the experience of her trials and the outlines of her career offer any indication as to how the accusers and accused alike viewed issues related to sexual equality and the status of women. They were in no more agreement on this than in other matters: Hutchinson thought women should be free to teach and possibly preach; Winthrop thought too much reading made women insane.

In *The World Turned Upside Down*, Christopher Hill's study of radical religious sects in Revolutionary England during approximately this same period of time, the author provides a fresh perspective on the Hutchinson case, and, incidentally, new insight on the sources of an American feminist intellectual tradition. Without claiming any direct link between the New World dissenters and the radical English sectaries, Hill's work makes it apparent that the two groups had much in common. He suggests that had their objectives been realized by such groups as the Ranters, the Seekers, the Diggers, and the like, they would have produced a dramatic transformation in society—one that would not only have had a "leveling" effect on the social classes, but would also have encouraged a greater acceptance of sexual equality. But, he says, that was "another revolution which never happened, though from time to time it threatened."[6] Although Hill's definition of what constituted sexual equality may be arguable, it does seem clear that the contentions of the radical sectaries held out the possibility of new, less confining, roles for women. The Hutchinsonians, not as specific about their economic aims as were their Old World counterparts, questioned existing political alignments and supported ideas and activities that would have led to a redefinition of sex roles. When Hutchinson tried to translate ideas into practice, she was

---

sion of the Hutchinsonian protest is Lyle Koehler, "The Case of the American Jezebels: Anne Hutchinson and Female Agitation during the Years of Antinomian Turmoil, 1636–1640," *Wlliam and Mary Quarterly* 31(1974): 55–78. I did not have the advantage of Koehler's work while writing this chapter since the article appeared after I had completed the final draft. His research on the backgrounds of some of Hutchinson's female supporters is very useful; his conclusion, however, seems inconsistent. Conceding that the Antinomian movement served as a vehicle for expressing women's discontent, he nevertheless concludes that the Hutchinsonians were neither conscious of their second-class status as women nor concerned about improving it. They recognized in Antinomianism, Koehler says, an ideology that would focus and express the resentments they intuitively felt. It seems questionable, particularly in Hutchinson's case, to argue that she was not conscious of the causes of her resentment and that her discontent remained nameless and unexamined.

6. Christopher Hill, *The World Turned Upside Down* (New York: Viking, 1972), p. 12.

checked by those who found her attempts contrary to "rule." She had visions of many things, including women as teachers-preachers, but that remained a visionary prospect, a revolution which threatened but did not happen.

The Hutchinson case came at a decisive time in the development of the infant colony and was both a cause and an example of the ferment that was threatening to reshape the future of the City Upon a Hill. The issues being raised by critics of the prevailing order—such as Hutchinson and Roger Williams before her—forced local leaders to take another look at their theological and political assumptions. So basic were these matters to the future of the colony that the controversy which developed around them has been described by historians as a turning point in the life of Massachusetts Bay. Simply stated, many of the theological arguments were hinged to the issue of how Puritanism could be adapted to their new situation now that Puritans themselves were controlling the state; the form of Puritanism that the Massachusetts divines had found so appealing when challenging the Established Church in England required modification in its New World setting. And again simply stated, the political implications of the questions asked by Hutchinson, Williams, and their supporters caused both electors and elected to reexamine their social compact theory of government, based on an agreement between God, the magistrates, and the people.

The resolution of these issues would have far-reaching effects on the life of the colony. But in matters relating to sexual equality there also existed the potential for changes that would have been equally far-reaching; Hutchinson's contention that salvation was an intensely personal experience that did not demand the assistance of clergymen contained within it the kernel of the argument in favor of sexual equality. If a woman professed such a saving experience, she not only ignored the authority of the clergy, but she also passed judgment on it. It was possible, she could contend, that her experience was authentic, while that of a particular minister was false, that he was not truly "saved" but was simply carrying out the appearance of salvation by engaging in good works.

For Hutchinson herself, the matter of her own sex became an issue in the case. It was introduced repeatedly during the course of her trials, though his sex had not been a matter for discussion during the previous trial of Roger Williams. Probably just as detrimental to Hutchinson's case was her personality: she was described in terms that made her appear to be haughty, abrasive, and outspoken, while Williams was characterized as a man with a sweet and amiable disposition. If outspokenness was sometimes a virtue in a man it was not so in a woman. She was suspected of being not only an Antinomian, but, far worse, a Familist, a radical group with roots in Europe and England that was presumed to encourage free love. Her own marital infidelity, she was warned, would inevitably follow from her opinions. She was obviously considered a social deviant for pursuing her particular course of action, and female social deviants, as she found out, could expect to have their activities ultimately described in terms of their sexuality. Thus it was that for Hutchinson, her abnormal pregnancy and her association with another dissenter who had a similarly unfortunate experience in childbirth, Mary Dyer, aroused the suspicion that both of them were witches. But at the time, of greater significance than the personal charges of Familism and witchery leveled against her were the unspoken, possibly unrecognized, fears that her views presented a potential threat to the Puritan concept of the family.

If, as Edmund Morgan[7] has observed, the marital relationship in Puritan society was initially and primarily based on a "rational" relationship—with conjugal love, if not romantic love, regarded as the desirable outcome of any union—then Hutchinson's elevation of revelation to a position of primacy could topple the marriage controlled by rationality from its accepted place. Hutchinson apparently did not see Familism as the only alternative to prevailing practice, nor did her accusers, but that was what they chose to focus attention on.

Hutchinson's role in the Antinomian controversy represents the most public aspect of her life, and it is from the period when the movement was at its height and appeared most threatening—that is, from about 1636 to 1638—that most of the information about her is drawn. Nothing written by her own hand concerning the movement is extant, making it difficult to determine on the basis of the records kept by those who had a partisan interest in the struggle what she actually believed and what was erroneously attributed to her. Yet such accounts provide the substance of what is known about her during this historically significant period in her career. The details of her early life, accumulated by her biographers, reveal some limited information regarding the external influences that may have motivated some of her decisions and shaped her views.

She was born in Alford, Lincolnshire, England, in 1591, the daughter of an outspoken and conscientious clergyman of the Church of England, Francis Marbury, and his wife, Bridget Dryden. One of thirteen children, she left home at the age of twenty-one to marry William Hutchinson, a fairly well-to-do merchant, who appears to have remained her constant

7. Edmund Morgan, *The Puritan Family* (Boston: Published by the Trustees of the Public Library, 1956), pp. 22ff.

supporter throughout the course of their married life. During the time they were married, Anne was pregnant at least sixteen times, witnessing the deaths of two, and probably three, of her children in childhood, and another in infancy, as well as the ill-fated final delivery. Yet despite the responsibilities of home and family—to which she attended faithfully— she managed to pursue other interests. She participated in the usual round of community and church activities common to women of her day, and advanced her theological education by traveling with her husband to hear the Reverend John Cotton, eminent theologian and Puritan sympathizer, preach at St. Botolph's Church in old Boston, (that is, Boston in England) some distance from their home. In addition, she practiced a form of folk medicine, serving frequently as midwife or nurse for those in childbirth or confined by illness. That she performed her work well was admitted even by Winthrop, who said some time later that she was "well furnished with means for those purposes,"[8] i.e., midwifery and nursing. But her very expertise in these areas left her open to new suspicions of witchcraft after the completion of her trials, since her detractors found it relatively easy to equate her nursing techniques and willingness to administer herbs and home remedies with the conjuring skills and mysterious potions they associated with witches. Still, her ability as nurse-midwife was never disparaged.

In 1634, after John Cotton had left old Boston for new, Anne, her husband, and children emigrated to the New World, where they were confident their religious life would flourish under Cotton's guidance. She continued to offer her medical assistance when it was needed, while also overseeing the construction of a new home for the family—across the street from Winthrop's. It was not long before she decided that she would follow the example of other church members in the community and open her home to friends and neighbors for a weekly discussion of the sermon preached the previous Sunday in Boston Church. Seated on a chair in the middle of the group, Anne would lead her visitors through an examination of the text and the conclusions that could be drawn from it. Initially her efforts were regarded approvingly by local officials of church and state, who saw them as an indication of the woman's piety. But they soon began to think otherwise, because of reports they heard of what appeared to be liberties she was taking in interpreting accepted Puritan tenets.

To discover what Hutchinson said it is necessary to rely on the records of her trials. She had been a serious student of Cotton's, and many of her conclusions were her own extrapolations of what she believed Cotton was saying. Both felt that of the two covenants God made with

8. Winthrop, "Short Story, etc." in Hall, *Antinomian Controversy*, p. 263.

humankind—first with Adam and then with Abraham—it was the second, a covenant of faith, rather than the first, a covenant of works, that took precedence in determining whether a person was truly saved or not. Hutchinson and Cotton both seemed to question the virtue of regarding outward signs and activities as manifestations of election. Doing good deeds and living a righteous life—sanctification—should indeed follow from the bestowal of God's saving grace—justification—but sanctification was not in itself confirmation of being one of God's elect. What Hutchinson said, however, sounded rather different to Bay Colony leaders than what they understood to be Cotton's position—that, as they themselves believed, the issue involved maintaining the two components, faith and works, in a very delicate balance. She had a naturally keen mind, although she had obviously never been to the university as Cotton had, and when she attempted to translate the finer points of theology into simpler terms for herself and her neighbors, she was misunderstood, misinterpreted, and accused of heretical tendencies. She acquired the name of Antinomian, which in theological circles was assignd to those Christians who, it was said, claimed that because they were under the law of grace they were relieved of the need to respect the more conventional laws of morality and government.

Neither Cotton nor Winthrop himself would have disagreed with Hutchinson's basic contention—that the law of grace took precedence over legalisms—indeed, that had been one of the Puritans' major claims when they had earlier challenged the Anglicans. But an overzealous emphasis on matters of faith, or piety, was linked in their minds with Antinomianism and with what they regarded as the disreputable behavior of groups like the Anabaptists, and particularly the Familists.

The growing popularity of Hutchinson's parlor sessions unsettled the magistrates and ministers in the community. From his vantage point across the street, Winthrop could observe what was taking place in the Hutchinson household, and what he saw was a woman of "ready wit and bold spirit" conspiring, he believed, to break down the sense of discipline he had struggled to maintain in the citizens of the colony. Her meetings, which invariably drew a full house, were beginning to exert a strong influence over the life of the community. Kai Erikson has described one of the functions that was associated with small group sessions: "The New England method of maintaining discipline was based on private conferences, public prayers, and a whole network of other pressures that were nonetheless compelling because they were unofficial."[9]

Hutchinson's weekly gatherings had become an integral part of that network, and Winthrop was displeased with the results, especially since

9. Kai T. Erikson, *Wayward Puritans* (New York: Wiley, 1966), p. 61.

they seemed to run counter to his concept of discipline. In May 1636, when the twenty-four-year-old Hutchinson sympathizer Henry Vane was elected governor rather than Winthrop, the struggle assumed a new, openly political dimension. An additional recruit to the Hutchinson ranks was acquired when Anne's brother-in-law, the Reverend John Wheelwright, joined them shortly after his arrival from England.

Vane's election and Wheelwright's arrival in 1636 pushed events closer to a confrontation. It proved to be a fateful year for Anne. In March she had given birth to a son, Zuriel, who presumably died shortly thereafter. Despite her personal problems, or perhaps because of them, she went on with her weekly meetings, encouraged by the support her views appeared to generate. Wheelwright, she told her listeners, was under a covenant of grace, as John Cotton was, and—so it was alleged—she hinted that it was possible that they were the only two ministers in the colony who were really saved. In October, the Hutchinson faction proposed that Wheelwright become the third minister on the staff of Boston Church, joining Cotton and John Wilson, the latter a clergyman who shared Winthrop's opinions.

Winthrop was able to block the appointment. Wheelwright was sent instead to a congregation in nearby Mount Wollaston, but Winthrop's negative vote on the issue served to widen the breach between what was developing into two rival factions within the church in Boston. When Winthrop took note of Hutchinson's opinions in his *Journal*, he concluded that she "brought over with her two dangerous errors: 1. That the person of the Holy Ghost dwells in a justified person. 2. That no sanctification can help to evidence to us our justification. —From these two grew many branches."[10] There may be some truth to the claim made by the nineteenth-century historian of the Antinomian controversy, Charles Francis Adams,[11] that the theological debate which grew up about the Hutchinson case considered obscure points of interpretation in a jargon now unintelligible, but that does not preclude the fact that the wider issues involved had immediate practical significance for the participants. In January 1637, when Wheelwright delivered a Fast Day sermon in Boston in which he urged his listeners to "prepare for battle and come out against the enemies of the Lord," his language was sufficiently direct to leave little doubt about what he was suggesting.

His listeners interpreted his meaning in terms of their own position

10. James K. Hosmer, ed., *Winthrop's Journal* (New York: Scribner's, 1908), I, 195.

11. C. F. Adams, *Three Episodes of Massachusetts History* (Boston, 1892), pp. 366–67.

vis-à-vis the Hutchinson movement. Anne Hutchinson and her friends could applaud the efforts of so able an advocate, one who could present their views to an audience much larger than the group she could gather in her parlor. But to Winthrop and those who sided with him, Wheelwright's sermon smacked of sedition, and they meant to deal with him. The General Court summoned him for a hearing in March, ostensibly to examine his sermon appeal for readiness for "battle," and as local ministers crowded in to listen to the investigation, they heard him judged guilty of sedition. The Hutchinsonians regarded the decision as a miscarriage of justice, and they proceeded to draft a petition to the Court appealing the verdict. The following May Winthrop was returned as governor, unseating Henry Vane, and while his election was not a popular one, he saw it as an opportunity to move against his opponents. During his tenure in office, he encouraged the Court to deal with those who had signed the petition, disfranchising some, banishing others, and relieving all of the weapons they possessed—and this at a time when there was a general feeling of alarm among the residents about a possible Indian "menace."

Anne's husband served briefly as a deputy to the General Court, and after he resigned his post in the fall of 1636, she had to rely on information from other political friends to learn the Court's business firsthand. A personal informant, however, was hardly required for her to appreciate the Court's intentions. It seemed obvious that by condemning her friends, the Court meant to frighten her into silence. To withdraw from public activity, to suppress beliefs she knew to be sound, would be to deny the revelation of the Holy Spirit within her, and that she knew she could not, or would not, do. The Court would inevitably have to confront her, as well.

But before the Court could try her in an open hearing, the church, in effect, put her views on trial at a synod convened in August 1637. The synod was an important event, the first in the life of the colony, and it attracted the kind of attention this significance demanded. The ministers who met together assumed as their responsibility the need to challenge the errors and to end the divisions that were threatening the peace of the colony, though participants and onlookers alike knew that their real business was to exorcise the devil disguised in the Hutchinson movement. The Hutchinsonians had lost their most prominent defender in civil proceedings when Henry Vane returned to England—he had sailed just a few days before the synod convened—leaving them with only John Cotton to protect their interests in ecclesiastical affairs. The delegates respected Cotton, but that respect did not relieve him of the need to appear before them to explain his position.

The convocation of clergymen ambitiously considered over eighty "errors," though to non-theologians and anyone unfamiliar with the subtleties of their theological system, many appear so repetitious that it seems as if one basic proposition could summarize the whole. And that was the question of whether a person who professed a personal revelation of the Holy Spirit was bound to respect the injunctions of Biblical and ecclesiastical authority. It appeared to the delegates that the Hutchinsonians answered that with a resounding "no." What the dissenters were asking, the ministers believed, was why someone who acknowledged the indwelling of the Holy Spirit as a personal reality should be judged by churchmen who may never have had such an experience, who may not be saved? Such a position called into question the whole system of constituted authority—both civil and ecclesiastical—because it implied the possibility of replacing corporate decisions with private judgment. Hutchinsonians might well claim that their personal experiences of salvation gave them the ability to discern whether or not the professions of others —regardless of their positions or social standing—were authentic. Hutchinson herself probably had no intention of becoming a lawbreaker, but the ministers deduced Antinomian conclusions from her opinions, and that suggested heresy.

What was worse, the ministers suspected that her views led directly to Familism, and the beliefs commonly associated, often erroneously, with the Familists, a radical sect known also as the Family of Love which originated in Holland in the sixteenth century. If individual inspiration took precedence over the monogamous injunctions of the church, where could it lead but to indulgence in sensuous desires and free love? Furthermore, since Familists held their property in common, it was easy for the ministers to accept the stories that they also engaged promiscuously and adulterously in the "community of women."[12] Cotton was questioned by the delegates to determine where he stood in relation to the "errors" being investigated, although there was no expressed concern that he was tainted with Familism. He tried to walk a theological tightrope, first leaning toward the Hutchinsonians and then toward the defenders of orthodoxy. It was an impossible position, but in the end the ministers seemed satisfied that he was at one with them.

Before the synod adjourned, the clergymen passed a resolution designed to silence Anne Hutchinson by prohibiting her meetings. They concluded:

12. Hill, *World Turned Upside Down*, p. 22.

"That though women might meet (some few together) to pray and edify one another; yet such a set assembly (as was then in practice at Boston,) where sixty or more did meet every week, and one woman (in a prophetical way, by resolving questions of doctrine, and expounding scripture) took upon her the whole exercise, was agreed to be disorderly, and without rule."[13]

A subsequent resolution condemned those who publicly questioned a preacher and debated his theological contentions—as the Hutchinsonians had done. Taken together, the decisions indicate that church leaders recognized in Hutchinson not just a troublesome church member, but the head of a faction that posed a danger to the stability of their society. And since it was not within their perogative to examine her politically, they would fault her on her failure to conform to the social behavior expected of women. Women could be permitted to meet together to pray and instruct each other, but they could not congregate in groups of sixty to hear the scripture interpreted by another woman. The resolution was therefore intended to do more than just silence Hutchinson; it was meant to disperse her female following. Hutchinson was attempting to usurp a role that custom assigned to men, and that was "without rule." To what appeared to be the Antinomian challenge to the whole system of rule she added yet another dimension.

The synod's decisions had apparently little direct effect on Hutchinson. She continued to convene her weekly discussions just as before and, as before, still arose and left if John Wilson preached what she regarded as his typically unenlightened sermons at Boston Church. And her followers remained loyal, despite the injunctions of the influential synod of ministers. Whatever risks were involved, the women who continued to meet with her seemed willing to accept them along with their teacher.

For John Winthrop, it was this direct appeal of the Hutchinsonians to women that made them especially dangerous. He observed:

"They commonly laboured to worke first upon women, believing (as they conceived) the weaker to resist; the more flexible, tender, and ready to yield: and if once they could winde in them, they hoped by them, as by an Eve, to catch their husbands also, which indeed proved too true amongst us there."[14]

13. *Winthrop's Journal*, I, 234.
14. Winthrop, "Short Story, etc.," in Hall, *Antinomian Controversy*, pp. 205–206.

By this admission, Winthrop confirmed the fact that it was the wives who converted the husbands to Hutchinsonianism, and not the other way around, suggesting that at least among some of the men in the movement there existed a considerable amount of respect for their wives' opinions.

In a study of family life in Plymouth Colony, *A Little Commonwealth*,[15] John Demos considered the question of sexual equality and concluded that it was relatively higher in the New World than the Old. He apparently did not include the views of radical religious groups in his assessment of the rights of English women. Within the limitations of the area Demos chose to examine, legal arrangements—a limitation, he explained, dictated by the types of sources available—he attempted to make a case for some evidence of sexual equality. But the legal concessions cited—such as the making of certain types of contracts, the "putting out" of children, the sale of land, and the granting of licenses—fails to explicate the kinds of problems faced by Hutchinson and the women who supported her. Even if one wanted to dismiss Hutchinson as a religious fanatic, it would still be necessary to consider the reaction of the women who felt denied the right of self-expression they associated with her meetings. The form of sexual equality they wanted was more personal than the contractual arrangements Demos discussed, which were, in any case, made possible because of the assumption of male dominance in the family as in the community. They were also frequently an expeditious way of dealing with certain practical problems, such as dividing an estate or arranging a marriage with a property-owning widow. For Hutchinson's friends, a narrow definition of sexual equality based on limited legal rights and protection from physical mistreatment was inadequate. Certainly the relative infrequency of incidents involving wife-beating is unconvincing evidence on which to build a case for sexual equality since, as the experience of Southern black slaves demonstrates, there is no correlation between the absence of physical violence and the acceptance of equality.

Winthrop's suspicions regarding the kind of woman he believed was attracted to Hutchinson's movement were confirmed when he heard of the case of Mary Dyer. He thought Dyer to be a bothersome Familist, yet despite his low opinion of her views, he referred to her as "a very proper and comely young woman," indicating that while he thought women had no talent for understanding books or politics, he still had an eye for a pretty face. He knew her to be a regular participant at Anne's

15. John Demos, *A Little Commonwealth* (New York: Oxford, 1970), pp. 94–95.

gatherings, and when he heard of her unfortunate experience in child-birth, he was quick to describe a cause-and-effect situation. It seemed that when Dyer went into labor, during the seventh month of her preg-nancy, she called on her friend Anne Hutchinson to assist with the de-livery. The event occurred on October 17, 1637, with Hutchinson and another midwife, Jane Hawkins, in attendance. According to the reports of her male contemporaries, Hawkins was a simple woman, a regular visitor at the Hutchinson weekly gatherings, who may have understood only a fraction of what she heard at the meetings. Dyer's delivery was a difficult one, presumably because the child was in a breech position until it was turned by one of the women. When the infant was finally delivered, it was dead and grossly malformed. If, from her long experience with such matters, Anne could respond calmly, perhaps even accepting what had happened, she was not sure that others could, so she attempted to conceal the condition of the stillborn child. She sought out John Cotton's advice on what she was about to do, and he agreed that it was the proper course of action. The infant was secretly buried, although probably not before one of the women who was among those milling about the house at the time of the delivery caught a glimpse of it. Months later, on the day Anne Hutchinson was excommunicated from the church in Boston, word leaked out that the woman seen comforting Anne was Mary Dyer, the one who had borne the "monster." Winthrop found it more than coincidental that the woman just banished as a "leper" was the associate of the mother of a monster, and he asked for an investigation of the birth the previous fall. The remains were exhumed, and Jane Hawkins was questioned. Winthrop, as unfamiliar as his contemporaries generally with the mysteries of premature birth, nevertheless described the fetus in al-most salacious detail:

> It had no head but a face, which stood so low upon the brest, as the eares (which were like an Apes) grew upon the shoulders.
>
> The eyes stood farre out, so did the mouth, the nose was hooking up-ward, the brest and back were full of sharp prickles, like a Thornback, the navell and all the belly with the distinction of the sex, were, where the lower part of the back and hips should have been, and those back parts were on the side the face stood.
>
> The arms and hands, with the thighs and legges, were as other chil-drens, but in stead of toes, it had upon each foot three claws, with talons like a young fowle.[16]

16. Winthrop, "A Short Story, etc.," in Hall, *Antinomian Controversy*, pp. 280–81.

Although he might not be expected to understand the causes and consequences of a premature delivery, Winthrop was apparently captivated by the circumstances surrounding it. He went on to report other unusual happenings:

> The occasion of concealing it was very strange, for most of the women who were present at the womans travaile, were suddenly taken with such a violent vomiting, and purging, without eating or drinking of any thing, as they were forced to goe home, others had their children taken with convulsions, (which they had not before, nor since) and so were sent for home, so as none were left at the time of the birth, but the midwife and two other, whereof one fell asleepe.
>
> At such time as the child dyed (which was about two houres before the birth) the bed wherein the mother lay shook so violently, as all which were in the roome perceived it.
>
> The after birth wherein the childe was had prickles on the inside like those on the childes brest.[17]

Winthrop's account, except for the disinterred remains which he admitted were "much corrupted," was based on hearsay and gossip five months old. The story came out after Hutchinson had twice been tried and the Dyer couple faced the prospect of being "admonished" for being Familists. And Jane Hawkins, midwife and friend to both women, was suspected by community leaders of being a witch, though her testimony was accepted at face value. Hawkins' vulnerability to the charge of witchcraft, like Anne Hutchinson's, was increased because of her association with midwifery and nursing skills. Winthrop reported that Hawkins left the Bay Colony shortly after the discovery of the remains, and he observed that, "it was time for her to be gone, for it was known, that she used to give young women oil of mandrakes and other stuff to cause conception; and she grew into great suspicion to be a witch, for it was credibly reported, that, when she gave any medicines, (for she practised physic,) she would ask the party, if she did believe, she could help her, etc."[18]

In the aftermath of the scandal that broke about the "monstrous birth," Cotton apologized for the part he had played in hiding the truth, and Jane Hawkins left for Rhode Island along with other Hutchinsonians, including the Dyers. But Mary Dyer had in store for her a fate that rivaled Anne's: adopting Quakerism, she was twice imprisoned for her

17. Hall, *Antinomian Controversy*, p. 281.
18. *Winthrop's Journal*, I, 268.

beliefs and eventually was hanged in Boston. As for Winthrop, he saw the events as a sign of divine judgment passed on those who would attempt to corrupt the saints of the Bay Colony.

Before the Governor ever learned of the unfortunate birth, however, he had committed himself to a plan designed to root out the troublesome Hutchinsonians. Despite the fact that his election the previous summer did not indicate an overwhelming vote of confidence, he proceeded to stack the General Court with deputies he knew to be inclined toward his position, dismissing the pro-Hutchinsonians William Aspinwall and John Coggeshall. Aspinwall was released ostensibly because his name appeared on the petition for Wheelwright, and Coggeshall then resigned in protest. With the Court then constituted in his favor, Winthrop began, in November 1637, to try and to judge those known to be Hutchinsonians, with the results mentioned above: banishment, disfranchisement, and disarmament. The ringleader was saved until last, presumably because her accusers believed that by then her spirit would be broken from witnessing the indictment of her friends, and she would be contrite. Their hopes proved to be misplaced.

Hutchinson was called before the Court in November 1637, to offer her own defense to the charges laid against her. The Court's immediate problem was that, as a civil body, it could not find legitimate political charges to bring against her; she had not signed the now-discredited petition, and she had not preached sedition. As Winthrop struggled to find a specific cause, he managed to develop two: disturbing the peace and continuing her proscribed weekly sessions. The Court accused her of being "one of those that have troubled the peace of the commonwealth and the churches" and of continuing a "meeting and an assembly in your house that hath been condemned by the general assembly as a thing not tolerable nor comely in the sight of God nor fitting for your sex."[19]

Although physically tired, Hutchinson was ready to match wits with her accusers. To Winthrop's unconvincing allegations she responded: "I am called here to answer before you but I hear no things laid to my charge." It was clear that, far from being penitent, she was going to be confident and aggressive. Winthrop, irritated by her answer, engaged in some verbal parrying with her, and then finally settled on the contention that she had transgressed the fifth commandment to honor father and mother. By continuing to receive in her home those whom the ministers and magistrates had found guilty of various offenses, she was dis-

---

19. "The Examination of Mrs. Anne Hutchinson at the Court at Newtown," in Hall, *Antinomian Controversy*, p. 312. All of the material relating to the civil trial was taken from this source.

obeying the fathers (but not the mothers) of the commonwealth, thereby "dishonour[ing] your parents." When Hutchinson challenged this line of reasoning, an exasperated Winthrop responded: "We do not mean to discourse with those of your sex but only this; you do adhere unto them and do endeavor to set forward this faction and so you do dishonour us." Throughout this initial stage of the confrontation, the discussion tended to focus on her apparent contravention of social custom, that is, her continued practice of convening large gatherings in her home, particularly since it was alleged that the meetings might have been sexually integrated.

Hutchinson remained firm but open, willing even to concede to the Court certain terms in dispute if the evidence could show she had violated a law. She defended her actions on several grounds: the Bible justified the practice of elder women teaching younger ones; the custom of convening religious gatherings in the home had been established in the colony before her arrival; the activity was one Winthrop himself was involved in; and the weekly gatherings at her home were separated by sex, with the men meeting apart from the women. Winthrop, undoubtedly annoyed by her persistence, tried to regain the offensive. Elder women, he said, should instruct their younger sisters "about their business, and to love their husbands and not to make them to clash." Instead, Hutchinson's supporters were causing disruption in the commonwealth because families were being neglected by women who were spending too much time at her theological discussions. Simon Bradstreet managed a grudging consent that he thought women's meetings were lawful, but the discussion, from the point of view of the examiners, was clearly not satisfactory.

They moved then into another area where they may have felt on firmer ground. They attempted to build a case for the charge that she had dishonored the fathers of the community around her alleged contention that all ministers save Cotton preached a covenant of works. It came as a logical progression in the argument: first she was charged with defying the synod by continuing her meetings even after they had been outlawed, and then she was accused of implying that ministers were false prophets not to be heeded.

Hutchinson held her own against the new charge until Hugh Peter revealed a conversation with her on the matter, one that she had presumed at the time to be confidential. Peter claimed that during a meeting a group of ministers held with her the previous December she disparaged the local clergy by saying they preached a covenant of works. His charges were supported by other ministers who had been present at the winter gathering, including John Wilson, who was undoubtedly still licking the wounds he had received from the Hutchinsonians during the Wheelwright controversy. Despite the fact that she stood virtually alone against this verbal barrage of the clergy, Hutchinson appeared unshaken, responding with logic and clarity to the new charge. Winthrop saw that the Court was making no progress and adjourned the meeting until the following day.

When the Court reconvened the next morning, it was confronted by a woman who had done some homework during the recess. Winthrop opened the session by repeating the charges against her—including the statements she allegedly made during the December conversation with the preachers. Hutchinson responded with her own report. During the recess, she had read over some notes in her possession which had been obtained from John Wilson's written account of her private meeting with the ministers. In looking over them, she said, she discovered that they differed in several significant respects from the verbal testimony given the previous day. Since that was the case and, further, since the ministers were witnessing "in their own cause," she desired to have their testimony given under oath. Her request for an oath struck like a bombshell. Winthrop saw no need for an oath; others thought it was unnecessary because the ministers were so well known. Yet when the Governor turned to those people gathered in the Court to ask if they were satisfied with the way the business at hand was proceeding, the record indicates their response as being, "Many say.—We are not satisfied." Anne could still count on the support of a loyal group of friends. But when John Coggeshall rose to raise a point tending toward her favor, he was admonished by John Endicott, who observed that "this carriage of your's tends to further casting dirt upon the face of the judges." Coggeshall was eventually intimidated into silence, though he had been scheduled to be one of her witnesses. Thomas Leverett, a ruling elder from Boston Church, did make a brief statement in her defense, but the fundamental task of affirming or challenging her claims fell to John Cotton, who was called from his place beside her to witness in her behalf.

During the course of repeated exchanges with the judges, Cotton held to his position that he could not remember her saying that all the ministers preached a covenant of works. The Court seemed to have no substantive charges on which to proceed against Anne, yet it was anxious to get on with the sentencing.

Hutchinson herself then asked to speak. What she said, the testimony of a believer compelled to witness to the truth when confronted with falsehood, assisted her prosecutors with their task of convicting her. The Lord, she said, had revealed his will to her by an "immediate revelation"; "By the voice of his own spirit to my soul." Though she should meet with affliction, God would deliver her as he delivered Daniel from the lion's den. Like the French Maid of Orleans, Hutchinson had it revealed to her that God would deliver her from her trials. She concluded her testimony with a warning:

> You have power over my body but the Lord Jesus hath power over my body and soul, and assure yourselves thus much, you do as much as in you lies to put the Lord Jesus Christ from you, and if you go on in this course you begin you will bring a curse upon you and your posterity, and the mouth of the Lord hath spoken it.

Her blast against the Court was thus double-barreled: Not only would the Lord deliver her, but he would bring a curse upon those who persecuted her.

Why would she say such things when she must have known that her own words would be used against her? Perhaps she so misinterpreted the sense of the Court that she believed her acquittal was already assured. Perhaps she was convinced that since the Court seemed determined to punish her as it had her friends, she would at least have the satisfaction of offering her own personal witness to the truth.

When she had finished, the Court resumed its questioning of Cotton, who, in an attempt to clarify her testimony, distinguished between two types of revelations or miracles. One, he said, was "above" nature and thus against Scripture, while the other was a manifestation of the providence of God, and was therefore scriptural and acceptable. But the judges were not satisfied with Cotton's explanation. The claims they had heard from Hutchinson's own lips about divine revelation were worse than those attributed to "The Enthusiasts and Anabaptists." The Deputy Governor, Thomas Dudley, probably summed up the hitherto unspoken fears of the Court when he recalled the example of the Anabaptists in Germany. It was reliance on revelation, he said, that inspired them who "have stirred up their hearers to take up arms against their prince and to cut the throats one of another." Anne Hutchinson, he was convinced, was "deluded by the devil." The woman who faced them, a keen-witted but bone-weary mother of eleven, was presumed to be plotting to overthrow the authority of the local magistrates, following the example of her co-religionists in Germany. The Court, without much further delay, voted to banish her because of "the troublesomeness of her spirit and the danger of her course amongst us." There were only two who dissented, Messers Coddington and Colborn, and Anne was accordingly banished as "a woman not fit for our society," imprisoned until the Court saw fit to send her away. When she asked the reason for her sentence, it was Winthrop who replied, "say no more, the court knows wherefore and is satisfied."

The case against her had been little more than a caricature of justice, based on the flimsy testimony of participants in a private conversation who could not even corroborate each other's account. The outcome was probably never in doubt. The Court had set itself the task of dealing with the Hutchinsonian critics in the colony, and did so in the months preceding and following Anne's trial, while she was detained in Joseph Weld's home. She was allowed to have visits from her family, but not from her supporters, though local ministers were allowed to come and go, virtually at will, presumably to bring her to an awareness of her "errors." She had been through a great deal, and she was languishing physically, but the clerical visits went on without interruption.

But the leaders of the Bay Colony were not through with Hutchinson, nor she with them. Before she was banished from the community, the church intended to have its say in the matter, and she was accordingly brought to trial before the church in Boston in March 1638. As the hearing opened, it was announced that Hutchinson was not well; "She is so weake that she conceaves herselfe not fitt nor able to have bine soe longe together."[20] Whatever the reasons for her indisposition, the hearing went on as scheduled, with her sharp comments to her examiners giving no hint of her disability.

That the civil authorities had already banished her did not cancel out the need for the church to try her as well. There were many compelling reasons for church leaders to proceed against her. The majority of her supporters were church members, and if the church did not condemn her views, it might be in danger of being disrupted from within by Hutchinsonian principles. Furthermore, some clergymen may have genuinely believed that by exposing her "errors" to her in open hearing, she would retract them, and thus dissolve the movement herself. And finally, for the church to remain silent regarding her could have been interpreted by civil authorities as a critical judgment of their handling of her case.

After passing a trying winter at Weld's home, she was faced with another ordeal in which she would now be clearly on the defensive. Already accused by the Court, she was to be questioned and cross-examined by a group of men highly skilled in the fine art of splitting theological hairs. Occasionally she was baffled by their very specialized vocabulary

---

20. "A Report of the Trial of Mrs. Anne Hutchinson before the Church in Boston," in Hall, *Antinomian Controversy*, p. 351. All of the material relating to the church trial was taken from this source.

and the particular meanings assigned to terms, but when that happened she was quick to admit the gaps in her education. The hearing took place in two parts, the second session being separated from the first by a week's time—time she spent confined in John Cotton's home. And although she renounced some of her opinions at the second meeting, she was not believed and was denounced as a liar.

The first session amounted to a theological debate, with accusers and accused alike liberally quoting Biblical texts to support their particular positions. Intricate, labored, and tedious, it revealed not only the extent to which seemingly minor points of theology could arouse an important segment of the religious community, but also Hutchinson's own rather extensive knowledge of the issues involved. The intention of the ministers seemed to be to force her to expose her sympathy for Anabaptist and Familist views. With that in mind, they pressed her on such issues as the physical resurrection of the body, something the Familists were suspected of denying. Cotton was cast in the role of chief inquisitor, primarily because he was acknowledged to be the best theologian among them, but also because they may have assumed that as her former teacher he would have an advantage in "reducing" her errors. When her son and her son-in-law came to her defense, they were rebuked for letting "naturall affection" interfere with the process of dealing with "damnable Errors." And one of these so-called errors was her contention that Christ came to the believer "in Union," resulting in a union of the person with Christ. For her examiners, such a view was not only inherently wrong, because unscriptural, but because it also implied a dangerous indictment of the church. For the person claiming the kind of experience she described, the church was unnecessary, or certainly peripheral, to his or her religious life.

The suspicion of Familism was present in the questions dealing with definitions of spirit and soul, with the ministers inferring that Hutchinson held to the mortality of the soul. John Davenport (or Damphord) observed that anyone who spoke for the mortality of the soul spoke for "Licentiousnesse and sinfull Liberty." He thought it was the chief sin of the Familists that they supported "the Communities of Weomen." Said Davenport: "it is a right principle for if the Resurrection be past than Marriage is past: for it is a waytie Reason; after the Resurection [sic] is past, marriage is past. Than if thear be any Union betwene man and woman it is not by Marriage but in a Way of Communities." Hutchinson repeated her earlier repudiation of the Familists, but the assumption appeared to remain that she was one of them. Thomas Shepard thought she was particularly harmful because "with her fluent Tounge and forwardness in Expressions," she was likely "to seduce and draw away many, Espetially simple Weomen of her owne sex."

The criticisms raised by Hutchinson's son and son-in-law created a special problem for those who were conducting the hearing. If the church was going to impose a sentence on the accused, it would require the unanimous approval of those eligible to vote, and not just a simple majority. Accordingly, it was decided to pass judgment on the outspoken dissenters, specifically her two male relatives, who were subsequently "admonished"—a form of church discipline that suspended them from participation in the Lord's Supper. Cotton, who pronounced the admonition, told the two men that their loyalty to their mother was actually a disservice to her because it only nourished her unsound opinions.

Hutchinson's confidant and theological mentor, Cotton had by this time come full circle for reasons not altogether clear. No longer her defender, he may have been persuaded by political as well as theological considerations to join with her attackers. He made some observations about his former pupil to the sisters of the congregation. He recognized, he said, that they may have drunk in some good things from Hutchinson, but they may also have taken in some of her "poyson." He continued: "she is but a Woman and many unsound and dayngerous principles are held by her." Then he turned his attention to the accused, admitting that she had "bine an Instrument of doing some good." Despite an impressive catalog of her virtues, however, he felt compelled to admonish her since the evil she expressed outweighed the goodness she demonstrated. He joined his voice to those of his colleagues in reviling the Familists and their "filthie Sinne of the Communitie of Women." And then he gave his warning to Anne that her personal infidelity would inevitably follow from her convictions, though he admitted he had no reason to suspect her of being unfaithful to her husband.

Before Cotton finished his charge, Hutchinson asked if she might interrupt him because, feeling overcome by weakness, she was afraid she might forget her comment before he concluded. He paused, and she said that she did not hold any of the views he charged against her before she was imprisoned. Shepard found her statement so offensive that he observed she was guilty not only of impudence—for interrupting Cotton's charge—but of misrepresentation, since she had held consistently to the very same positions. Shortly after his cutting comment, the meeting adjourned for a week.

It was undoubtedly a restless week for Anne Hutchinson: ill, alone, concerned about the conduct of her case, she was counseled by Cotton. When the hearing resumed and she was permitted to speak, she admitted that she had been deceived on several important points and now wished to retract her errors. She listed the opinions she concluded were false and her new views on the matters in dispute. Whether or not her retraction was authentic may indeed be debatable; Christopher Hill has suggested that it was common practice among the Familists to recant when apprehended, only to reaffirm their old opinions once any immediate danger had passed.[21] Perhaps she had more sympathy with the Familists than she realized or cared to admit. Certainly the ministers were not put off by her "confession." They found new charges to level against her, with someone remembering that she had said there are "no distinct graces inherent in us," and others noticing her physical appearance. The conclusion was soon forthcoming that "Repentance is not in her Countenance," and that her retraction was a lie. Hugh Peter said she had once spoken approvingly of a woman preacher in England—probably from the diocese of Ely where Familists were strong—and John Wilson thought she was trying to "be a greate Prophites."[22] And it was Wilson who probably summed up the prevailing attitude of the clergymen when he commented that her sinful disrespect for the magistrates was exceeded only by her far greater transgression of "slightinge of God's faythfull Ministers and contemninge and cryinge downe them as Nobodies." She had seemingly conveyed the impression she thought they were "Nobodies." Hugh Peter observed that her fundamental problem was that she had "rather bine a Husband than a Wife and a preacher than a Hearer; and a Magistrate than a Subject." It was obvious he knew which side of that equation he preferred for himself. Wilson called her a "dayngerus Instrument of the Divell," while another examiner advised the women present to take notice of the enormous evils that had been exposed in the one on whom they had "doted soe much."

The case was sealed, and it was left to Wilson to pronounce the excommunication. With perhaps some sense of personal satisfaction, he announced that she was cast out and delivered "up to Sathan," labeled a "Hethen and a Publican," and a "Leper." As Anne Hutchinson got up to leave, with the brutal benediction sounding all too clear, she was joined by Mary Dyer, who took that timely moment to comfort the accused. Her simple gesture undoubtedly helped Hutchinson, but it determined Dyer's future in the colony. For it was then that news reached Winthrop of the "Monster" that Mary had produced, and served to remind him of the "monstrous opinions" held by her husband William. William Dyer was, "by an unexpected occasion," called before the church the following Sunday, questioned about his allegedly Familist views, and subsequently "admonished." The Dyers eventually followed the same route traveled by

21. Hill, *World Turned Upside Down*, pp. 22–23.
22. "Report of Trial of Mrs. Anne Hutchinson," in Hall, *Antinomian Controversy*, p. 381; Battis, *Saints and Sectaries*, pp. 43–44.

the Hutchinsons and many others accused by the Court and the church: leaving behind friends, property, businesses, and old ties, they made new homes for themselves in Rhode Island.

A few days after Anne's sentence was pronounced, the Hutchinsons left Massachusetts with their dependent children. Winthrop later wrote that after her excommunication, Anne's "spirits, which seemed before to be somewhat dejected, revived again, and she gloried in her sufferings, saying that it was the greatest happiness, next to Christ, that ever befel her."[23] She rested and tried to recover from her ordeal in the crudely built house her family had quickly constructed on Aquidneck. As other exiles from Massachusetts joined them, her spirits understandably rose, until late summer, when the child she was carrying aborted. At what stage in her pregnancy the miscarriage occurred is unknown: Dr. John Clarke, the physician and friend who attended her, said that she had been so ill for six weeks before the delivery that she was "doubtful of her life."[24] Like Mary Dyer earlier, Hutchinson delivered a deformed, premature fetus, attributable in part, perhaps, to her age—she was then forty-six.

When her accusers back in the Bay Colony heard of her misfortune, they exploited it with sordid interest. Even Cotton preached a sermon about the Hutchinson "monster," while Winthrop collected testimony from Clarke which he willingly passed on. According to the account, what Anne Hutchinson produced was "30. monstrous births or therabouts, at once; some of them bigger, some lesser, some of one shape, some of another; few of any perfect shape, none at all of them (as farre as I could ever learne) of humane shape."[25] What modern medical opinion suggests is that Hutchinson's "monster" was a hydatidiform mole, the "end stage of a degenerating pregnancy,"[26] although that diagnosis depends on accepting as valid the descriptions of Clarke and Winthrop. For her accusers, it was a sign of the hand of God at work:

"And see how the wisdome of God fitted this judgment to her sinne every way, for looke as she had vented mishapen opinions, so she must bring forth deformed monsters; and as about 30. Opinions in number, so many monsters."[27]

23. *Winthrop's Journal,* I, 264.
24. John Winthrop, *History of New England,* edited by James Savage (Boston, 1825), I, 271–73.
25. Winthrop, "A Short Story, etc.," in Hall, *Antinomian Controversy,* p. 214.
26. David N. Holvey, ed., *The Merck Manual of Diagnosis and Therapy,* 12th ed. (1972), pp. 817–19.
27. Winthrop, "A Short Story, etc.," in Hall, *Antinomian Controversy,* 214.

It all fitted neatly together into a rational whole, even to the number of "monsters." As misery piled upon misery for Anne, her detractors were convinced that she was paying the price for having consorted with the devil. A few fruitless gestures were made by some determined officials of Massachusetts to "reduce her errors," but she remained unconvinced and unrepentant.

After her husband died in 1642, she and her children still at home moved again, this time to Long Island. The following summer, in 1643, with apparently no warning or indication of hostility, she and all but one of her children were murdered by the Indians. In the preface to Winthrop's account of the Antinomian controversy, *A Short Story, etc.,* Thomas Welde says of their deaths, "Gods hand is the more apparently seene herein,"[28] by making such a shocking example of her and her family.

Hutchinson's case could therefore be satisfactorily dismissed by her accusers, who found their treatment of her vindicated by the judgment of God. But if they had wanted to view her life as an example of Calvinistic predeterminism, they might have developed an argument more convincing—to her supporters and perhaps to recent observers—if they had chosen to focus on her personal qualities rather than her tragic misfortunes. It would have been relatively easy to suggest that because of her personality, specifically her vivid imagination, she was predisposed to conflict with any constituted authority, regardless of the circumstances or location. Her imagination made it possible for her to envision important realignments in all areas of the society of her day, changes the more prosaic might regard as sheer fantasy at worst or wishful thinking at best. According to Perry Miller, she and Roger Williams were both banished because "they were altogether too gifted with imagination."[29] It was also a quality that Christopher Hill believes was common to the radical religious groups in England, and he refers to Herbert Marcuse's observation that "In the great historical revolutions, the imagination was, for a short period, released and free to enter into the projects of a new social morality and of new institutions of freedom: then it was sacrificed to the requirements of effective reason."[30] Both Hutchinson and Williams may well have been banished because they possessed all too active imaginations. Anyone, whether man or woman, faced such a prospect if they managed to attract a sizable group of supporters whose visions of change challenged the prevailing order.

28. Hall, *Antinomian Controversy,* p. 218.
29. Perry Miller, *The New England Mind; The Seventeenth Century* (New York: Macmillan, 1939), p. 259.
30. Herbert Marcuse, *An Essay on Liberation,* p. 37; quoted in Hill, *World Turned Upside Down,* p. 336.

But Hutchinson's problems were compounded because she not only possessed imagination, but she also appeared as the embodiment of the changes she anticipated. For her, the arguments of the ministers and magistrates that a woman should neither teach nor preach were unconvincing. Since God bestowed his grace freely on believers, irrespective of their sex, the local officials should be similarly blind to the matter of sexuality when those same believers felt compelled to bear witness to their faith. That was the most radical change in sex roles that she personally advanced, although the potential for other changes was also present. For within the Hutchinsonian movement, as within the radical English sectarian movement, it appeared that some women, at least, sensed opportunities to develop new forms of self-expression, some of which would inevitably have had an effect on the marital relationship and the family structure.

To regard the Antinomian controversy as a turning point in the history of Massachusetts Bay because of the significance of the political and religious issues involved—matters of dissent, freedom of conscience, and limited political authority—is a valid, but incomplete way of viewing the event. Hutchinson brought into focus questions that bore directly on issues of sexual equality and the role of women, and any consideration of the controversy must also encompass them. There were women among her supporters who recognized in her appeal the possibility for a fundamental change, but that was a revolution that did not happen.

2

Eighteenth-Century Theorists of Women's Liberation

MARGUERITE FISHER

$\mathcal{A}$T a time when the women's liberation movement has gained widespread attention, and its arguments are regularly disseminated throughout the communications media, it is worth noting that almost two centuries ago some of its basic tenets were being expressed by European social theorists. These theorists of the late eighteenth century outlined some of the essential principles of the Age of Reason and Enlightenment. Thus modern feminism first emerged as an integral part of eighteenth-century social and political liberalism, which continued to provide the ideological frame of reference for subsequent feminist activity. In the nineteenth century, the American feminists Elizabeth Cady Stanton, Susan B. Anthony, and Matilda Josyln Gage acknowledged their debt to Revolutionary liberalism in their *History of Woman Suffrage:* not only did they include the names of some eighteenth-century theorists in their dedication of the work, but they generously sprinkled the work itself with quotes and paraphrasing from those who helped frame a feminist intellectual tradition.[1]

1. *The History of Woman Suffrage* (New York: Fowler and Wells, 1891–1922), six volumes of documentary materials on the history of the suffrage movement in the United States, edited by Elizabeth Cady Stanton, Susan B. Anthony, and Matilda Joslyn Gage, was dedicated to the memory of nineteen feminists, including Mary Wollstonecraft, "whose earnest lives and fearless words in demanding political rights for women" had been an inspiration to the editors. Elizabeth Cady Stanton wrote in her diary of the London Anti-Slavery Convention of 1840: "She [Lucretia Mott] had told me . . . of Mary Wollstonecraft, her social theories, and her demands for equality for women," I, 421.

A basic concept of the eighteenth-century philosophy of the Enlightenment was that people were creatures of society, products of their social environment. Education and experience moulded the human personality. The Age of Reason and Enlightenment discarded the notion that the human being came into the world with a predetermined, innate character. Humankind was believed to be capable of indefinite potentialities, if only the prevailing system of society made possible the free and full development of the individual. Advancing upon this premise, a few of the more intrepid eighteenth-century theorists argued that the dependent and supposedly inferior condition of women was due not to predestined and innate nature, but to training and experience.

Eighteenth-century women, brought up to accept the customary subordinate role, were denied a reasonable education but were trained in social artificialities. Wives were regarded in the law as the chattels of their husbands and prohibited from claiming either their own property or their own earnings.[2] They were not even recognized as the equal guardians of their children. The prevailing attitude of society was summarized by that father of revolutionary theory, Rousseau, who said: "The education of women should always be relative to that of men: To please, to be useful to us, to make us love and esteem them, to educate us when young, to take care of us when grown up, to advise, to console us, to render our lives easy and agreeable; these are the duties of women at all times, and what they should be taught in their infancy."[3]

In Europe, the first important voice to be raised in protest against the subjection of women was that of the social and political philosopher, Baron Holbach, a German who became a naturalized French subject and who later was ranked as one of the most prolific writers among the Encyclopaedists. In his *Système Social*, published in 1774, he included a chapter on the status of women. Women throughout the world, he said, were forced to submit to tyranny. The "savage" makes clear his contempt for his mate by his subjection of her and his cruelty toward her. But is it not true, asked Holbach, that the European man is equally contemptuous of women, relying only on more subtle means to mask his true feelings? In an indictment subsequently reaffirmed by nineteenth-century American feminists, Holbach accused men of subordinating women by denying them access to a sensible education, by offering empty flattery

2. See *Blackstone's Commentaries* on the laws of England, first published in 1765: "By marriage the husband and wife are one person in law: that is, the very being or legal existence of the woman is suspended during the marriage, or at least is incorporated and consolidated into that of the husband. Book I, Chapter 15, p. 441.
    3. Rousseau, *Emile* (New York: Appleton, 1901), Book V, p. 105.

for frivolous accomplishments, and by substituting deference for real respect.[4]

In accordance with the eighteenth-century assumption that human beings were the product of social environment, Holbach proposed giving women the opportunity for a better education and doing away with marriages of convenience. He even went so far as to advocate that women should share with men in the tasks of government, after their minds had been emancipated and developed through freedom and education.

Soon after Holbach had dared to apply the fundamental tenets of eighteenth-century theory to women, an Englishman who had emigrated to America indicated that he was thinking along similar lines. Within a year after his arrival in America in 1774, Thomas Paine was settled in Philadelphia and had become the editor of the *Pennsylvania Magazine*. In August 1775, an article entitled "An Occasional Letter on the Female Sex" was published in this periodical. There is some question whether the "Occasional Letter" was actually written by Thomas Paine, the editor, or by a little-known contributor.[5] At any rate, the letter was accepted by the editor as an expression of his own thinking on the subject of the status of women.

Two hundred years after it was written, "An Occasional Letter" still sounds fresh and provocative. Like Holbach, the author of "An Occasional Letter" observed that women everywhere are enslaved, seduced and oppressed by their judges who, "after having prepared their faults, punish every lapse with dishonor." Polygamy in some countries forces women into rivalry with their sisters; indissoluble marriage ties in others often join the "gentle with the rude"; and unjust laws, even in fairly enlightened countries, rob women of freedom of expression. Man historically has been "either an insensible husband or an oppressor." The result, says the author, is that in over three-quarters of the world, women are consigned by nature to a place somewhere between "contempt and misery." They are nothing when they are not loved, and tormented when they are. "Who does not feel for the tender sex?" he asked.[6]

The hopes and aspirations of the Age of Reason and Enlightenment were synthesized at the end of the eighteenth century in the writings of Marie-Jean, Marquis de Condorcet (1743–94). His confidence in humankind, his assumption of an individual's rationality and capacity to create

4. *Système Social* (London, 1974), 3 vols.
5. See the article by Frank Smith, "The Authorship of 'An Occasional Letter on the Female Sex,'" *American Literature* 2(1930):277–80.
6. "An Occasional Letter on the Female Sex," in *The Complete Writings of Thomas Paine*, collected and edited by Philip S. Foner (New York: Citadel Press, 1945), II, 36–37.

a better world, his firm belief in equality and a person's right to self-development, his expectations of social progress—these were reflections of his optimistic faith not only in people but in the future of society.

But while Condorcet's eighteenth-century contemporaries expounded their beliefs in man and his natural right to liberty and equality, most of them did not recognize the claim of females to these same rights of nature. Condorcet was a major exception, however, and he may be justly regarded as one of the fathers of European feminism. He carried the political and social theory of the French Revolutionary period to its logical conclusion and applied its tenets to all men, regardless of social class or color, and to women as well. The societal role of both men and women was to be founded on the freedom of the individual. Condorcet maintained that men and women alike should have the opportunity to live their lives as distinct personalities and to express their innate potentialities in all ways not harmful to society.

The French Revolutionary ideologists argued for a political system based upon popular sovereignty and the right of all men to choose their public officials. Manhood suffrage was provided for in the Constitution of the Year One, which was drawn up by the Convention in 1793 but never put into operation. Condorcet raised his voice in the Convention to support universal suffrage, irrespective of the issue of sex. In two pamphlets—*Lettres d'un Bourgeois de New-Haven a un Citoyen de Virginie* and *Sur l'Admission des Femmes au Droit de Cite*[7]—Condorcet outlined his arguments in favor of woman suffrage. His position was comprehensive and without qualifications, supporting the complete legal and political equality of men and women. His arguments sound today like well-worn platitudes, made familiar in American history by the feminists during their years of organized agitation from 1848 to 1920. In fact the American leaders in the woman suffrage movement in the pre–Civil War period utilized Condorcet's pamphlets, which were brought to America by such European feminists as Frances Wright and Ernestine Rose.[8]

Legal and political equality for women were inherent, in Condorcet's reasoning, in the natural rights philosophy accepted by the revolutionary theorists. "Is it not in their character of sensible beings, capable of reason and with moral ideas, that men have rights?," asked Condorcet. "Women, therefore, should have absolutely the same. . . . Either no in-

7. Found in *Oeuvres Complètes*, edited by A. C. O'Connor and M. F. Arago (Paris, 1847–49), 12 vols.

8. See, for example, the references to Condorcet in Stanton *et al., History of Woman Suffrage*, I, 35; 825–26.

dividual member of the human race has any real rights, or else all have the same; and whoever votes against the rights of another, no matter what his religion, his color or his sex may be has henceforth abjured his own."

Condorcet maintained that not only should women be granted the suffrage but they should also be eligible to hold public office.[9] In answering an argument which became familiar and timeworn during the following century—that the enfranchisement of women would lead to neglect of the home—Condorcet replied with pungent irony that the right to vote would not induce women to forget their homes and families any more than it would lead their farmer and artisan husbands to leave their plows and shops.[10]

In a society in which freedom and equality prevailed, the philosophers contended, men might be expected to develop as free and rational beings concerned with the welfare of humanity. Condorcet applied this same reasoning to women. If women seemed at times less rational and more impulsive than men, this was a product of their social background and education. The customs and expectations of society were predicated on a training and education for women, both formal and informal, that differed from that of men. As a consequence, the behavior of women reflected these environmental differences. Thus, said Condorcet, "It is as reasonable for a woman to be concerned about her physical charms as it was for Demosthenes to be concerned with his voice and gestures."[11]

Condorcet went on to argue that women had the same natural mental capacity as men. Their failure to demonstrate this mental equality in practice was due to lack of opportunity as well as to inferior education. Hence Condorcet advocated equal opportunities for women with men in all grades of education, from the highest to the lowest.[12] In common with modern feminists, he contended that equality in formal education is not sufficient in itself to overcome the subtle psychological effects of a social environment which regarded women as inferior. The development of a woman's innate capacities could be frustrated just as effectively by social attitudes which crushed her belief in herself as by the lack of formal education. "The kind of constraint imposed on women by traditional views regarding manners and morals," said Condorcet, "has influenced their

9. *Sur L'Admission des Femmes au Droit de Cité. Oeuvres Complètes*, X, 122.
10. *Lettres d'un Bourgeois de New Haven à un Citoyen de Virginie. Oeuvres Complètes*, IX, 17–18.
11. *Sur L'Admission des Femmes au Droit de Cité. Oeuvres Complètes*, X, 125.
12. *Sur l'Instruction Publique. Oeuvres Complètes*, VII, 215–16. This work was a report and draft bill on national education, prepared for the Revolutionary Convention in 1792.

mind and soul almost from infancy; and when talent begins to develop, this constraint has the effect of destroying it."[13]

Condorcet's championship of equality for women led him to turn a critical eye on the institution of the family. Divorce, he maintained, should be granted to either husband or wife, after the recommendation of an advisory council consisting of the relatives of both parties. The legal indissolubility of marriage and the prohibition of divorce, he argued, created such social evils as prostitution, illegitimacy, and adultery. Illegitimate children should not be denied their natural rights as citizens. The prevailing laws which stigmatized and deprived the illegitimate of their natural rights had originated in "the class division of society, in the great inequality of wealth, in the system that prevents children from marrying without their parents' consent, and, above all, in the indissolubility of marriage."[14] And it was the practice of birth control, he believed, that was a necessary pre-condition to the emancipation and free development of women and the welfare of children. It was the responsibility of parents to assure the well-being of their children as well as to bring them into the world. Children should not be born into a family or social situation that denied them a fair chance to develop as enlightened and rational beings.

Condorcet entertained liberal views concerning sexual morality as it pertained to women. Individual freedom was to be shared by women as well as men, and women should be free to conduct themselves in all ways not harmful to society. Women, like men, were human beings first and foremost, and their sexual and biological role should be subordinate to their role as citizens in a free society.

Many of Condorcet's contemporaries were shocked by his willingness to extend the French Revolutionary ideology to women. The eighteenth-century intellectuals continued for the most part to share the point of view expressed by Rousseau in his *Emile,* that woman was naturally inferior to man and should be assigned a restricted role as wife and mother.

That was not true, however, for William Godwin, the eighteenth-century English writer who subscribed with enthusiasm to the natural rights theory of the Revolutionary period. His political and social philosophy was founded upon a background of reading in Helvetius and Holbach, Rousseau and Voltaire. Godwin's basic conceptions concerning the nature of humanity and the general world process included a deep regard

13. *Lettres d'un Bourgeois de New Haven à un Citoyen de Virginie. Oeuvres Complètes,* IX, 19.

14. *Esquisse d'un Tableau Historique des Progrès de l'Espirit Humain. Oeuvres Complètes,* VI, 523.

for the intrinsic worth of every human being. His ideal political system assumed the development of the reason latent in all people and the social potentialities inherent in the individual personality.

Godwin's novels, *Caleb Williams* (1794) and *St. Leon* (1799), indicate that he, like Condorcet, was willing to accord to women the rights to freedom and self-development which the Revolutionary philosophy proclaimed for men. His one significant work of political theory, an essay entitled *An Enquiry Concerning the Principles of Political Justice*, first published in 1793, referred indirectly to the status of women. A considerable proportion of the essay is devoted to a discussion of the deleterious effects of existing institutions on human character. Four of the institutions in the contemporary social environment which Godwin condemned with particular vigor were government, law, property, and marriage. Thus marriage was criticized for both men and women, because "it checks the independent progress of the mind." Since marriage entailed the economic dependence of women, he argued, it contributed to their moral perversion. "Marriage," said Godwin "is an affair of property, and the worst of all properties." Marital ties, he believed, were unnatural constraints that inevitably created feelings of hostility by foreclosing the possibility of pursuing individual interests. When a man claimed a woman for his exclusive partner, he denied his neighbor the chance of "proving his superior desert," and created a perpetual jealousy. Godwin thus regarded marriage as "the most odious of all monopolies," which, because of the antagonisms it generated, inhibited social progress and philanthropy. What he proposed as a replacement was a kind of continual renewal of commitment; a relationship would be maintained only as long as both partners agreed to continue the arrangement.[15] Such freedom, he said, would not degenerate into license. Most people would continue to prefer one partner. At any rate, inconsistency was to be preferred to the deceit and intrigue engendered by monopolistic ownership of one person by another.

Godwin's sympathy with feminist emancipation was intensified by his association with Mary Wollstonecraft, whom H. N. Brailsford has called "the one woman of genius who belonged to the English revolutionary circle."[16] Disdaining the legitimate bonds of marriage, Godwin and Wollstonecraft lived together until the imminent birth of their child induced them to bow to convention. They were married in 1797, but tragedy followed soon afterwards. Mary Wollstonecraft died a few days after the

15. *Political Justice* (London: Swan Sonnenschein, 1896), pp. 103–104.
16. H. N. Brailsford, *Shelley, Godwin and Their Circle* (New York: Henry Holt, 1913), p. 147.

birth of her daughter Mary, who was later to become the wife of the poet Shelley.

In 1792, Wollstonecraft had published her famous plea for the recognition of women as creatures of human dignity and rationality, *A Vindication of the Rights of Woman*. In it she argued vigorously for the right of women to participate as equal citizens in society; it was the first systematic exposition of women's rights to come from a woman's pen. The *Vindication* was, in addition, the first work in which a woman dared to analyze the problems of her sex by suggesting that women were, first of all, a part of humanity rather than creatures described only in terms of their sex.

Having been forced to earn her living and help support her family, Mary Wollstonecraft soon learned at first hand the social and economic injustices which were the lot of women unprotected by privileged status. Earning her living by writing and translating, she struggled to achieve economic independence, and in this struggle she forged her arguments against the subjection of women.

Anticipating the insight of later social psychologists, she based the theme of the *Vindication* on the contention that the subjection of women lies in their own attitudes toward themselves, as well as men's attitudes toward them. The eighteenth-century faith in reason and belief in freedom could not logically be denied to women. Women should have the same opportunity as men to develop their minds. Women, she said, have been stripped of virtue and given artificial graces that enable them "to exercise a short-lived tyranny." Since "liberty is the mother of virtue," enslaved women everywhere are forced to "languish like exotics and be reckoned beautiful flaws in nature." Wollstonecraft, somewhat less skeptical about marriage than Godwin, thought that the institution would succeed only if both partners possessed the same educational background and were able to be self-sustaining, enlightened citizens of society.[17]

Mary Wollstonecraft envisioned a perfect companionship of men and women, a relationship founded upon an equality of educational and intellectual opportunity. Such equality also assumed the right to earn a living, which would then give women self-respect and remove them from their degrading dependence upon men.

Thus, in the thinking of Holbach, Paine, Condorcet, Godwin, and Mary Wollstonecraft, the eighteenth-century concern for the intrinsic worth of the individual and the right to self-development was extended to women. Progress toward the ideal of a democratic society, these writers maintained, was to be accompanied by the social and political emancipa-

17. *A Vindication of the Rights of Woman* (London: Walter Scott, 1891), p. 78.

tion of women. No artificial barriers of sex were to deny one half of humanity the benefits of freedom and equality on which the new society was to be founded. The reasoning of these eighteenth-century theorists furnished inspiration and argument for later American feminists who freely acknowledged their debt to their predecessors, in particular to Condorcet, Paine, and Mary Wollstonecraft. All social movements are typically indebted to an earlier generation of thinkers; in the case of American feminism, it would be difficult to imagine its growth and development without the infusion of Revolutionary political and social liberalism. American Puritanism also influenced the direction of feminism, but it posed a confusing contradiction for women: supporting the equality of all people before God, it served as a socially powerful restraining force against the desires of women to act on the basis of the promise it affirmed. There were no similar hobbles attached to Enlightenment feminism; the practices it proposed were consistent with the theory it espoused. It is not surprising, therefore, that nineteenth-century American feminists quoted more liberally from their European ancestors than from their American ones.

3

The Puritan Ethic in The Revolutionary Era:
Abigail Adams and Thomas Jefferson

RALPH KETCHAM

$\mathcal{A}$BIGAIL ADAMS was the quintessential Puritan—purposeful, pietistic, passionate, prudish, frugal, diligent, courageous, well-educated, and self-righteous. Thomas Jefferson, on the other hand, was the quintessential Enlightenment Man—reasonable, serene, restrained, optimistic, urbane, tolerant, learned, many-sided, and self-possessed. In studies of early American history these "types" are often set in opposition to each other; that is, one flourished especially in the seventeenth century and in New England while the other flowered forth in such eighteenth-century secular figures as Franklin, Jefferson, and Madison. Furthermore, the dynamic of colonial history has often been pictured as a "progression" from a narrow-minded, intolerant, guilt-ridden, Puritanism to a more liberal, expansive Age of Reason that happily dominated the American Revolution and introduced the new nation into a more modern era. Though this view is seldom offered by scholars in a straightforward or simple way today, it still infuses much popular and textbook understandings and is still commonly the point from which even rather serious students begin an intensive search for the meaning of our early history. In fact, of course, many Puritans revered reason, and the Enlightenment developed its own dogma and vision of a "Heavenly City." Also, as Franklin showed in moving from a Puritan childhood to a "free-thinking" maturity while retaining a serious attitude toward life, the two world views shared much more than is apparent if one attends only to the theological polemics that divided Calvinists and Arminians. The relationship between Abigail Adams and Thomas Jefferson reveals much of the ambiguity, complexity, and, in the end, essential agreement between the spirit of Old South Church, Boston, and that of Independence Hall.

Abigail Adams, granddaughter of wealthy, influential Colonel John Quincy, daughter of the Reverend William Smith, wife of a signer of the Declaration of Independence, and mother of the premier diplomat of the first seventy years of our national history, was certainly the leading woman of the American Revolution. And, surely, if her letters and the influence she had on others are any indication, and if women had been allowed an equal place in public life in her day, she would herself have been among the greatest of the "founding parents." Some wag has observed that the Adams family, though it had been in the New World since the 1630s, never amounted to anything until a then obscure John married Abigail Smith in 1764.

She had by inheritance all the advantages a century-old Puritan culture in New England could provide. Through her maternal grandparents, John and Elizabeth Norton Quincy, she knew the grace, self-esteem, and sense of authority of the first families of Massachusetts Bay. In their manor house, Mount Wollaston, overlooking Boston Bay, young Abigail spent her summers responding to the wit and humor of her grandmother and absorbing from her grandfather his sense for politics. She loved his fine library and read with him from Plato's *Republic*, More's *Utopia*, and Locke's *Essay Concerning Human Understanding*. Though as a woman there could be no thought of Abigail's receiving a formal education, adults around her who saw her bright and inquisitive mind encouraged her to enlarge and refine it as a priceless gift from God.

Her father, earnest and learned, also encouraged Abigail to learn by using his own considerable library filled with works of the ancient authors as well as books on the ethics and divinity of the eighteenth century. By joining Charles Chauncy to oppose Jonathan Edwards and the tumults of the Great Awakening, the Reverend Smith showed himself to be part of the strong Puritan strain following John Wise and others into the Age of Reason. Eventually this theological leaning found institutional expression in the transformation of many Congregational churches into Unitarian Societies, including the Church in Braintree, Massachusetts, attended by John and Abigail Adams. Puritans of this persuasion found no incongruity between their ancient faith and the dictates of reason. Rather, they saw logic and rationality and the harmony of nature as strong evidence of the workings of Providence in the world. By accepting this version of Puritanism, then, Abigail Adams was able to retain the ways and habits of her forebears without feeling in the least that she had to "set faith over reason" or in any other way resist all she could learn from the new books surrounding her.

In fact, as she read eagerly and sharpened her mind in a bright and learned family circle, Abigail came honestly and forthrightly to opinions that left her ready for revolution. Furthermore, in meeting and marrying John Adams, she found a kindred spirit who not only was attracted by the intellectual qualities already evident in Abigail, but who rejoiced that his wife continued to grow in learning, in insight, and in solid conviction. Their correspondence was always that of intellectual equals exploring each other's minds earnestly, joyfully, and critically. One of their court-ship games was to each ask the other for "a Catalogue of Faults." With mock seriousness John upbraided Abigail for her "Habit of Reading, Writing and Thinking" and her way of "sitting with the Leggs across" which, John supposed, was caused by her "fault" of doing "too much thinking." In reply Abigail observed that while "a gentleman has no busi-ness to concern himself about the Leggs of a Lady," she intended to persist in her faults "at least till I am convinced that an alteration of them would contribute to" the happiness of her husband-to-be.[1]

In 1764 Abigail Smith and John Adams began a marriage that lasted fifty-four years. A portrait of Abigail taken two years after her marriage at age twenty-two shows her as a bright, serious woman with dark eyes, a straight nose, and small mouth that make her a strikingly handsome woman—an impression sustained in portraits taken both twenty and fifty years later. The marriage produced five children in eight years, the first a daughter (another daughter died in infancy) and then three sons, all of whom lived to maturity and had numerous children themselves. To a degree remarkable in the eighteenth century John and Abigail shared in the rearing of their children. John took a deep interest in their day-to-day growth and Abigail helped (and in John's long absences from home en-tirely managed) their intellectual development. Their way seems to have been moderately strict without being overbearing or unloving, but most apparent was the high expectations they had for their children. Each in-sisted upon diligence, industry, piety, study, uprightness, and growth in wisdom. The Adams children were taught that life was serious, that they must excel in all they did, and that people were given talents to use for the glory of God and the benefit of the human race. The Puritan ethic undergirded Adams family life from start to finish.

Though Abigail accepted the traditional roles of helpmate, keeper of the home, rearer of children, and supporter of her husband's career, she

---

1. John Adams (hereafter JA) to Abigail Adams (hereafter AA), May 7, 1764, and AA to JA, May 9, 1764; L. H. Butterfield et al., Adams Family Correspondence, 2 vols. (Cambridge: Harvard University Press, 1963), I, 44–47; all correspondence between these two is taken from these volumes and will be identified in the text by date.

did so with a fullness and independence far beyond the convention of the day—one Boston area squire, for example, thought "girls knew quite enough if they could make a skirt and a pudding." On August 14, 1776, a month after the Declaration of Independence, Abigail lamented that "the poorer sort of children [in Braintree] are wholly neglected, and left to range the streets without schools, without business, given up to all Evil." But, she added "if you complain of the neglect of Education in sons, what shall I say with regard to daughters who every day experience the want of it." She hoped, therefore, that the new Constitution of Massachusetts would provide a "liberal plan" to encourage "Learning and Virtue" in *all* children. "If we mean to have Heroes, Statesmen and Philosophers" to sustain republican government, Abigail insisted, "we should have learned women. . . . If much depends as is allowed upon the early education of youth and the first principals which are instilled take the deepest root, great benefit must arise from literary accomplishments in women." John responded on August 25 that Abigail's sentiments "are exactly agreeable to my own."

If this expressed in part the old nostrum about "what a boy learns at his mother's knee," Abigail added enormously to its conventional content. In 1774, for example, while John attended the First Continental Congress, Abigail read books on history and politics, posing for her husband the question: "did ever any Kingdom or State regain their Liberty, when once it was invaded, without Blood shed?" She corresponded with another mind-honing New England female, Mercy Otis Warren, about the lessons one could learn from the tribulations of Sparta, Macedon, and Rome. Abigail developed such "a very great fondness" she reported, for Charles Rollins' *The Ancient History*, which dramatized the classical heroes, that she "perswaided Johnny to read me a page or two every day, and hope he will from his desire to oblige me entertain a fondness for it." Johnny, of course, was seven-year-old John Quincy Adams who by this time had not only learned from his mother to read and write, but had also begun the study of the ancient languages with her. As John and Abigail Adams thought about education, they made no distinction whatever between men and women on topics to study, the capacity to understand, and the benefit to socity of a thorough education. In fact, their life-long friendship with Mercy Otis Warren, despite strenuous disagreements over the nature of the American Revolution, manifested their respect for keenness of mind in both sexes. Abigail took a special pleasure in correspondence with this exceedingly intelligent woman.

Jefferson lacked the constant companionship of a brilliant Abigail to make a sense of female equality commonplace, and he lived in a society more acquiescent in the view of women as empty-headed adornments. He confessed late in life, too, that "a plan of female education has never been a subject of systematic contemplation with me," and his own proposals for the University of Virginia made no provision for women (but probably because he knew such an inclusion would vastly increase the always strong political opposition to the University as a whole, rather than because he himself would not have wanted it).

His assumptions about human nature and his education of his own daughters, furthermore, leave little doubt that he welcomed and encouraged female accomplishment. His inclination to think highly of human capacities and the critical need for such capacities in his overall social philosophy eventually even eroded his deep prejudices about black inferiority. The much less degraded condition of the females around him enabled his empirical mind to accept more quickly female equality. He insisted in France that his daughter Martha attend a school of high standards and that she cultivate "music, drawing, books, invention, and exercise [as] so many resources to you against ennui," and learn to sew and keep house. But she was also to study Latin, history, natural philosophy, and other basics in "male" education so that she might fully develop her faculties and would be able to properly educate her children should her husband be unable to do so—and Martha did in fact participate importantly in the schooling of her dozen children when their father proved too unstable to help much. Jefferson's faith in human potential and Abigail Adams' puritan horror at the waste of talents each resulted in unusual disdain for discriminatory education or for female repression.[2]

Though Jefferson's enlightened views left him clear on the moral injustice of slavery, its deep roots in Virginia society, and his acquiescence in the conventions of gentry life, kept him from ever doing anything effective about slavery and left him unable to conceive of blacks as equal members of society. Abigail, on the other hand, reared in more egalitarian New England, saw more quickly and more profoundly the incongruity of both slavery and racial oppression in revolutionary America. She wrote to John Adams on September 22, 1774, that she wished "most sincerely there was not a slave in the province. It always appeared a most iniquitous scheme to me—fight ourselfs for what we are daily robbing and plundering from *those who have as good a right to freedom as*

2. Thomas Jefferson (hereafter TJ) to Nathaniel Burwell, March 14, 1818; Adrienne Koch and William Peden, eds., *The Life and Selected Writings of Thomas Jefferson* (New York: Modern Library, 1944); all correspondence between Jefferson and persons other than JA or AA is taken from this volume and will be identified in the text by date.

we have" (italics added). "You know my mind upon this subject," she continued to her husband, probably shedding intense light on both the topics and dynamics of countless earnest conversations.

Less than a month before her husband's inauguration as president, Abigail showed she retained her revolutionary ideals and also had a keen sense of how to nourish them amid compromising prejudices. She had sent a black servant boy (kept in her house on the same sort of apprentice basis, probably, as her white servants) to the local Quincy primary school. A neighor came by anxiously asking Abigail to withdraw the lad lest the school fold up because other parents objected to a Negro being in school with their children. "Pray" Abigail asked him, "has the boy misbehaved?" No, the embarrassed neighbor replied, it was just. . . . He added that *he* had no objection, it was the others. Abigail asked why "they" didn't come to complain themselves. She went on to lecture that his request "is attacking the principle of liberty and equality upon the only grounds upon which it ought to be supported, an equality of rights." Her servant's black face should be no barrier to education, she insisted, since he had as much right and need to earn a living as any white person. As the discomfitted neighbor left the house Abigail called after him to send the squeamish people to her if they muttered any more about blacks, and added that she hoped "we shall all go to heaven together."[3] Understanding the Puritan requirement that every human being become all he or she could for the glory of God, and offended at blatant oppression of any group—perhaps especially because she felt the sting of prejudice against women—Abigail Adams believed that the principles of the American Revolution held for all people. Neither the Puritan ethic as she lived it day by day nor the new Enlightenment creed she learned reading into the night left room for discrimination and slavery.

Abigail Adams and Thomas Jefferson met rather accidently for the first time in Boston in 1784 as each made ready to embark for Europe. Prepared by John Adams to like and respect each other, they were unable to arrange passage on the same ship, but they eagerly made plans to meet in Europe. In Paris, as Jefferson and John Adams attended to their diplomatic business, the families often dined or traveled together and developed strong bonds of affection. Abigail mothered twelve-year-old Patsy Jefferson, and Jefferson admired and instructed handsome, brilliant John Quincy Adams. After nine months, when the Adamses left for London, Abigail wrote Jefferson she was "loth . . . to leave behind me the

3. AA to JA, Feb. 13, 1797; quoted in Page Smith, *John Adams*, 2 vols. (New York: Doubleday, 1962), II, 926.

only person with whom my companion could associate with perfect freedom, and unreserve." Jefferson replied simply that "the departure of your family has left me in the dumps." Abigail told her sister that Jefferson was "one of the choice ones of the earth."[4] It was perfectly clear, after a year of closeness, that the Virginia diplomat and the New England lady had discovered they were kindred spirits.

The personal ties strengthened further when nine-year-old Polly Jefferson, attended only by a slave girl, arrived in London after a lonely, frightening voyage from Virginia. Abigail at once took over, kindly caring for Polly and quickly coming to love the girl. Abigail wrote Jefferson that Polly was "a child of the quickest sensibility, and the maturest understanding I have ever met with for her years." After two days under Abigail's care, Polly "was restored to the amiable lovely child which her aunt [in Virginia] had formed her, . . . [and] she was the favorite of every creature in the [Adams] house." With a thoroughness and precision that could only have delighted Jefferson, Abigail had both Polly and her servant properly outfitted, and sent Jefferson a detailed account of the expenses. Characteristically, before Jefferson reimbursed Abigail, he checked her arithmetic and discovered that Abigail had cheated herself by more than a pound. Abigail, perhaps eager to give Polly the same intellectual stimulation she had craved as a child, furnished Polly books "out of a little library," which the youngster "reads to me by the hour with great distinctness, and comments on what she reads with much propriety."[5] Made secure and buoyed in self-esteem by the kind, loving family, Polly was able to bear another journey with a strange servant to join her father in Paris.

What had happened, of course, is that Abigail Adams and Jefferson had discovered they shared the deepest and most profound values: those of personal relationships, family matters, habits of life, and day-to-day morality. Jefferson revealed his intense devotion to the pattern (properly called the Puritan ethic even though many who subscribed to it were not formally Puritans) in his letters to Patsy about her education. Her future happiness, the father wrote, depended upon "contracting a habit of industry and activity" while she was young. "Of all the cankers of human happiness none corrodes with so silent, yet so baneful a tooth, as indolence. . . . Exercise and application produce order in our affairs, health of body,

4. AA to TJ, June 6, 1785, and TJ to AA, June 21, 1785; AA to Mrs. Richard Cranch, 1785; L. J. Cappon, ed., *The Adams-Jefferson Letters*, 2 vols. (Chapel Hill: University of North Carolina Press, 1959), I, 28, 33, 14.

5. AA to TJ, June 27, 28, July 6, 10, 1787, and TJ to AA, July 1, 10, 16, 1787; *ibid.*, I, 178–88.

cheerfulness of mind, and these make us precious to our friends," he added.[6] John or Abigail Adams could surely have written that letter, or, as Edmund Morgan has remarked, so could Cotton Mather. Valuing much the same things in the most important relationships in life, it was easy for Jefferson and Abigail Adams to respond warmly to each other as human beings.

As intellectuals concerned with issues far beyond those of family and child-rearing, though, the two Americans readily exchanged views on the public events transpiring around them. They had first to understand and reflect upon the people and cultures of the two great nations to which they had come. Surprisingly, in view of Jefferson's reputation as a Francophile and Abigail's as an Anglophile, their overall reactions to the two countries, as they exchanged visits and letters during the years 1784–1788, were much the same. Like most people with entree to aristocratic circles in France, Jefferson and Abigail were awed and thrilled at the splendor of the arts and the grace and amiability of society. "The roughness of the human mind is so thoroughly rubbed off with [the French], that it seems as if one might glide through a whole life among them without a jostle," Jefferson wrote an American friend. He was also pleased at the "little sacrifices of self, which really render European [i.e., French] manners amiable, and relieve society from the disagreeable scenes to which rudeness often subjects it. In the pleasures of the table, they are far before us, because with good taste they unite temperance. They do not terminate the most sociable meals by transforming themselves into brutes."[7] Altogether there was an ease and artfulness and gaiety in human relationships in Parisian society that entirely delighted both the Adamses and the Jeffersons.

Upperclass life in England reflected some of the splendor and politeness of that in France, but two further qualities distinguished it. The English countryside was more prosperous, more tidy, and better regulated than that of France, and was thus peculiarly pleasing to people with Puritan propensities. Abigail and Jefferson also liked the solid, elegant, disciplined feeling of London, as compared to the disordered and im-

6. TJ to Martha Jefferson, March 28, 1787, *Selected Writings*, p. 17; E. S. Morgan, "The Puritan Ethic and the American Revolution," *William and Mary Quarterly* 24(1967):7. In this chapter I use the term "Puritan Ethic" as Morgan defines it in this article: the pattern of values woven together most cogently by the Puritans of New England but widely accepted as well by many Anglicans, Presbyterians, deists, and others, that derived from the Reformed (Puritan, Calvinist) religious movements of the sixteenth and seventeenth centuries but which in the eighteenth century had become for many people principally an "ethic" to guide everyday life.

7. TJ to Eliza Trist, Aug. 18, 1785, and to Charles Bellini, Sept. 30, 1785; *Selected Writings*, pp. 372, 383.

poverished appearance of so much of France. On the other hand, a certain harshness, coldness, and arrogance so infused the very air of Britain, it seemed, that life there simply lacked *amiability*, a word both Americans used again and again in trying to capture the essence of their fascination with France. They noted, for example, that the stern discipline imposed in English schools, and the violent reaction against it, perhaps to be expected in training soldiers or haughty officials, hardly improved the grace of English society. "The peculiarities of English education," Jefferson observed scornfully, were such that school boys learned mainly "drinking, horse-racing, and boxing."[8]

Abigail and Jefferson also thought the life of the common people in England, though poor in comparison to yeoman and artisan life in America, was vastly better than the degraded life of the peasants and urban poor of France. They ascribed the superior conditions in England to less oppressive government and better common morality than prevailed in France. "Of twenty millions of people supposed to be in France," Jefferson wrote, "I am of opinion there are nineteen millions more wretched, more accursed in every circumstance of human existence than the most conspicuously wretched individual of the whole United States."[9] Furthermore, the same dreadful government that degraded the common people of France also poisoned the aristocracy, when one looked below the gay and glittering surface. Infidelity, deception, degeneracy, foppery, waste, and indolence abounded everywhere, arousing Abigail's horror and scorn, and Jefferson's disgust.

A kind of balanced and revealing evaluation emerges, then, from the traumatic exposure to French and English society. Regarding France, its refinements and grace could by no means redeem the the oppression, poverty, and moral decay. England, on the other hand, seemed chained to a sternness and arrogance required by its military pre-eminence and perhaps even by its economic progress. These ironies and paradoxes posed serious problems for the observant Americans. As for the French, Jefferson counselled one time "nourish peace with their persons, but war against their manners;" that is, admire their skill in human relations, but avoid their customs and their immorality. But neither French elegance or English power could compensate for the attendant evils and make the Old World seem preferable to the New. "I am really surfeited with Europe," Abigail wrote after eighteen months in Paris and London, "and most heartily long for the rural cottage, the purer and honester manners of my native land, where domestic happiness reigns unrivalled, and vir-

8. TJ to J. Bannister, Jr., Oct. 15, 1785, *ibid.*, p. 386.
9. TJ to Eliza Trist, Aug. 18, 1785; *ibid.*, p. 372.

tue and honor go hand in hand." Jefferson made the same point when he observed that "an American, coming to Europe for education, loses in his knowledge, in his morals, in his health, in his habits, and in his happiness."[10]

These reactions, of course, are exactly what one would expect of so-journers who had built the Puritan ethic into their sense of revolutionary purpose as Abigail Adams and Thomas Jefferson had done. This ethic was for them the basic substance of the "national character" they saw in America and which was necessary to replace the British character from which they had declared themselves independent in 1776. They sensed strongly, furthermore, that *statements* of national purpose and *frames* of government were mere skeletons—a full, vital nationhood might grow on them, but for that to happen a pattern of values, habits, and attitudes guiding everyday life would have to emerge. It was this pattern, grounded for both Abigail Adams and Jefferson in substantial measure on the Puritan ethic, that they came to sense so much more strongly as they saw the contrasts of the "alien" cultures of France and England. As Franklin, Crèvecoeur, and others were also observing during the 1780s, American republican principles made it impossible for the new United States to define itself in terms of the accomplishments and high life of the aristocracy as nations had traditionally done. Rather, if America had any distinctive meaning or character, it was to be found in the situation and way of life of its common people. It was at this level, of course, that Abigail Adams and Jefferson came to see the starkest contrast between the Old and the New Worlds, and came most to admire the "purer and honester" ways they saw, or at least *hoped* to see, in the American countryside.

The Puritanism of Abigail Adams and Jefferson manifested itself somewhat differently as each responded to the tumults caused in Massachusetts by yet another Puritan, Daniel Shays. John Adams himself rather surprisingly set the tone of discussion as he received the first reports. "Don't be alarmed at the late turbulence in New England" he wrote Jefferson on November 30, 1786. "The Massachusetts Assembly had, in its Zeal to get the better of their Debt, laid on a Tax, rather heavier than the people could bear; but all will be well, and this commotion will terminate in additional Strength to Government." By this he meant not strength achieved through suppression, but a greater firmness in the public councils as governors and governed came better to understand the needs of each other. Jefferson received this evaluation optimistically, glad for his part, he replied on December 21, to see "the people

10. AA to TJ, Feb. 11, 1786, *A–J Letters*, I, 119; subsequent correspondence between AA and TJ is from these volumes and is identified in the text by date. TJ to J. Bannister, Jr., Oct. 15, 1785, *Selected Writings*, p. 387.

awake and alert." Their "good sense," he was sure, would "lead them back, if they have erred in a moment of surprise." Abigail's next letter to Jefferson, on January 29, 1787, revealed the darker side of her Puritan nature: the rebellion had been "carried to so alarming a Height as to stop the Courts of Justice in several Counties. Ignorant, wrestless desperadoes, without conscience or principles, have led a deluded multitude to follow their standard, under pretense of grievances which have no existence but in their imaginations." She was horrified at their demands for paper money, equal distribution of property, canceling of debts, and abolition of the State Senate. Rebellious as Abigail was in some ways, her sense of human weakness and of the need for order in human society gave her, like an eighteenth-century John Winthrop, grave misgivings about the likes of Daniel Shays. It was not the watchful spirit of liberty that guided the rebels, she informed Jefferson. Rather, the "mobish insurgents are sapping the foundation, and destroying the whole fabrick at once." She was confident, nonetheless, that "these people make only a small part of the state," and that the trouble might "prove sallutary . . . by leading to an investigation of the causes which have produced these commotions." "Luxury and extravagance" among the rich had led to debts they couldn't discharge. The unwise tax passed by the legislature laid too heavily on small landholders, while the wasteful rich refused to lend money to a government they feared would repudiate its debts. The signs of decadence and immorality so dangerous in independent Massachusetts in 1786 were, to Puritans like Abigail, exactly the same qualities, rampant among British office-holders in America before the Revolution, that had led to the rupture of 1776. But Abigail hoped this new round of selfishness, waste, distrust, and exploitation would be corrected by good sense among the people and a responsiveness in the government.

Jefferson's reply on February 22 overlooked Abigail's forebodings and anxiety for order to emphasize the virtues of rebellion, which he likened to "a storm in the atmosphere." He hoped the rebels would be captured but then pardoned (Abigail had supposed the leaders would be made examples of) because he thought "the spirit of resistance to government is so valuable on certain occasions, that I wish it to be always kept alive. It will often be exercised when wrong, but better so than not to be exercised at all." The exchange, of course, reveals no simple case of Abigail Adams, the stern New Englander, petrified with fear of mobs and disorder and determined to maintain order even if that required suppression, and Jefferson, the liberal Enlightenment man, serenely countenancing the spirit of revolution. Each admired, indeed insisted upon resistance to injustice and oppression (as had Puritans since their earliest struggles in sixteenth century England), and each was fully aware of the benefits of peace and order in society—surely no one more valued those qualities than the supremely methodical and civilized master of Monticello. In reacting as they did to Shays' rebellion they in fact defined the limits of the amalgam of puritan and Enlightenment ethos that ungirded American revolutionary thought. In a paradoxically English combination, Abigail Adams and Thomas Jefferson added to a sober, serious, viligant, morally earnest puritanism, a more tolerant, more serene, more liberal neoclassic view inherent in the earlier, English phase of the Enlightenment. They sought, following Joseph Addison, to have puritan moral zeal without its fanaticism and to have Restoration wit and elegance without its degeneracy. This *combining* of outlooks, tempering rather than repudiating the Puritan ethic, furnished the pattern of habits and values needed to give life to the frames of government fashioned in the United States between 1776 and 1789—and *both* Abigail Adams and Thomas Jefferson embodied the outlook.

A final revelation of the workings of these two remarkable minds occurred in 1804, following the bitter political wars that had divided the Adams and Jefferson families. Mary Jefferson Eppes, the nine-year-old Polly whom Abigail had so loved in London in 1787, died at Monticello after a lingering illness on April 17, 1804, at the age of twenty-five. Knowing the president's feeling for this beloved daughter, and unable despite the bitterness left over from the election of 1800 to be silent in the presence of her own grief, Abigail Adams took pen in hand to console her former friend. "Powerful feelings of my heart," she wrote Jefferson on May 20, "have burst through the restraint [of public differences], and called upon me to shed the tear of sorrow over the departed remains of your beloved and deserving daughter, an event which I most sincerely mourn. The attachment which I formed for her, when you committed her to my care upon her arrival in a foreign land, has remained with me to this hour." Thinking of the death of her son Charles in 1800, Abigail added that she knew "how closely entwined around a parent's heart, are those chords which bind the filial to the parental Bosom, and when snapped asunder, how agonizing the pangs of separation." She acknowledged the ill-will separating the families only by noting Jefferson's public office and "reasons of various kinds" that had kept her from writing. She concluded ambiguously with "sincere and ardent" wishes from one "who once took pleasure in subscribing Herself your Friend."

Jefferson wrote back politely on June 13, 1804, appreciating Abigail's condolences and recalling "with gratitude and friendship" the kindnesses to little Polly. Then he opened himself about their former relationship, remembering it fondly and stating he had no personal reason for any change of feeling. His private affections, he added, were not changed by differences in political philosophy or even in public policy because "each party [was] conscious they were the result of an honest conviction in the other." Then, in a note of rancor in an otherwise entirely gracious letter, Jefferson could not resist mentioning "one act of Mr. Adams' life, and one only, [that] ever gave me a moment's personal displeasure. I did consider his last appointments to office as personally unkind." Those appointments of my "most ardent political enemies," Jefferson complained, robbed him of loyal colleagues and placed on him the "odium" of extensive removals from office. "Common justice," Jefferson thought, demanded that he be "free to act by instruments of [my] own choice." Jefferson declared, however, that he had long "cordially" forgiven John Adams and that his personal feeling toward both the Adamses was once again as it had been in Europe in the 1780s.

Abigail, of course, was insulted at the charge her husband had been "personally unkind" and at Jefferson's presumption in "forgiving." In a letter of July 1 she defended John Adams's midnight appointments, upbraided Jefferson for "public approbation" of the wretched James Callender who had written "the basest libel, the lowest and vilest Slander, which malice could invent, or calumny exhibit against the character and reputation of your predecessor," and complained bitterly that Jefferson had even removed John Quincy Adams from his office as Commissioner of Bankruptcy in Boston. Not content to argue particular grievances, though, Abigail tackled Jefferson on basic questions of republican government. The President, she felt, betrayed his high office when he "gave countenance to a base calumniater" because he was accountable "for the influence which his example has upon the manners and morals of the community. . . . When such vipers [as Callender] are let loose upon Society, all distinction between virtue and vice are levelled, all respect for character is lost in the overwhelming deluge of calumny—that respect which is a necessary bond in the social union, which gives efficacy to the laws, and teaches the subject to obey the Majestrate, and the child to submit to the parent."

In reply on July 22, Jefferson tactfully and satisfactorily explained the personal misunderstandings, but he also took up the challenge on sedition and free speech. "I discharged every person under punishment or prosecution under the Sedition law, because I considered and now consider that law to be a nullity as absolute and palpable as if Congress had ordered us to fall down and worship a golden image." His oath to protect the Constitution, he insisted, required that he relieve everyone, including even such an unworthy person as Callender, whose rights had been "violated by an unauthorized act of Congress." This only further aroused the sterner side of Abigail's Puritan nature, as she revealed in her letter of August 18, 1804: "If a Chief Majestrate can by his will annul a Law, where is the difference between a republican, and a despotic Government?" she retorted. If there were "no checks to be resorted to in the Laws of the Land" against calumny and slander, soon "truth and falsehood [would] lie in one undistinguished heap." Then each man would have to become "the judge and avenger of his own wrongs, and as in a late instance [the Burr-Hamilton duel], the sword and pistol [would have to] decide the contest." In such a society "all the Christian and social virtues will be banished the Land. All that makes life desirable, and softens the ferocious passions of man will assume a savage deportment, and like Cain of old, every Man's hand will be against his Neighbour." To Abigail, the bonds of society and the need to positively encourage virtue, order, and stability entirely justified laws restraining iniquity.

Both parties realized by this stage, of course, that they had trespassed so far into deeply decisive political questions that they had hindered rather than hastened the repair of their personal relations. Yet neither could desist. Jefferson responded on September 11 to Abigail's charge of executive despotism with one of judicial tyranny should the courts have an exclusive power to determine the constitutionality of laws. He upheld the Republican idea of "co-ordinate" responsibility in all branches of the government to assess constitutionality. Furthermore, though he agreed with Abigail on the need to restrain "the overwhelming torrent of slander which is confounding all vice and virtue, all truth and falsehood in the U. S.," he insisted that the Constitution gave the States, not the Federal Government, this responsibility. Abigail fired back one final retort on October 25: "I cannot agree, in opinion, that the Constitution ever meant to withhold from the National Government the power of self defence, or that it could be considered an infringement of the liberty of the press, to punish the licentiousness of it." She then asked that the correspondence be terminated, and Jefferson acquiesced.

At one point in the exchange, in an effort to make the dispute a merely theoretical one, Jefferson had observed that the "honest portion" of each political party in the United States had "the same object, the public good: but they differ essentially in what they deem the means of promoting that good. . . . One fears most the ignorance of the people: the other the selfishness of rulers independent of them." In so putting the issue Jefferson did, of course, properly identify a difference in emphasis between the parties and likely between Abigail and himself as well, but more importantly he revealed his acceptance of centuries-old axioms of classical and Puritan political thought. "The public good" was preeminent and included substantive notions, as Abigail had put it, of "all the Christian and social virtues . . . that make life desirable." There was, for all practical purposes at least, a definable, absolute idea of "the good society" embodying ideas of morality and everyday life that found its fullest expression, in the Anglo-American world in the seventeenth and eighteenth centuries, in what we have called the Puritan ethic. This good life, however, did not arise spontaneously in nature, nor was it inherent in humanity. Rather, it required both steady nourishment of virtue-building institutions (as much a mania with Jefferson as with John Winthrop) and skillful guardianship against the corruptions of human nature whether in the people at large or in those who held political power.

Demonology fills the social thought of both Abigail Adams and Thomas Jefferson. The New Englander feared an unhinged public unsupported by vital schools and churches and led astray by slandering editors and unscrupulous demagogues. In such a society, life would scarcely be worth living, and that was exactly what she saw being encouraged by the libertarian doctrines of Benjamin Bache, James Callender, and other radical Republican editors in 1798. The Virginian, on the other hand, feared an uneducated, rootless proletariat, accumulating in vast, sinful cities, that would either be bamboozled and enslaved by priests, princes, and other pettifoggers, or be enlisted by a Caesar or a Robespierre in campaigns of fanaticism or aggrandizement. Either horror subverted his cherished ideal of the yeoman republic.

To their strong sense of the good society and the dangers to it of febrile institutions and a corrupted public, both Abigail Adams and Jefferson added the revolutionists' determined zeal to resist tyranny—something as utterly unbearable to the Puritan as to the Enlightenment philosopher. Each accepted the obligation, despite the hazards to order and stability in society, of steady, lawful opposition to oppression as long as that seemed effective, and finally of armed rebellion. Neither valued the status quo for its own sake, nor would either flinch from the challenge vice and tyranny raised before them.

Abigail's position is perhaps best seen in her enthusiastic endorsement of her husband's signature on both the Declaration of Independence and the Alien and Sedition Acts. Far from being inconsistent or even paradoxical, Abigail would have seen them as two sides of the coin of good government. The Declaration of Independence was proper and necessary because, she was sure, Britain intended to fasten upon America the same sort of corrupt, unresponsive government George III and his ministers conducted in London. Under such a system, the growth, freedom, and virtue Abigail valued would be destroyed. After independence and the establishment of stable, republican governments, however, the chief concern was not of external tyranny but of social malignancy at home. It was as necessary and proper to take action against one as against the other. Girding one's self in 1798 was no less needful than in 1776. Abigail Adams saw no need to apologize for a law that aimed directly at slanderers and calumniators—they were undermining the rational discourse vital to republican government, destroying public morality, and perhaps even rendering the federal government defenseless against its enemies. It would be naive and faint-hearted not to act against such threats. In yet another era, one feels sure Abigail would have approved her son's defiance of the slaveholders in Congress, and would even have admired William Lloyd Garrison's fiery denunciations of slavery—and of course esteemed his defense of women's rights. She always responded favorably to courageous assaults on evil.

Jefferson agreed with a surprising amount of this view, as his libertarian critics have pointed out. He valued rational discourse, public morality, and stable government as much as did Abigail Adams. His tirades against the vituperative press and his measured support of *state* action against "libellers" do indeed mark him as not in the school of J. S. Mill and Justice Holmes with regard to freedom of expression. As a practical matter, though, he felt that, especially as the public improved in education and sophistication, its critical judgment was a sufficient antidote to licentiousness, and that the almost certain abuses of any laws abridging freedom of expression were so palpable that they were to be avoided as the plague. He took virtue as seriously as Abigail Adams, but, as his remark about the difference between the parties shows, he emphasized the dangers to it from abusive rulers at a time when Abigail saw the main threats from public confusion and social disarray.

What one finds, then, in a comparative view of Abigail Adams and Thomas Jefferson is a richer and more complex sense of the underlying values of the American Revolution than is evident in the interpretation that places them in opposite positions or in a preoccupation with the formal statements of purpose and frames of government. Their deep agreement on the validity of the Puritan ethic in large measure accounts for the warmth of their personal friendship and is also a critical part of their concern for the emergence of an American national character. To each, mere independence was but the barest beginning. New governments meant nothing unless they were used to encourage the attitudes and habits of life implicit in the Puritan ethic. The difference in emphasis between them—principally on the degree of government direction or even compulsion useful in sustaining public virtue—arose not from a basic polarity in their world views but from Abigail's use of Enlightenment confidence in freedom and openness to temper her basic Puritan righteousness and sense of social cohesion, and Jefferson's continuing acceptance of Puritan habits even as he absorbed the faith of the Age of Reason. They combined the same streams of thought, but in different measure. To see how much each accepted of the outlook conventionally associated with the other, we need recall only Abigail's worship for the last thirty years of her life in a church that had become Unitarian, and Jefferson's Calvinist injunction to his daughter, "if at any moment, my dear, you catch yourself in idleness, start from it as you would from the precipice of a gulf."[11] The American Revolution in this view, then, found its intellectual dynamic in the meeting of the Puritan and Enlightenment world views, often in the same person. Moreover, the first manifestation of the national character had at its base the values and daily habits that Abigail Adams and Thomas Jefferson shared, and that made them respond so warmly to each other when they met as human beings and before they could be caricatured into political stereotypes.

11. TJ to Martha Jefferson, March 28, 1787, *Selected Writings,* p. 417.

SECTION II

The "Cult of True Womanhood"

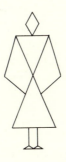

IN THE NINETEENTH CENTURY, the Victorian image of woman was endowed with the aura of universality and divine sanction. It was then seemingly pervasive and has remained so tenacious that people have ignored the fact that it was a historically determined view of woman. Even into the twentieth century, the New Victorian image of woman was simply an adaptation of an old stereotype designed to conform to a different historical setting. Only recently have the qualities of the Victorian lady been re-examined, as both men and women express their realization that the view of woman idealized by their parents was the product of history rather than divinity.

The "Cult of True Womanhood," the cultural expression of the Victorian stereotype, was, in the second quarter of the nineteenth century, ironically juxtaposed against the emergent woman's rights movement. While supporters of the cult were urging women to be pious, pure, domestic, and submissive, feminists were making plans to demand the suffrage and rewrite the Declaration of Independence at the Seneca Falls Convention of 1848. The middle-class consensus that defined the attributes of the "true" woman also maintained the nineteenth-century concept of the family. Yet it was paradoxically from this middle-class environment that the reform crusade, which included the woman's rights movement, drew most of its adherents. That was true for the two women who laid the plans for the Seneca Falls Convention, Elizabeth Cady Stanton and Lucretia Mott. Both from middle-class families, they were antislavery activists who had confronted discrimination and prejudice against women while supporting the emancipation of Negroes. According to social convention, political involvement was inconsistent with female submissiveness.

Besides offering the opportunity to express long-suppressed aspirations, the Seneca Falls Convention was a response to the prevailing stereotype of woman. Victorian commentators typically idealized the religious wife and mother who willingly sacrificed her own ambitions for her husband's. But very few, and they were usually feminists, mentioned the legal limitations that were as confining as her whalebone corsets; denied equal opportunity for advanced education, the Victorian woman could not claim her own children in case of marital separation, and at least until mid-century, had no legal right to property and then only very limited. It was, in part, a reaction to such restrictions that prompted the participants at Seneca Falls to revise the Declaration to read: "We hold these truths to be self-evident: that all men and women are created equal. . . . The history of mankind is a history of repeated injuries and usurpations on the part of man toward woman, having in direct object the establishment of an absolute tyranny over her." It was not only vocal feminists who rejected the image of true womanhood. Black women, "factory girls," working-class women, and women without husbands lacked the time, opportunity, and, in most cases, the inclination to cultivate such qualities as domesticity and submissiveness.

Organized feminism, quiescent during the Civil War, dissipated its effectiveness by dividing into two rival factions when the war ended. When finally reunited in the last decade of the century, the feminist movement became a single-minded campaign to gain the vote. Radical feminists demanded an attack on the traditional role of woman preserved in the domestic system, but the more moderate wing of the movement feared that such a wide-ranging assault would jeopardize their fight for the ballot. Like their male allies among the Progressives, the moderates said that women deserved a place in politics because their perception of injustice uniquely equipped them for the task of eliminating corruption from government. Social changes—in dress, mores, and behavior—came with the advent of the Flapper in the 1920s.

Until the last decade of the nineteenth century, the nativist movement appeared as the natural enemy of organized feminism. Antagonistic toward most reform efforts except temperance, nativists directed their hostility toward blacks, Jews, Roman Catholics, and immigrants generally. The anger and anxiety that supported their racial and ethnic prejudice, according to David Bennett, also shaped the nativist view of woman, a view inconsistent with feminist goals. Nativists could be found in the North as in the South, in the city as in the country. And in the "convent literature" that the movement spawned, anti-Catholicism and sexism merged. Purporting to be the recollections of young women who had been tortured and debauched by Roman Catholic clerics, convent literature qualified as nineteenth-century pornography. Roman Catholic priests, long suspected of being magicians and heretics, were now described as sadistic lechers who seduced innocent young women. Throughout much of the nineteenth century, nativism and the cult of true womanhood were able to play mutually supportive roles.

For middle- and upper-class physicians, nativism might have sounded like the raffish ravings of farmers and shopkeepers. Association with such unsophisticated expressions of prejudice would have tarnished the professional image that most physicians hoped to project. But as Jane Donegan indicates, physicians made few modifications in the stereotypic image of woman which nativists endorsed. Not only did male midwives or obstetricians discriminate against women as potential colleagues; they also discriminated against them as patients. Licensing restrictions and educational requirements kept women from the practice of medicine, except in the secondary role of nurses. And the prudish concern for propriety associated with the cult of true womanhood dictated the nature of the medical care available to pregnant women and those in need of gynecological treatment.

If, as Donegan's chapter suggests, the practice of medicine was one of the props that helped support the stereotype of white women, slavery served a similar function for black women. To the extent that the cult of true womanhood applied to black women at all, it was only within the context of slavery. It was the plantation owner who defined for black women the meaning of piety, purity, domesticity, and submissiveness. While some planters found it useful to encourage sexual purity through conventional marriage arrangements, others found it advantageous to assign certain women as "breeders," choosing themselves the men deemed best able to sire healthy babies. Harriet Tubman, as Otey Scruggs indicates, was a black woman who rebelled against both racism and sexism. A runaway from slavery, she returned South repeatedly, at the risk of her own life, to assist other fugitives to reach free soil. Nurse, social worker, wartime scout, she supported the suffrage for women for the same reason she supported it for black people—as a means for securing liberation.

There were, of course, many nineteenth-century feminists, from Sarah Grimké to Margaret Fuller to John Stuart Mill, who described the married woman's status in society as analogous to that of a slave. But Grimké demanded no special favors for women; she asked only that men "take their feet from off our necks." John Stuart Mill, in his essay *On the Subjection of Women,* published in England in 1869, explored the nature of authority and subjection and concluded that "marriage is a monstrous contradiction to all the principles of the modern world." From 1865 until his death, Mill served as the political voice of the British women's suffrage movement.

4

Women and the Nativist Movement

DAVID H. BENNETT

> A nation can rise no higher than the spirit and virtue of its womanhood. Our land, after all, owes its eminence to the fine women at whose knees we learned life's first lessons and its first prayers. . . .
>
> No finer spirit of chivalry touches the Klansman than his pledge to protect womenhood. She is today the victim of lust and selfishness. . . . Klansmen demand that all men treat women fairly and honestly. We stand pledged to protect her and claim to be champions of her interest and her welfare.[1]

*T*HE Klansman's pledge to protect woman and to champion her interests has an antique sound in a period long removed from the age in which nativist fraternities were an important part of the American political and social scene.

From the Know Nothing movement and its antecedents in the mid-nineteenth century to the rise of the modern Klan in the 1920s, nativism periodically had offered American men a vision of brotherhood and a taste of community, a sense of service and a missionary ideology—all of it based on the politics of exclusion. The particular objects of the nativists' wrath were Roman Catholic immigrants, especially Irish Catholic immigrants. They were considered alien intruders, foreign minorities who could not assimilate into the national culture because their background and training were incompatible with unique American institutions.

1. E. H. Lougher, *The Kall of the Klan in Kentucky* (Greenfield, Ind., 1924), p. 75.

Women were never offered membership in the anti-alien movements. In later years, women's auxiliaries were thrown together for some nativist societies, but the struggle against the foreign foe was conducted by the fraternity, a fitting unit to carry the "Americanist" banner in the male-centered politics of the nineteenth century and the early decades of the twentieth.

But if women were not involved in the central drama of nativist activity, they figured prominently in the fevered imaginations of nativism's apologists. "Victims of lust and selfishness," they must be protected from the evil exploitation fostered by a sinister enemy. In supporting the cause which defended pure womanhood against sexual degradation, true American men could prove their virtue and their manhood. If women made mild gestures at independence, they might be praised for "realizing their potential," but nativism rejected equality of the sexes as anathema to the traditional American model of hearth and home, where the female had a special moral role to play in creating and preserving American institutions. Women were seen as both delicate and precious, essential to national health and well-being, but incapable of protecting themselves, created by a distinctive American environment to be "help-meets" for the men who would shield them from dangers posed by the unAmericans.

The nativist movements which presented the image of such a threatened womanhood were not marginal organizations on the lunatic fringe of American politics. Nativists in America were never fascists plotting to overthrow the government and replace it with some new order, nor were they monarchists dreaming of a new aristocracy of the estates. They were instead, Americanists *par excellence*. Their overriding ideals, including their vision of women, reflected widespread prevailing attitudes, passions, and fears.

"Our mission is to restore America to the Americans," a Know Nothing publicist wrote in 1850, "to purify and strengthen this nation . . . to keep it clean from corruption." In dozens of books, pamphlets, and broadsides issued by nativists over two centuries, the theme was repeated and refined. They pictured the United States as a unique and gifted land, a garden of Eden to be preserved against the encroachments of the sinners: "America has done and is doing the world's work, in establishing the only true principles of liberty the world has ever known. . . The hand that guides this light is a Divine one. . . . It is the hand of God. America has a mission to teach the world."[2]

2. Frederick R. Anspach [An American], *The Sons of the Sires* (Philadelphia: Lippincott, Grambe, 1855), pp. 18–20; Frederick Saunders and T. B. Thorpe, *A Voice to America* (New York: Edward Walker, 1855), pp. 207–210; and Anna Ella Carroll, *The Great American Battle* (New York: Miller, Orton and Mulligan, 1856), pp. iii–iv.

This "mission," a variation of the more conventional American Dream, was celebrated in the stirring words that filled even the earliest nativist oratory: freedom, opportunity, individualism, and equality—all for true Americans. But how could aliens, and particularly Roman Catholic aliens, flourish in a democratic ethos, since they came from class-bound states and knew nothing of political freedom? Worst of all, as Catholics, they were disciples of an authoritarian church, the instruments of a power-hungry clerical hierarchy which cast envious eyes on the glorious American subcontinent.

From the first settlement of the colonial period anti-Catholicism was a familiar theme in America. But it was in the nineteenth century that the animus was reawakened by waves of immigration from Catholic Ireland and Germany. During the 1830s nativists and immigrants clashed on numerous fronts. Anti-alien, anti-Catholic activity erupted in violent convent burnings, in political organizing, in the creation of missionary societies, and in the proliferation of "American" and "protestant" newspapers and journals. Later, when the potato famine in Ireland and on the Continent helped to spur a wider exodus to the New World, nativist fraternal orders produced the American or Know Nothing Party. The young party's meteoric rise to national power was accelerated by the political chaos of pre–Civil War years, when the issues of slavery and free soil ruptured old alliances.

As nativism prospered in a setting of social and economic upheaval and political crisis in the period 1830–56, it would emerge again three decades later in another period of rapid change and stress. In the decade and a half before the turn of the century, dozens of patriotic societies—some newly organized, others newer versions of older orders—responded to the themes of earlier movements and excoriated the same villains. And a quarter of a century after the most prominent of them, the American Protective Association, had reached its peak, there would be another and still more powerful nativist fraternity recruiting members across much of the nation: the modern Ku Klux Klan. The ceremony for administering the oath of membership in the Know Nothings would be found at the ritualized heart of this twentieth-century secret society: "A sense of danger," the Klansman would read, "has struck the heart of the nation . . . and hence true men have devised this order as a means of disseminating patriotic principles, of keeping alive the fire of national virtue, of furthering America and American interests."[3]

What tied all these movements to one tradition was the common vision of alien intruders in the promised land. But another and more sug-

3. Carroll John Noonan, *Nativism in Connecticut, 1826–1860* (Washington: Catholic University, 1938), pp. 199–200.

gestive connection is found in the secret, fraternal organization which was the prominent feature of the most successful groups. The ritual for admission to the local chapters of the Order of the Star Spangled Banner (from which the American Party was to emerge) included elaborate raps and special handclasps, muttered passwords, the flashing of bizarre signs. The Klan carried such fraternal secrecy to the brink of absurdity. Only the sheer power of the order kept more Americans from dismissing its garb and organizational structure with contemptuous laughter: cheap white robes and grotesque masks, titles like Kligrapp and Klabee, Cyclops and Knight Hawk, Grand Dragon and Imperial Emperor.

The flamboyant ritual and exalted titles, the claims to roots in antiquity, characterized a fraternalism which the nativist orders shared with other secret societies. One historian[4] has suggested that they were evidence of men's desire for permanence, stability, and community in a world of change. It might also be noted that such permanence and stability—the status quo—are vital ingredients in maintaining sexual inequality in society.

Georg Simmel wrote in the *Web of Group Affiliations* of the "common purpose" of such organizations "to compensate for that isolation of the personality which develops out of the breaking away from the narrow confines of earlier circumstances." In the post-Jacksonian years of growing social and physical mobility, in a landscape of burgeoning towns and rudimentary new factories, in an era offering not only opportunity but also the omnipresent risk of personal failure, there was greater need than ever for men to seek the brotherhood of the definable group. Peril went beyond the personal: breakup of union, specter of civil war, vision of destruction for the "America" whose promise shaped the prideful posture of generations of men. Later, in other years of almost unparalleled economic development, the fraternity again served as refuge for those who feared change. It was to re-emerge once more in the "roaring twenties"—a time of political passivity but striking social upheaval, a time in which countless rural Americans felt displaced, discarded, shamefully cast away, in which many others in the booming cities grappled with the assault on older mores that had long governed relationships between parents and children, men and women, citizen and government.[5]

The nativist movement offered safe haven to men pressured, angered, and confused by the turmoil of their age. The members fancied them-

4. Rowland Berthoff, *An Unsettled People: Social Order and Disorder in American History* (New York: Harper & Row, 1971), pp. 272–74.

5. Georg Simmel, *Conflict & The Web of Group-Afflictions* (New York: The Free Press, 1956), pp. 19, 65, 163.

selves as "protectors" of imperiled America—and indeed they were not imagining the disorder of their time. But their frenetic political activity, their calls for sanctions against the alien and repression of "unAmerican" ways, could not ameliorate any serious societal ills. Nativism was not a solution but another symptom of America's problems. And in nativism's vision of the role of women we see how these anti-alien fraternities offered American men another way to handle their anxieties.

In the literature of the Know Nothing movement, there is little reference to women as social or political figures but constant allusion to the image of the terrorized girl, victim of clerical lust and alien, Catholic degeneracy. A bizarre spate of books about the sexual underground of Roman Catholicism emerged in America a few years earlier, in the 1830s. It was not by accident that the symbolic burning of a Catholic institution in this decade would occur at the famous Ursuline Convent in Massachusetts. The "convent literature" of the day was painting an incredible portrait of life behind "nunnery" walls.[6]

Published in New York in 1836 was a slim volume which would become an immediate sensation, *The Awful Disclosures of Maria Monk: As Exhibited in a Narrative of Her Sufferings During a Residence of Five Years as a Novice and Two Years as a Black Nun in the Hotel Dieu Nunnery at Montreal*. It sold 20,000 copies within a few weeks; sales were to reach over 300,000 in subsequent years as *Awful Disclosures* became the best-selling book in American history until surpassed by *Uncle Tom's Cabin*. Maria Monk claimed to be a Protestant girl who had converted to Catholicism and entered a convent to be educated, only to be abused by both nuns and priests, one of whom she claimed was the father of her baby, born after her escape. Her mother was to testify that Maria was mentally unstable—the victim of a brain injury—and that she was a prostitute who probably had conceived in an asylum. Some researchers have suggested that she was the dupe of several nativist ministers, who shared profits from the book that they had written and/or edited. But whatever the truth about Maria, there is no question that the book bearing her name had great celebrity and helped create a new genre of American literature. Convent exposés would be a staple for booksellers in subsequent years.[7]

6. Robert H. Lord, John E. Sexton, and Edward T. Harrington, *History of the Archdiocese of Boston* (New York: Sheed & Ward, 1944), pp. 206–22; and "Burning of Ursuline Convent" in *American Violence: A Documentary History*, edited by Richard Hofstadter and Michael Wallace (New York: Vintage, 1971), pp. 298–301.
7. Maria Monk, *Awful Disclosures of Maria Monk as Exhibited in a Narrative of Her Sufferings During a Residence of Five Years as a Novice and Two Years as a Black Nun in the Hotel Dieu Nunnery at Montreal* (New York: Howe & Bates,

One of the first of the nunnery books was Rebecca Reed's *Six Months in a Convent*. Published in Boston in 1835, a year after the great fire, it purported to be the story of life in the Ursuline Convent and served as an apologia for the destruction of the buildings on Mount Benedict. The author told a story of brutal authoritarianism and sinister conspiracy, of starvation and humiliation, of physical abuse and intimidation.[8] Reed's book was basically a nativist political tract, but Monk's *Awful Disclosures*, published a few months later, focused almost wholly on sex and sadism.

Maria Monk wrote of corrupt priests, living in the nunnery day and night, terrorizing innocent young women who believed claims that Jesuits could read minds and would "strike dead at any moment" the girl who struggled against their "abominable deeds." Moving through secret passageways between seminary and convent, priests enlisted corrupt Mother Superiors to arrange "criminal intercourse." And deep in the cellars were bleaching bones of the infants born of these illicit affairs, strangled immediately after baptism. The descriptions of the sexual assaults were graphic; more than a century after publication, versions of *Awful Disclosures* would appear in "adult" bookstores. In a rival convent exposé, published in New York in 1836—*Rosamond: A Narrative of Captivity and Sufferings of an American Female Under the Popish Priests in the Island of Cuba*—some of the most obscene passages were printed in Spanish or Latin, for Samuel B. Smith (the man who discovered "poor, broken-hearted Rosamond" Culbertson and matched her against poor Maria) explained that certain things were too shocking for the average reader. But such "sensibilities" were the exception; in most places the books were clear enough in their descriptions of priest's "seizing and satiating their appetites . . . only on the young and pretty" women.[9]

Mixed with and often dominating the tales of sexual conquest were bizarre "revelations" of sadistic behavior in the inner sanctums of the convents. Maria Monk wrote of "secret places of internment. . . . Hear the shrieks of helpless females in the hands of atrocious men." Now the reader is told of young, fair girls dragged to dimly lit rooms where they

---

1836), pp. 19–22; Allen Churchill, "The Awful Disclosures of Maria Monk," *The American Mercury* 27 (January 1936): 94–98; and Reuben Maury, *The Wars of the Godly* (New York: Robert T. McBride, 1928), p. 64.

8. Rebecca Theresa Reed, *Six Months in a Convent* (Boston: Russell, Odiorne and Metcalf, 1835), pp. 76–180, 186.

9. Monk, *Awful Disclosures*, pp. 56–58, 62–73, 90, 167–175; and Rosamund Culbertson, *Rosamund: A Narrative of Captivity and Sufferings of an American Female Under the Popish Priests in the Island of Cuba* (New York: Leavitt, Lord, 1836), pp. 6–7, 15–32, 133.

are beaten and stomped to death by Superior and priest. Again and again the same images appear: girls "crushed to death" or "maimed" or "garotted" or "trampled to death," while brutal clerics laughed. But torture, not murder, is the mainstay of these stories, and the descriptions are suggestive of the "velvet underground" of a later day. Innocents are "branded with hot irons" or "whipped on naked flesh with rods before private altars." Leather apparatus of various kinds are described in careful detail: straps binding arms and mouth, belts "sinking into the very flesh." The torturers stick pins in victims' cheeks for penance, force them to go barefoot in the cold dungeons for months, flagellate, punch, and choke. "Well paid" priests, "cruel and cold blooded," they are in it for the sheer pleasure it brings them. No scenarist for Hollywood horror films could create more despicable villains. They are caricatures of Catholic deviltry.[10]

What can be said of these incredible books, which had such a wide currency in their day? Surely, they did not picture reality. The famous "nunnery committee" in Massachusetts failed to find even a scintilla of supporting evidence when the state legislature commissioned its curious investigation of the "secret places" in the convents. Clearly, the political motives of the anti-Catholic authors and their obvious financial interest suggest that they were up to something more than informing public opinion in an earnest effort to root out hidden evils. Of course, such exposés did not appear for the first time in the 1830s. Long a staple of anti-Catholic literature, some of the more lurid European contributions to the genre were reprinted earlier by nativist editors as part of the concerted assault on the Church. Two particular favorites were Scippio de Ricci's *Female Convents: Secrets of Nunneries Disclosed* and Englishman Richard Baxter's *Jesuit Juggling: Forty Popish Frauds Detected and Disclosed.*[11]

In their shocking journeys behind convent walls, enemies of "popery" could play upon one of the themes they liked best—the dangers of secrecy and secret organizations, the "unAmerican" nature of Roman Catholicism. This was ironic, since many of the nativist critics were themselves members of secret societies. Their harsh focus on the secrecy of convent and seminary was aimed at attacking and weakening the image of moral-

10. Culbertson, *Rosamund,* pp. 101–102, 197–217; Monk, *Awful Disclosures,* pp. 14, 111–20, 186, 196–210; and *American Protestant Vindicator,* May 10, 1837, August 16, 1837.

11. Theodore Dwight, *Open Convents or Nunneries and Popish Seminaries Dangerous to the Morals, and Degrading to the Character of a Republican Community* (New York: Van Nostrand and Dwight, 1836), pp. 38–39, 73–89, 99–114, and Ray Allen Billington, *The Protestat Crusade, 1800–1860* (Chicago: Quadrangle, 1964) pp. 67, 104–107, 114–17.

ity, rectitude, and service associated with religious orders. Smash down the doors to these sinister repositories of dark secrets, Theodore Dwight demanded in *Open Convents: Or Nunneries and Popish Seminaries Dangerous to the Morals and Degrading to the Character of a Republican Community;* for if they operate in private, who will believe verbal denials made in public? The way was clear for defenses of the most notable exposés, as in the publication of *Decisive Confirmation of the Awful Disclosures of Maria Monk* and *Further Disclosures by Maria Monk Concerning the Hotel Dieu Nunnery of Montreal; also, Her Visit to Nuns' Island, and Disclosures Concerning that Secret Retreat.*[12]

Convent literature described gross deviance, made very clear who perpetrated it, and on this basis served the cause of militant Protestants. Kai T. Erikson has noted how deviant outsiders create a sense of community by supplying a focus for group feeling, how "the excitement generated by the crime . . . quickens the tempo of interaction in the group," producing a climate in which private sentiments of many individuals can be "fused together into a common sense of morality." This was a central goal of a movement which sought to unify "real" Americans so they might effectively meet the threat posed by the enemy within.[13]

It was no coincidence that women were the victims of this enemy. David B. Davis reminds us that the literature was issued in a period of "increasing anxiety and uncertainty over sexual values and the proper role of woman." Anti-Catholics shared with anti-Mormons and anti-Masonics a feeling that one of the greatest threats to Christian civilization lay in the "desexing" of women; they shared a "romantic belief that morality can be secured only by sanctification of women." Woman's role as moral authority was accentuated in an age of socio-economic upheaval, when national values were under pressure and traditional relationships threatened. Were women offered their sanctified role as a sop for being denied access to opportunity in the competitive marketplace? The first stirrings of a revived woman's consciousness were expressed at this time in Lydia Maria Child's *History and Condition of Women* (1832) and Sarah Grimke's *Letters on the Equality of Sexes and the Condition of Women* (1837). Many men tended to respond to feminist demands with

12. Maria Monk's story was attacked from many quarters; particularly damaging was a report by Colonel William L. Stone, a Protestant and editor of the *New York Commercial Advertiser,* who investigated the convent at Montreal.

13. Kai T. Erikson, *Wayward Puritans: A Study in the Sociology of Deviance* (New York: Wiley, 1966), pp. 4–19. On the function of the "criminal act" as integrator and unifier of societies, see Emile Durkheim, *The Division of Labor in Society* (Glencoe, Ill.: The Free Press, 1947), p. 102, and Lewis Coser, *The Functions of Social Conflict* (Glencoe, Ill.: The Free Press, 1964), p. 127.

even greater insistence on female delicacy, dependence, sensitivity, and sensibility. Yet their same idealized women, the guardians of moral authority, were then pictured as abused, degraded, and shamefully exploited by the enemy. What a heroic setting for the true patriot. How better to defend the American way? If the symbolic "woman" is raped by "them," certainly she must be saved by "us" in a crusade against the lustful monsters of conspiracy.[14]

But while *Awful Disclosures* and its emulators brought anti-Catholics to the banners of militancy by manipulating the image of threatened womanhood, perhaps these books served another, latent function as well. This was a time of religious awakening, when ministers harped on the breakdown of moral standards and called for a return to more temperate behavior. This was a period of rapid mobility and economic opportunity, when men poured energy and hope into their job, farm, business. Could the repression of sexual energies—called for by authoritative religious figures and necessitated by the demands of a production-minded world in crisis—lead to a peculiar fascination with a pornographic literature legitimized only because it damned the very sexual activity it described in such exciting detail? Steven Marcus, writing of *The Other Victorians* (a study of sexuality and pornography in mid–nineteenth-century England), observes that "literature is, after all, as much a deflection of impulses as it is a representation of them and of action. We cannot let it pass as an accident that a great age of concerted and organized social growth and social action should also have produced such a literature. . . . That may, among other things, demonstrate part of the price we pay for social advancement." In 1838, in *Humbugs of New York,* a doctor named David M. Reese agreed that Catholicism was a world conspiracy but loathed the convent books because they had a "deplorable moral influence upon the young." He may have overlooked these subtler relationships between pornography and sexual repression.[15]

And what of the function of sadism in these startling books? The appalling violence coloring almost every page in them is replete with picture images, so finely detailed in the descriptions of the instruments

14. David Brion Davis, "Some Themes of Counter Subversion: An Analysis of Anti-Masonic, Anti-Catholic, and Anti-Mormon Literature," *Mississippi Valley Historical Review* 47(September 1960):219; David Brion Davis, "Some Ideological Functions of Prejudice in Ante-Bellum America," *American Quarterly* 15(Summer 1963):119; and William R. Taylor, *Cavalier and Yankee* (Garden City: Anchor, 1957), pp. 144–51.

15. Bernard Weisberger, *They Gathered at the River* (Boston: Little Brown, 1948), pp. 155–56; Alice Felt Tyler, *Freedom's Ferment* (New York: Harper, 1944), pp. 318–19; Steven Marcus, *The Other Victorians* (New York: Bantam, 1967), pp. 265–66.

and techniques of torture that they cannot be dismissed merely as powerful indictments of a mythical Catholic bestiality. How is the enormous
popularity of these books explained? It is perilous to speculate on the
fantasies of those long dead, but some ideas demand tentative exploration.

The tantalizing tales of sexual appetites of ostensibly celibate priests
may have served as an acceptable projection of the hidden fantasies of
those constrained in their own sexual activities, and so too might the
reading of lurid narrations of pain (and pleasure through inflicting pain)
have served latent needs—the release of anger. There were, of course,
other outlets for violent feelings. These were violent times and not a
little destructive rage was channeled into overt anti-Catholic, anti-alien
displays. But there were enormous burdens borne by those who struggled
with the paradox of a competitive ethos which they may have celebrated
yet which carried with it such a high price in frustration and failure.
Anger inevitably accompanies failure, and in the accounts of brutality
made acceptable through attribution to the enemy, one could vicariously
enjoy expressions of unbounded rage.

Again, it is noteworthy that the victims of the sadists inevitably were
women, not young priests or innocent young seminarians. Were women
to be blamed for the anxieties that plagued men? If so, it would not be
the first time in the history of relations between the sexes. Psychoanaly-
tic literature suggests an inextricable alliance between sadism and maso-
chism. Both seem to represent means of defense against castration anxiety;
by performing symbolic castration on others, the sadist gains assurance that
he is the castrator and not the castrated.[16] There were many reasons why
men should seek reassurance that they were still masterful in these years
of social and economic challenge and uncertainty. The nativist's "way of
life" imposed rigors against which the convent literature provided release
through projection and reaffirmation of manhood.

But what of women readers? We have no data on the number of
women who purchased these remarkable tracts or those who discovered
them when they were brought into nativist households. Was there widespread fear of rape by evil, "foreign" prelates in the American Protestant
community? The setting for the sinister deeds alleged in the literature—
deep within convent walls—makes this seem unlikely. Perhaps some of
those women who did find the plight of Maria and her sisters fascinating
reading were caught up in their own kind of fantasy. If so, they might be
responding to the same social forces affecting men in these years.

16. See, for example, Paul Friedman, "Sexual Deviations," in *American Handbook of Psychiatry*, edited by Silvano Arieti (New York: Basic Books, 1959), I, 603.

In the early 1850s, as the Know Nothing Party swept to victory after victory, nativism emerged as a major force in American life with the appeal of "convent books" undiminished. Sex and sadism were still principal themes. Josephine Bunkley's *Testimony of an Escaped Novice,* produced by Harper & Brothers in 1855, was replete with tales of "discipline, . . . whips with leather thongs struck on naked backs, . . . [and] females buried alive." And nativists continued to be prime consumers. Charles W. Frothingham's *The Convent's Doom* (1854) was dedicated to "the Know Nothing fraternity throughout the United States," and went through at least five editions (more than 50,000 books); in 1855 a "Native American" (E. Hutchinson) issued a broadside called *Startling Facts for Know Nothings,* decrying the "licentiousness and debauchery" of the Catholic clergy. The subject was political dynamite, and it was hardly coincidental that the famous Hannah Corcoran Riots erupted in Charlestown, Massachusetts, after a young Irish immigrant girl who had become a Baptist was spirited away to Philadelphia by her mother and a Catholic priest. Her Protestant guardians called it kidnapping and talked darkly of rape and murder, and a huge nativist mob attacked police and militia companies. The nativist image of woman remained that of a dependent, defenseless creature. While women were organizing the first women's rights convention in upstate New York (good Know Nothing country), nativism continued to use women as symbolic victims of male rage. And in the brotherhood of the anti-alien order, women could never be members and never be equals, but their virtue and delicacy must be preserved.[17]

The men who first joined the nativist fraternities were not from marginal groups at the extremes of the social and economic scale. There were some prosperous businessmen—real estate and insurance brokers —and a few professionals well placed in society. And there were numerous farmers (although later nativist movements would have a stronger rural base). But the majority would form a cross section of mid-nine-

---

17. Josephine M. Bunkley, *The Testimony of an Escaped Novice* (New York: Harper & Brothers, 1855), pp. 37, 41–42, 59, 91–154, 225–312; E. Hutchinson, *Startling Facts for Native Americans Called 'Know Nothings'* (New York: American Family Publication, 1855), pp. 75–88; William Hogan, *Auricular Confessions and Popish Nunneries* (Hartford: Silas, Andrus, 1850), II, 212; *Pilot* (Boston), April 9, 16, 1853; "Declaration of Sentiments and Resolutions, Seneca Falls Convention," in *Up From the Pedestal: Selected Writings in the History of American Feminism,* edited by Aileen S. Kraditor (Chicago: Quadrangle, 1969), pp. 184–88; and Andrew Sinclair, *The Emancipation of the American Woman* (New York: Harper & Row, 1965), pp. 59–64. A few women did operate on the fringes of the movement as pamphleteers and publicists; the author of *The Great American Battle* was Anna Ella Carroll.

teenth-century Protestant urbanites: masons and painters, machinists and seamen, butchers and grocers, ship smiths and carpenters. It was the "average man," not some desperate fanatic, who was responding to the call. He believed in what Barbara Welter has called "the cult of true womanhood," which had such wide currency in these days: women's true virtues being piety, purity, submissiveness, and domesticity. Nativists liked to believe that they were defending these exalted qualities, protecting "true woman" from the sinister plans of the alien enemy, and so preserving the American way of life.[18]

Forty years later, a new nativism of the nineties expressed similar themes. The passing years brought some changes in the nativists' vision of women, but convent literature continued to fire the anti-alien imagination. Advertisements for reprints of Maria Monk's work appeared in many publications of the American Protective Association, and APA cited other old favorites: Edith O'Gorman's *Convent Life Unveiled*, Madam D.'s *Priest and Nun*, Leyden's *Secret Confessions to a Priest*, and Miss Cueak's *Life Inside the Church of Rome*.[19] The APA Magazine of March 1896 featured such stories as W. J. Phillips' "Convent Horrors," filled with old-time sado-masochism. In "A Priestly Liar," in June 1895, readers learned of the "libidinous, rapist priest with lust in his heart" who "disgraced his victims . . . these trusting women." In the Omaha *American,* November 12, 1892, wild, sadistic fantasies of "Romish violence" were focused on the fate of women: "the priest swears that he will wage relentless war against the heretics . . . that he will burn, waste, boil, flog, strangle . . . rip up the stomachs and wombs of women and crush the heads of their infants."

The new movement had its own "convent heroine," a latter-day Maria Monk. Margaret Shepard, author of *My Life in the Convent*, was on the lecture circuit for a number of patriotic societies, including the APA, in the late 1880s and 1890s. Shepard's book related a strange tale of a girl whose first lover was a priest who ran off after fathering her child. The baby died after the broken-hearted young woman was imprisoned when she turned to petty crime to sustain herself. In desperation, the author claimed, she entered a convent, only to be victimized by "licentious and lecherous priests . . . seeking to lure young and innocent girls into sin." Coerced into believing it "her duty to submit," the "helpless" female faced a "hell upon earth." She told of beautiful girls tortured

---

18. *Directory, Alpha Chapter No. 1, OUA, August 1848* (New York: R. C. Root Anthony, 1848); and Barbara Welter, "The Cult of True Womanhood: 1820–1860," *American Quarterly* 18(Summer 1966):151–74.

19. J. J. Tighe, The *A.P.A.* (New York: D. P. Murphy, 1894), p. 36.

and disfigured in grotesque ceremonies, and of orgies of sex and sadism in which girls were raped and brutalized.[20]

The fate of Margaret Shepard was seen as the fate of all women under alien, Catholic power. All Americans should note how Roman Catholicism "deifies a woman (Mary) but holds women so loosely in its esteem" that when the Church ruled the European world, "nowhere were women educated." But in the United States, boasted *The Patriot: An Advocate of Americanism*, published in Chicago in 1891, "We are glad woman is not merely a favored slave of man. . . . Protestantism treats woman with respect and she is educated here, not degraded."

In the nativism of the nineties, the image of women was slowly changing. While the popularity of convent literature still attested to the continuing need to depict women as helpless victims, it was now possible to point with pride at how much better women were treated here than in those despised, alien lands across the ocean. It was now fashionable to call for women's nativist orders, sister groups to the mainline nativist fraternities. Along with the National Association of Loyal Men of American Liberty and the Patriotic Order of Sons of America there was established the National Daughters of Liberty. Alongside the Loyal Orange Institution of the USA (for émigrés from Protestant Ireland) came the Ladies Loyal Orange Association dedicated, said the *Patriot*, to "those desiring to perpetuate principles of true Americanism and Protestantism . . . , to defending families and friends from the deep intrigues of Popish mercenaries."[21]

Even the American Protective Association, the nativist organization which was to wield a measure of political power in these years, had its women's affiliate, the WAPA (Women's American Protective Association). William J. Traynor, president of the order, was willing to support women's suffrage and laced his argument for expanding the franchise with a mixture of paternalistic pride at how "we" treat "our" women in America and back-handed praise of American women's abilities as compared to inferior immigrant men. In this presidential address, carried in the July 1895 edition of the *APA Magazine*, he noted, "The grand women

20. Margaret L. Shepherd, *My Life in the Convent* (Toledo, Ohio: Protestant Book House, 1938), pp. 5, 88–126, 162–79, 182–200, 245–56.

21. *The Patriotic Order Sons of America: Platform of Principles* (Cincinnati: Johns, Rinbach, 1889); *National Association of Loyal Men of American Liberty* (Boston, 1890); *Constitution of the National Council Daughters of Liberty* (New York: G. Burton, 1887); James Ray to Henry Baldwin, January 6, 1891 in Henry Baldwin Papers (New York Public Library Division of Manuscripts); and Donald L. Kinzer, *An Episode in Anti-Catholicism: The American Protective Association* (Seattle: University of Washington Press, 1964), pp. 47–48.

of America are . . . as worthy to cast a vote . . . as those pauper and criminal riffraff of Europe . . . every ignorant dago and mick . . . ignorant Pole . . . Hun and Slav . . . Bavarian and Italian."

In fact, the franchise issue brought nativism into a curious alliance with some elements of the movement for women's rights. In 1894, Carrie Chapman Catt declared in a speech in Iowa that "this government is menaced with great danger . . . in the votes possessed by the males in the slums of the cities and the ignorant foreign vote. . . . There is but one way to avert the danger—cut off the vote of the slums and give to woman the power of protecting herself that man has secured for himself—the ballot. Put the ballot in the hands of every person of sound mind in the nation." Earlier, Olympia Brown told the convention of the National American Woman Suffrage Association in 1889 that "women are well educated; they are graduating from our colleges; and yet they are the political inferiors of all the riffraff of Europe that is poured upon our shores." In the past, suffragists had based their claim to the ballot principally on the inalienable rights of every human being, as Aileen Kraditor has observed, but in the period of great immigration, many middle-class women shared the nativist anxieties of some anti-suffragist males of the same social stratum. Now, it was argued, women deserve the vote not because all human beings are equal, but because native Americans and foreign-born Americans were not equal, and the inferior should not rule the superior. Furthermore, the suffragists' new strategy of favoring an educational requirement for the vote (which would strike at "illiterate" immigrants) directly helped their cause by disenfranchising many newcomers with conservative views, men who came from patriarchal societies with traditional ideas about the role of women.[22]

But if it seemed that nativists were coming together with the most vociferous advocates of women's rights, their common ground was more illusion than reality. There might be women on the fringes of the movement, women writing for major nativist journals, there even might be common cause in calls for the franchise for native women. But there was no acceptance of equality of the sexes by nativist men—they believed that the vote would not make women equal but would make America more "democratic"—most of whom recoiled at the notion of strong and

22. Carrie Chapman Catt, "Danger to Our Government," and Olympia Brown, "On the Foreign Menace," in Kraditor, *Up From the Pedestal*, pp. 257–62; Aileen S. Kraditor, *The Ideas of the Woman Suffrage Movement, 1890–1920* (New York: Columbia University Press, 1965), pp. 123–29; and William L. O'Neill, *The Woman Movement* (Chicago: Quadrangle, 1971), pp. 72–73.

aggressive females threatening the traditional relationships between the sexes.[23]

A remarkable piece in the *Wisconsin Patriot,* May 18, 1895, showed how frightening nativists found this prospect. The newspaper usually devoted itself to stories about prominent men and some frequent "convent" features. But this issue offered a long "fictional" article entitled "Women in the Next Century." Set in 1945, it pictured a dramatic reversal of sex roles in marriage. Wife and husband live in a large "Pacific Heights" mansion. She is the dominant, driving force, a successful businesswoman. He stays home all day with "the men," is concerned about hair styles and frilly drapes while his wife swings wheat deals and buys gold mines. His wife buys him rings for Christmas, he gives her suspenders, for she literally wears the pants, while he is attired in slippers and skirts, silk dresses and ruffles. The husband is lectured by his wife on economy, although she urges him to get his whiskers curled and his head manicured for she wants him to "look nice." They live in an age of total woman power (the chauffeur is a uniformed woman) and when they go to the theatre, the talk is all of politics among the wives, who mention women gubernatorial and Congressional candidates, with hated Irish politicians suddenly taking new shape—"Bridget O'Flaherty for Attorney General." Cigar-smoking, tough-minded women control everything—Shakespeare is even rewritten to feature tragic heroines. At intermission, men sit alone in the theatre in their patent boots and colored coats while wives speak of the important affairs of the world. Afterwards, the wife takes her husband to a restaurant and "gives him some supper before taking him home." She goes to sleep "little dreaming that her meek and humble husband is planning and developing a 'New Man' Movement."

The emerging feminism of the 1890s was clearly a frightening prospect to the defenders of the American Way. Women must know their place and stay in it lest the whole structure of society crumble and the heroic American male be emasculated. Nativists as protectors of the nation must now fight this dangerous development even as they organized to meet the foreign Catholic foe.

Two and a half decades later, nativism's worst fears had not been realized, but its image of women remained unchanged. In the age of the Flapper, in the years after the suffragists had won their battle for the franchise, the growing Ku Klux Klan cherished the image of the vulnerable and virtuous female as the conservator of American values.

23. Lucinda Chandler, "Lessons in Americanism," *The Patriot: An Advocate of Americanism* (Chicago) 1(March 1891):40.

Another generation of nativists meant another resurgence of convent tales. *Dawn* (a major Klan paper in Chicago) offered "Convent Cruelties—the True Story of Ex-Nun Helen Jackson," and advertised offprints of the sado-masochist piece for months after initial publication. Other Klan papers featured, among many, such works as "Behind Convent Walls" and "Roman Priest Alienates Women's Love."[24]

In Dallas in 1921, hundreds of men marched through the streets under banners reading "Our Little Girls Must Be Protected" and "Pure Womanhood." Two years later, at a meeting of state leaders of the Klan, the Grand Dragon of the Realm of Arkansas read "A Tribute and Challenge to American Women": At the "very mentioning of the word 'women,' true men at once come to attention, for whatever else the human heart may forget in the rough experiences of life, it cannot forget its mother." The Constitution and Laws of the order, Klansmen were reminded, instructs initiates to "shield the sanctity of home and the chastity of women . . . to protect the weak, innocent and defenseless."[25]

It was in the name of such protection that local Klans engaged in notorious terrorism. Brandings, floggings, and tar and featherings occurred in numerous states in the South, Southwest, and lower Midwest. The victims of the masked nightriders often were accused adulterers and wife-beaters, men who were said to be not supporting their families or had deserted their women. The enemies of "pure womanhood" must be punished, and for modern nativists of the Klan that meant sinners of both sexes. "Fallen women" were the targets in many rural bastions; young women accused of prostitution or bigamy were stripped, tarred and feathered, left half-conscious with hair shorn. One can speculate on the sexual frustrations of these bands of white-robed, small-town men, envious of the freedom of millions of more liberated urbanites in the "roaring twenties," finding perverse pleasure in their crusade for "morality," in their efforts to preserve the old order.[26]

But for "true women"—women who knew their role and understood

24. *Dawn* (Chicago), June 2, 1923, December 8, 1923; *The National Kourier* (Washington, D.C.), October 1, 1925; and Bishop Alma White, *Klansmen: Guardians of Liberty* (Zarephath, N.J., 1926), pp. 127–38.

25. Henry P. Fry, *The Modern Ku Klux Klan* (Boston: Small, Maynard, 1922), pp. 185–91; Kenneth T. Jackson, *The Ku Klux Klan in the City, 1915–1930* (New York: Oxford University Press, 1967), pp. 66–67; *Papers Read at the Meeting of Grand Dragons, 1923* (Atlanta: Ku Klux Klan, 1923) pp. 89–91; and W. C. Wright, *Religious and Patriotic Ideals of the Ku Klux Klan* (Waco, Tex., 1926), p. 13.

26. Fry, *The Modern Klan*, pp. 185–91; Charles C. Alexander, *The Ku Klux Klan in the Southwest* (Lexington: University of Kentucky Press, 1966), pp. 43, 52, 65; "The Reign of the Tar Bucket," *The Literary Digest* 70(August 27, 1921):1–12; and American Civil Liberties Union Archives (1912–50), Vol. 231.

their place—the Klan offered its own brand of liberation. Like the APA in an earlier generation, it scorned the "abuses of women" in Catholic Italy, Spain, and South America where "ecclesiastical domination has rendered their seclusion semi-oriental," where women "suffer educational, social and political disadvantages." "Suppression of sex" might be the rule in foreign lands, but true Americans all know that "woman should not be a slave of man." The time has come, one Grand Dragon announced, for women to "take their places in the broad activities of national life."[27]

What this meant was that the Klan would offer membership in affiliate groups to "patriotic" women. Of course, one woman had played a key role in the movement from its outset. Mrs. Elizabeth Tyler, a shrewd public relations consultant, joined forces with another promoter named Edward Clarke Young to turn the order founded by William J. Simmons into a national organization. Simmons, sometime minister, garter salesman, and fraternal organizer for the Woodmen of the World, gave Tyler and Clarke's Southern Publicity Association a free hand to build the Klan. Mrs. Tyler and her associate profited by the arrangement but Simmons soon found the growing movement beyond his powers of management, and Hiram Wesley Evans, a clever and ambitious Klan leader from Texas, moved in to grasp power from the founder. It was out of this struggle for power that the first women's auxiliary was founded. Simmons, having lost control of the male Ku Klux Klan, organized a women's branch called "Kamelia" and proclaimed himself its "El Magnus" or chief officer. Evans soon countered with the "Women of the Ku Klux Klan." After lengthy court battles, Simmons accepted a cash settlement to leave the order, and Women of the Klan emerged as the single membership organization for klanswomen everywhere. It absorbed such local groups as the Order of American Women in Ft. Worth, the Ladies of the Invisible Empire in Louisiana and Arkansas, the Ladies of the Cu Clux Clan in Oklahoma. It established its own imperial palace (national headquarters) in Little Rock, sent its own Kleagles (organizers) into the field, called on Klansmen to influence wives and sisters to join up. Soon Mrs. Lula A. Markwell, first Imperial Commander, was claiming a membership of 200,000.[28]

---

27. *Dawn*, December 8, 1923; *The National Kourier*, August 14, 1925; "American Women," *The Kourier Magazine* (Atlanta) 1 (April 1925):11–15; and *Papers Read at the Meeting of Grand Dragons*, pp. 91–92.

28. Charles O. Jackson, "William J. Simmons: A Career in Ku Kluxism," *The Georgia Historical Quarterly* 50(December 1966):351–65; William J. Simmons, *The Klan Unmasked* (Atlanta: William F. Thompson, 1923); Robert L. Duffus, "Salesmen of Hate: The Ku Klux Klan," *The World's Week* 46 (May 1923):33–36; Alexander, *The Klan in the Southwest*, pp. 102–105; and *Dawn*, November 17, 1923.

Why did these women join? Were they denying their traditional role of moral guardian of the home to become what some anti-Klan editorialists would call "nativist Amazons?" Of course, they were not. These were merely auxiliaries to the real Ku Klux Klan, the fraternal order charged with responsibility for carrying the protectors creed into the twentieth century. These women's units attracted wives and sisters of real Klansmen, and the members performed customary housewifely chores by preparing food for the numerous Klan outings, picnics, and clambakes.

In fact, the women's Klan was little more than the instrument of one man's authority. James Comer, Evans' early ally and Grand Dragon of the Arkansas Klan, had originally put up the money to start the "Women of the Ku Klux Klan." He completely controlled its activities, even forcing the resignation of Mrs. Markwell and (after bypassing her Vice Commander) installing Miss Robbie Gill as the new "leader." Within a year, Comer married Miss Gill and they moved into the pillared mansion which served as headquarters. Later, many disgruntled members charged him with using their order to further a variety of money-making schemes.[29]

With such "leadership" in their sister organization, it was little wonder that Klansmen would not be threatened by the speeches of Imperial Commander Gill. She told the Second Imperial Klonvokation, "God gave Adam woman to be his comrade and counselor. . . . Adam was lord and master. . . . Eve's name meant life, society, company, . . . and I know you men have long since bowed before women's power and . . . marveled at your inability to get along without her." Men do "not tolerate abuse of her. . . . Instead they receive the greatest inspiration from her" and so are helped to "perform noble deeds."[30]

The nativists of the twenties wanted women to help protect America against the alien menace, but she could do that best by playing her traditional role. At the top of a list of women's priorities in an article in *Dawn*, January 19, 1924, entitled "The Fate of the Nation is in the Hands of its Women," was the injunction to "preserve the sanctity of the home." In another publication, *The Fiery Cross*, July 6, 1923, the headline announced "Women's Loyalty Will Fulfill a Manifest Destiny," for "even in the midst of all the pressing duties of maternal care and home making, women have found time to keep the spiritual fires of the nation burning on the altar. She has been the conscience-keeper of the race." And the women of the Klan knew their place. The American flag, they were told,

29. Alexander, *The Klan in the Southwest*, pp. 217–21; and David M. Chalmers, *Hooded Americanism* (Chicago: Quadrangle, 1965), pp. 240–41.
30. Robbie Gill, "American Women," *Inspirational Addresses Delivered at the Second Imperial Klonvokation* (Kansas City: Knights of the KKK, 1924), pp. 51–60.

spoke directly to them. Red stood for blood shed "for women's protection." White represented purity and blue the loyalty of men to women and women to the "men who are dependent upon her." Grand Dragon Comer, that authority on women's rights, explained that "American women have as much to do with shaping the destiny of America as the man . . . for they have the burden of rearing children."[31]

For all their posturing in hooded garb, women on the margins of the Klan were relegated to second-class citizenship in a movement which embraced a sexist ideology of classic dimensions. Like nativists in earlier years, Klansmen insisted that women served their nation best as housewives and parents, the religious and moral force in home and society. These nativists thought they were paying their highest tribute to women by identifying women's virtues and women's plight with America itself— both were threatened by aliens, ignorant or malevolent foreigners who would rape and despoil Mother Earth (both the nation and its "womanhood") unless heroic protectors rose to the defense. Nativists never questioned their assumptions of male dominance, for the American Dream that they sought to protect had no room for sexual equality. The image of threatened womanhood was essential to their own search for masculine validation, their own effort to handle the problems of a changing society.

In the years after the sudden collapse of the Klan in the late twenties, new conditions militated against another rebirth of traditional nativism. Immigration restrictions shut off the flow of newcomers, the frequent objects of anti-alien anger, and the raw hostility focused on Irish Catholics lost its force with the passing years. Economic depression, world war and protracted international conflict gave rise to other forms of political and social protest in the name of "protecting America." Soon the nativists would be remembered in most parts of the country, if at all, as spooky boys in costume, seeking escape from the concerns of the real world. But a closer examination of their ideology reveals how clearly these angry and fearful men reflected prevailing attitudes in the society, and not the least significant part of their ideology and their rich fantasy life was their image of women in America.

31. *Ibid.*, pp. 51–53; *The Kourier Magazine* 1: 11–15; and James Comer, Grand Dragon, Realm of Arkansas, "A Tribute and a Challenge to the Wonderful Womanhood of America," *The Imperial Night Hawk* (Atlanta) 1 (October 3, 1923):2.

5

Man-Midwifery and the Delicacy of the Sexes

JANE B. DONEGAN

*T*HE practice of midwifery had been the unquestioned province of women in colonial America. Midwives, while lacking formal training in their craft and ignorant of the principles of anatomy and physiology, nevertheless ruled supreme. The very presence of men in the lying-in chamber was regarded as indecorous; therefore, male physicians were summoned only as a last resort, when abnormal cases required more help than the midwives alone could give. In the eighteenth century, significant advances in British medicine led to the development of the new obstetrics, with its greater understanding of the mechanics of parturition, the classification of labors, and the use of obstetrical instruments. In the 1760s, the new obstetrics spread to America, and traditional midwifery practices began to change.

The transition of midwifery from an art practiced by untrained women to a legitimate branch of medicine had as one important consequence the decline of the midwife and the accompanying growth in popularity of the general practitioner as accoucheur. Some women, out of habit or modesty, continued to resort to the midwives. Upper-class women in Philadelphia, Boston, and New York, however, had begun to believe that the superior training of doctors equipped with instruments could be equated with safer and shorter parturition. These women set the trend for employing the accoucheur, so that by the second decade of the nineteenth century, those who could afford the services of a general practitioner hardly ever employed a midwife.[1]

Despite this fact, the doctors' hold upon the practice of midwifery remained a tenuous one throughout the period following the Revolution. There were only a few specialists in obstetrics. The majority of deliveries among the upper classes in northern cities were attended by general practitioners who recognized the rewards accruing to the accomplished accoucheur. Midwifery, in itself, was not especially lucrative, although physicians probably received higher fees for this service than had the midwives. Greater financial rewards could be obtained from a varied practice ranging from vaccinations and minor ailments to the treatment of serious diseases and surgical operations. Midwifery's attraction was that it fed this general practice; the man who acquitted himself well in the lying-in chamber earned the enduring gratitude of patient and husband. As one Boston physician succinctly observed: "Women seldom forget a practitioner who has conducted them tenderly and safely through parturition—they feel a familiarity with him, a confidence and reliance upon him, which are of the most essential mutual advantage in all their subsequent intercourse as physician and patient. It is this which ensures to [doctors] the permanency and security of all their other business."[2]

Obstetrics, reported a committee of the Philadelphia College of Physicians a few years later, had become a highly competitive field precisely because it led "to the highest success in medicine, more certainly than any other department of practice." Even physicians who opposed man-midwifery despaired of accomplishing reform, owing to the common boast of the doctor "that if he can attend one single case of midwifery in a family, he has ever after secured their patronage."[3]

1. The generalizations and conclusions in this article are based primarily upon an examination of the contemporary medical literature published in Philadelphia, Boston, and New York. Specific references not cited may be found in the author's unpublished doctoral dissertation, "Midwifery in America, 1760–1860; A Study in Medicine and Morality," Syracuse University, 1971.

2. [Walter Channing], *Remarks on the Employment of Females as Practitioners in Midwifery* (Boston: Cummings and Hilliard, 1820), pp. 19–20. In the three cities considered in this chapter, physicians in New York received the highest midwifery fees. The New York City Fee Bill of 1816 set fees of $25–$30 for common cases, and $35–$60 for tedious or difficult ones. In 1817, the Boston Medical Association established fees of $12 for day cases and $15 for night cases, without apparent regard for the nature of the cases. In 1834, the fee table for the College of Physicians in Philadelphia listed $8–$20 for midwifery. Detailed discussion of fees appears in Henry B. Shafer, *The American Medical Profession, 1783–1850* (New York: Columbia University Press, 1936), pp. 154–60.

3. *Report of the College of Physicians, November 15, 1835*, in W. R. Penman, "The Public Practice of Midwifery in Philadelphia," *Transactions of the College of*

Consequently, most physicians were eager to add normal midwifery cases, which constituted the majority of deliveries, to the abnormal ones for which they would almost always be called. To accomplish this, they attempted to reinforce the growing acceptance of the idea that the parturient woman's best prospect for eliminating the hazards of childbirth and post-partum complications lay in the employment of the accoucheur. Working in the doctors' favor was the fact that man-midwifery was no longer strictly an innovation. In 1826, William Dewees, adjunct professor of Midwifery at the University of Pennsylvania, prefaced his textbook by exhorting medical students to learn the theory of midwifery thoroughly. In general practice "everyone almost" was called upon to attend deliveries. "A change of manners, within a few years," he observed, "has resulted in the almost exclusive employment of the male practitioner," a change chiefly realized "by a conviction, that the well-instructed physician is best calculated to avert danger, and surmount difficulties."[4]

It would have been strange, indeed, had physicians not played their strongest suit. They emphasized the element of safety and stressed the potential for danger that accompanied every normal case. In contrast to the midwives, who lacked opportunities to gain training, the doctors held a virtual monopoly on the use of the forceps, the lever, and other obstetrical instruments. The pregnant woman, vulnerable in her understandable wish for a shorter and safer delivery, permitted the accoucheur to be called because she believed he always offered the best chance for both.

Despite the repeated claims and promises of the profession, evidence suggests that this belief was not always warranted. In the better medical colleges—such as the University of Pennsylvania, the College of Physicians and Surgeons in New York, and the Massachusetts Medical College (Harvard)—midwifery and the diseases of women and children constituted one separate department. Yet even these schools did not always require completion of this combined course for the medical degree. Medical students studied anatomy and physiology of the female, but often had little or no clinical experience in obstetrics. In 1832, Dr. Daniel Drake, surveying medical education, noted that the young practitioner would embark upon his career with less practical knowledge in obstetrics than in any other branch of medicine. He urged that the student be especially

---

Physicians of Philadelphia 37 (October 1869):129; W. Beach, An Improved System of Midwifery adapted to the Reformed Practice of Medicine . . . with Remarks on Physiological and Moral Elevation (New York: Scribners, 1851), p. 13.

4. William P. Dewees, A Compendious System of Midwifery, Chiefly Designed to Facilitate the Inquiries of those Who May be Pursuing This Branch of Study (Philadelphia: Carey & Lea, 1826), pp. xiv–xv.

diligent in acquiring theoretical information in midwifery, in order to avoid being "thrown into situations of responsibility most harrowing to his feelings, if not fatal to his patient."[5]

Then, as now, most obstetrics cases were normal ones, and the actual services performed by a knowledgeable physician should not have differed appreciably from those which a competent midwife was capable of providing. These were limited to making the patient as comfortable as circumstances permitted, lending encouragement without giving false hope of a rapid delivery, supporting the perineum at the moment of birth to prevent rupture of the tissue, tying off the umbilical cord, and supervising the expulsion of the placenta.[6] That physicians were equipped with obstetrical instruments, however, held a potential for disaster. There was a marked tendency for doctors to resort to mechanical aids in cases where their use was completely unnecessary. Many men poorly trained in midwifery and lacking in experience did not hesitate to use the lever or forceps with an appalling disregard for the consequences. Indiscriminate "meddlesome midwifery" persisted, despite the repeated warnings of authorities that such interference was potentially harmful to mothers and infants.

The eminent New York physician, Samuel Bard, who maintained his interest in obstetrics for over fifty years, prefaced the third edition of his *Compendium of the Theory and Practice of Midwifery* with a warning. He had, he said, added a chapter on the use of instruments "rather to recommend caution and repress temerity, than to encourage confidence and presumption" on the part of the youthful practitioner. His work extolled the virtues of caution and patience which permitted nature to accomplish its course unimpeded. Bard vividly traced the consequences

---

5. Daniel Drake, *Practical Essays on Medical Education and the Medical Profession in the United States* (Cincinnati: Roff & Young, 1832), pp. 40–41.

6. The use of anesthesia in childbirth was advocated by Walter Channing in his *Treatise on Etherization in Childbirth*, which appeared in 1848. American obstetricians resisted this innovation, and it was many years before either ether or chloroform won acceptance. In 1851, Dr. Augustus K. Gardner promoted the use of chloroform in "simple and natural as in difficult and instrumental deliveries." He observed that anesthesia was commonly used in Boston, but in New York its use was "exceedingly limited." Augustus K. Gardner, *A History of the Art of Midwifery: A Lecture Delivered at the College of Physicians and Surgeons, November 11, 1851* . . . (New York: Stringer & Townsend, 1852), p. 24. Charles D. Meigs, a prominent Philadelphia obstetrician who opposed anesthesia, observed in 1849 that it had made no real progress in his city, and added, "it is quite . . . true that a lying-in room is, for the most of the time, a scene of cheerfulness and gaiety, instead of one of shrieks and anguish and despair which have been so forcibly portrayed." In Lewis C. Scheffey, "The Earlier History and the Transition Period of Obstetrics and Gynecology in Philadelphia," *Annals of Medical History* 3rd series, 2 (May 1940):221.

that followed the physician's hasty resort to instruments: "He will probably fail at first, for want of judgment, to discriminate accurately between one case and another, as well as for want of skill and dexterity in the application of his instruments; and finding himself foiled in the use of the safer lever and forcep, he will become alarmed, confused and apprehensive for his patient's safety, as well as for his own reputation. And now, deeming a speedy delivery essential to both and . . . having taken the case into his own hands . . . he thinks he must not desist before he has accomplished it, he flies to the crotchet, as more easy in its application and more certain in its effect—with this he probably succeeds; and although the poor infant is sacrificed, yet he persuades himself, perhaps honestly believes, this was necessary."[7]

William Dewees' *Compendious System of Midwifery* also stressed the importance of non-interference. "It is a vulgar prejudice," wrote Dewees, "that great and constant benefit, can be derived from the agency of the accoucheur; especially, during the active state of pain; and this feeling is but too often encouraged by the ignorant, and the designing to the injury of the patient, and to the disgrace of the profession. When all things are doing well, the *active* duties of the accoucheur, are limited indeed—it is but where the contrary obtain, that he can be said to be actively useful."

Another physician, comparing American and French obstetrical training in the *Eclectic Journal of Medicine* for November 1836, was convinced that the American medical schools placed undue emphasis on abnormal cases. The result was that students gained the mistaken impression that such abnormalities were the rule rather than the exception. The physician could do much to contribute to the parturient woman's comfort, safety, and her post-partum recovery, but not, warned this author, "by any instrumental display, or the exhibition of medicine to hasten labour; or by hasty extraction of the placenta."

John Metcalf, who recorded more than three hundred obstetrical cases he had attended, said that experience had taught him that despite the professional attention given to the kinds of delicate manipulations which could be employed, in actual practice the need for them was very rare. The secret of success in obstetrics, he stressed in the *American Journal of the Medical Sciences,* October 1843, lay in "letting the patient alone" so long as the physician could reasonably assume that the natural machinery of parturition could accomplish its end without help.

7. Samuel Bard, *A Compendium of the Theory and Practice of Midwifery* . . . (New York: Collins, 1819), pp. iv–vi; 240.

In 1845, Gunning S. Bedford, who held the Chair in Midwifery and the Diseases of Women and Children at the University of New York, warned his students that unrestrained and "unpardonable" use of instruments was still widely prevalent. A young practitioner, discussing operative midwifery with Bedford, had mentioned that he brought to his practice great familiarity with instruments. The preceptor with whom he had studied had averaged sixteen embryotomies a year! Dr. Bedford was horrified, but not surprised, for as he observed to his class, "I have myself witnessed in this city scenes of blood sufficient to satisfy my mind that this is not an exaggerated picture."[8]

Another physician, Augustus K. Gardner, lecturing in New York on operative midwifery in 1851, warned that it was the shortsightedness of the medical profession that threatened obstetrical practice in that city. The average medical student could graduate without ever having attended a delivery. The resulting ignorance led either to meddlesome midwifery on the one hand, or to the equally dangerous doctrine of absolute non-interference on the other. If a doctor encountered only uncomplicated cases at the outset of his career, he was likely to believe that "all the talk of position, presentation, rotation, and such like is all nonsense, or at best theoretical, and he joins the 'expectant' practitioners, trusts to the *vis mediatrix naturae* . . . and by a dull inactivity . . . loses the child, and not unfrequently the mother also, and injures the reputation of the profession."[9]

Had these deficiencies been common knowledge, women might have shown greater reluctance in employing male physicians. As it was, doctors faced a more formidable obstacle to continued dominance in obstetrics in the form of the cultural mores of the period. With the growing urbanization of American life that accompanied nascent industrialism, upper- and middle-class women were confined to a narrow sphere of home and family. There they were expected to cultivate the virtues of "true womanhood,"[10] and warned of the dire consequences of immodesty. A society

8. In John Stevens, *Man Midwifery Exposed, or the Danger and Immorality of Employing Men in Midwifery Proved; and the Remedy for the Evil Found* (London: Horsell, 1850), p. 41.

9. Gardner, *Art of Midwifery*, p. 30. The poor preparation of medical students in midwifery was still being criticized as late as 1912. J. W. Williams, professor of obstetrics at Johns Hopkins, noted that there was a professor of obstetrics who admitted that he had never seen a woman deliver prior to assuming his professorship! See J. Whitridge Williams, "Medical Education and the Midwife Problem in the United States," *Journal of the American Medical Association* 58 (January 6, 1912): 1–7.

10. See Barbara Welter, "The Cult of True Womanhood: 1820–1860," *American Quarterly* 18 (Summer 1966):151–74. For an example of advice typically given

that grew increasingly prudish as the century progressed, could not be expected to look with equanimity upon the presence of accoucheurs in the lying-in chamber, regardless of their training.

The doctors themselves were well aware of the conflicting demands of modesty and safety. Even the physician who argued against a proposal to restore midwives in Boston felt constrained to admit that the honor, virtue, and dignity of women greatly depended upon their feelings of delicacy. "There can be no doubt," he observed, "that the attendance of a female must be more grateful to these feelings, and that they must be somewhat wounded at first by the presence of a physician."[11] He hastened to add, however, that the employment of a doctor did not constitute an indelicacy, and had come to be accepted in Boston as a matter of course.

Other physicians were more sensitive to propriety. In 1835, Edward Cutbush, delivering an address before a mixed audience at the opening of the new medical school at Geneva College, commented at length on all branches of medicine except obstetrics. The speaker explained that "delicacy has thrown a veil around this subject which precludes all remarks before this audience."[12] Cutbush confined himself to lavishing praise on William Shippen, whose "suavity of manner and correct deportment" in the eighteenth century had contributed much to obviating the prejudice against accoucheurs. Neither Shippen's students, nor those of the succeeding generations, Cutbush assured his audience, had been guilty of violating strict propriety in the course of their professional obligations.

The eminent Charles D. Meigs, who for many years held the Chair in Obstetrics and the Diseases of Women and Children at Jefferson Medical College in Philadelphia, once described to his students the embarrassment with which his own teacher had approached the topic of midwifery. Thomas Chalkey James was so modest, Meigs recalled approvingly, that as he lectured, the delicate nature of his subject "frequently sent the mantling blood over cheeks and brow to testify that he had the deepest sense of the delicacy of the task assigned to him—that of exposing to hundreds of young men, those trembling secrets of the lying-in chamber, which he had blushed to learn and which he more redly blushed to tell!"[13]

---

to women see "W.," *The Ladies Magazine and Repository of Entertaining Knowledge* 1 (June 1793):36.

11. [Channing], *Remarks*, p. 16.

12. Edward Cutbush, *A Discourse Delivered at the Opening of the Medical Institution of Geneva College, State of New York, February 10, 1835* (Geneva: Greves, 1835), p. 9.

13. Charles D. Meigs, *Introductory Lecture to a Course on Obstetrics Delivered*

Meigs had overcome his own youthful inclination to regard mid-wifery as an occupation "fit *only* for old women," as his long and pro-ductive career in obstetrics attests. Still, he retained the gentleman's respect for womanhood. In order to be successful, Meigs believed, the accoucheur must fully comprehend those traits that were unique to the female. In 1847 he favored his students with an entire lecture built around these "distinctive characteristics." Woman elevated and civilized mankind. The arts, literature, and science all flourished under her spell; her smile was the propelling force that made man's achievements possible. Natur-ally prone to be religious, she exerted a salutary effect upon society's morals, setting the tone and willingly martyring herself for religion, coun-try, and family. But, of all her attributes, observed this physician, the most charming was her modesty. This modesty stemmed from her "na-tural" inclination to timidity and dependence, and served as one of her strongest attractions as well as one of her most powerful aids. It bound her to home and family, where she transmitted to her children those positive values which elevated mankind. It made her "Come out from the world, and be separate from it."[14]

This idealized concept of delicate American woman—modest, docile, submissive, and gentle—found wide acceptance among both the men and the women of the period. Even when feminist reformers sought greater equality for women, many were careful to couch their demands in terms of usefulness within "woman's sphere."[15] Of chief interest here is the incongruity of the situation in which, despite the "innate" modesty and delicacy of her character, the enciente woman was encouraged to suspend her prejudices and inhibitions—at least temporarily—in order to obtain a safe and rapid delivery at the hands of an accoucheur. The physicians' task in overcoming woman's timidity was made all the more complex by their own recognition of the need to bow to propriety and decorum. One solution, of course, was to provide society with medically trained women attendants. The same cultural attitudes, however, that bound women to their natural "sphere" made it increasingly difficult to accept the notion that "true" women could be competently trained to

in Jefferson Medical College, November 4, 1841 (Philadelphia: Merrihew & Thomp-son, 1841), p. 8.

14. Charles D. Meigs, *Lecture on some of the Distinctive Characteristics of the Female, Delivered Before the Class of the Jefferson Medical College,* January 5, 1847 (Philadelphia: Collins, 1847), pp. 6–16.

15. William O'Neill demonstrates how this trend became more pronounced later in the century, as feminists soft-pedaled earlier radical positions in favor of more acceptable socially oriented objectives. See William O'Neill, "Feminism as a Radical Ideology," in *Dissent: Explorations in the History of American Radicalism,* edited by Alfred F. Young (De Kalb: Northern Illinois University Press, 1968), pp. 275–300.

perform the delicate tasks of the obstetrician and still retain their modesty, and physicians capitalized on this in their determined efforts to keep women out of medical practice.[16]

Anxious to attract obstetrical cases, yet mindful that they were always subject to criticism, the doctors endeavored to strike a balance that would permit them to control the field, yet not offend the sensibilities. In 1838, Hugh L. Hodge, Professor of Midwifery at the University of Pennsylvania, put the problem in focus. Deploring the continued presence among women of "prejudice" against the accoucheur, he asserted that medical students must not only totally qualify themselves in obstetrics, but must also "diffuse, in every direction a knowledge of the great value of obstetrics, as a practical science." In so doing, they must inculcate the view that parturition was *always* dangerous. This must be the goal, insisted Hodge, for if these facts can be substantiated; if this information can be promulgated; if females can be induced to believe that their sufferings will be diminished, or shortened, and their lives and those of their offspring, be safer in the hands of the profession; there will be no further difficulty in establishing the universal practice of obstetrics. All the prejudices of the most ignorant or nervous female, all the innate and acquired feelings of delicacy so characteristic of the sex, will afford no obstacle to the employment of male practitioners.[17]

While they admitted to the "delicacy of the sexes" and acknowledged what Meigs called "the embarrassments of the practice," doctors nevertheless belittled objections to the obstetrician by charging that women were cultivating a "false delicacy." The American edition of Hugh Smith's *Letters to Married Ladies* (1829) cautioned women against withholding information from their physicians. Pointing out that a doctor

16. Many of the early women physicians of the 1850s were attracted to medicine because they recognized the need to provide an alternative to the accoucheur. Elizabeth Blackwell stated that her interest in medicine had been stimulated by the remarks of a friend who suffered from a painful disease, "the delicate nature of which made the methods of treatment a constant suffering to her." The friend had added that her misery would have been reduced greatly had she been able to consult a woman physician. See Elizabeth Blackwell, *Pioneer Work for Women* (New York: Dutton, 1915), p. 21. As the movement for women physicians gained ground, the profession insisted that women who studied medicine were immodest and "unsexed" themselves. See, for example, John Ware, "Success in the Medical Profession," *Boston Medical and Surgical Journal* 43 (January 22, 1851):509–22; *New York Medical Gazette* 1 (July 13, 1850):23; Daniel Holmes, "An Essay on Medical Education," *Transactions of the Medical Association of Southern Central New York 1854* (Auburn: Moses, 1854), pp. 36–52.

17. Hugh L. Hodge, *Introductory Lecture to the Course on Obstetrics and the Diseases of Women and Children, Delivered in the University of Pennsylvania, November 7, 1838* (Philadelphia: Auner, 1838), p. 11.

could not prescribe properly without full knowledge of his patient's symptoms, the physician as author warned women against deciding for themselves what they would reveal and what they would not. "True modesty," observed the author, "never interferes, in any respect, with health; it must be nothing less than mock modesty, bearing no alliance to that lovely charm which sheds such lustre over every female grace." He scorned the exhibition of "mere pretence of character," and assured his readers that doctors were not deceived by it.

As doctors expanded their treatment of women to include not only parturition but also that wide range of disorders included in the term "diseases of women," the problems multiplied. Frequently, the woman who could be persuaded to call a doctor to deliver her was loathe to have him treat other "female complaints." If she did consult him, she was reluctant even to describe her symptoms, and more often than not would absolutely refuse to submit to a physical examination. Charles Meigs warned that the woman who was less than candid, or who steadfastly refused to permit more than a partial and superficial examination, invited grave consequences. Yet physicians, too, must recognize their own responsibilities. Meigs observed that many practitioners were constrained by their sense of delicacy from examining women patients thoroughly. To illustrate his point, he cited the case of a patient who had suffered for twenty years from an abnormal condition of the uterus. Although she had been examined repeatedly during that time, not one of these partial examinations revealed the actual source of her complaint. As a consequence, she had suffered unnecessarily for years from a condition that could have been remedied if one of the attending physicians had persisted in obtaining the requisite information.

But even Meigs's genuine concern about the medically injurious effects of modesty did not prevent his making this astounding observation: "It is perhaps best, upon the whole, that this great degree of modesty should exist even to the extent of putting a bar to researches. . . . I confess I am proud to say that, in this country . . . there are women who prefer to suffer the extremity of danger and pain, rather than waive those scruples of delicacy which prevent their maladies from being fully explored. I say it is an evidence of the dominion of a fine morality in our society."[18]

Yet, it would certainly be erroneous to consider Meigs's comment as representative of the views of the entire medical profession. The majority of physicians were inclined to draw a fine distinction between "false"

18. Charles D. Meigs, *Females and Their Diseases* (Philadelphia: Lea & Blanchard, 1848), pp. 20–21, 19.

and "genuine" modesty. As Dr. John F. Holston put it in the *New York Medical Gazette* of May, 1854, intelligent women, when not blinded by "modern reform notions," recognized the difficulties involved in training women as obstetrical attendants, and wisely agreed that the "bulk" of obstetrical practice should be in the hands of male practitioners. In 1855, John Quackenbush, of the Albany Medical College, remarked to students that most doctors could expect to be called upon to practice midwifery during their careers. The public, he noted, had learned that childbirth was a risky business, and had been persuaded to employ the accoucheur "almost" exclusively. "The natural delicacy of the woman exists *now;* but she permits the knowledge of her danger to override this delicacy of her feelings and the modesty of her nature."[19]

These observations notwithstanding, physicians were vulnerable to the charge of exciting "improper feelings" among their women patients. Professors at the medical colleges were conscious of this fact, and repeatedly urged students and colleagues to take every possible precaution to avoid censure. It was essential for a doctor to cultivate a climate of mutual respect with his patient. No true gentleman, asserted one doctor, would commit the error of infringing on the delicacy "which should ever attach itself to the almost sacred office in which he is engaged."[20] Although Caspar Wistar, midwifery professor at the University of Pennsylvania, considered it a "self-evident truth" that women should be attended by accomplished male obstetricians, this was not always so apparent to the public. In asking woman to sacrifice some degree of modesty by employing the accoucheur, the doctor incurred a special obligation. He must not betray her trust in him, and must strive always to "repay woman's confidence . . . by diligence and . . . [devotion to] duty."[21]

The need to observe strict propriety in the lying-in room made it awkward for physician and patient when it was necessary to conduct a vaginal examination. The young physician was cautioned to examine only when it was essential, and warned against unnecessary repetition. Above all, such examinations must always be conducted with decorum and preferably in the presence of a married woman or nurse. William Dewees suggested that even questioning of a delicate nature be accomplished

19. John Van Pelt Quackenbush, *An Address Delivered Before the Students of the Albany Medical College, Introductory to the Course on Obstetrics, November 5, 1855* (Albany: B. Taylor, 1855), p. 7.

20. [Channing], *Remarks*, p. 20.

21. Caspar Wistar, *Eulogium on William Shippen . . . delivered before the College of Physicians of Philadelphia, March, 1809* (Philadelphia: Dobson, 1818), p. 30; and Quackenbush, *Address*, p. 8.

through the intermediary nurse or elderly female friend. This third person should be the one to propose a necessary examination to the patient, and to urge it upon her. Permission granted, further precautions were called for. "Before you proceed," advised Dewees, ". . . let your patient be placed with the most scrupulous regard to delicacy, as the slightest exposure is never necessary."[22] Only when all light was excluded from the room could the exclusively tactile examination proceed. Finally, when delivery was imminent, the decorous physician left the room while the nurse positioned the patient. He returned when she was covered entirely except for her head, at which time he delivered the child under the blanket or sheet.

The post-partum mother frequently has difficulty excreting urine. To effect elimination in such cases, a catheter must be passed through the urethra to the bladder. Physicians and patients alike found this procedure unpleasant and offensive. Consequently, doctors could not agree about who was responsible for performing catheterizations. Samuel Bard believed it could be done by a woman attendant, who should introduce the device "under the bed-clothes."[23] Thomas Ewell concurred. He emphasized the fact that the passing of the catheter was a simple matter, and insisted that it was a "disgrace to the [female] sex" for a man to perform this "odious" task.[24] William Dewees, who believed that the physician should perform the operation, nevertheless was aware of the potential offense to dignity it involved, and carefully advised the young practitioner on correct procedure. Once the patient had been positioned properly at the side of the bed, the doctor lubricated his finger with sweet oil or lard. Then he carefully placed his hand beneath the bedclothes, "so as not to occasion the smallest exposure" of the patient, and inserted the catheter. Relying solely on the sense of touch might be awkward, but it was considered infinitely preferable to offending etiquette. Charles Meigs favored teaching the patient to insert the catheter herself. "There is," he wrote, "scarcely a more disagreeable operation to be performed than that of catheterism of the female; an operation which, I should think, every gentleman would be glad to commit to other hands than his own."[25] At mid-century, Chandler R. Gilman, professor of obstetrics at the College of Physicians and Surgeons in New York, stated that he never used the

22. Dewees, *Compendious System,* pp. 190–91.
23. Bard, *Compendium,* p. 26.
24. Thomas Ewell, *Letters to Ladies, Detailing Important Information Concerning Themselves and Infants* (Philadelphia: W. Brown, 1817), p. 96.
25. Meigs, *Females and Their Diseases,* p. 572.

catheter if he could avoid it. When forced to it, he normally avoided exposing his patient, although he admitted that in some cases, "delicacy must yield to necessity."[26]

The "diseases of women" presented additional challenges to decorum. Gynecology was in its infancy in the early years of the nineteenth century. For the most part, doctors treated gynecological disorders medically rather than surgically, prescribing pills and pastes. Digital examination, even when permitted by a reluctant patient, provided doctors with little accurate information and left much to conjecture until the vaginal speculum began to find favor. This instrument, developed in France by Joseph Claude Anthelme Recamier, made possible the inspection of the cervix and uterus, greatly enhancing the possibilities for treating diseased parts effectively. After many years of experimentation, and subsequent modification of the speculum to widen the field of vision, Recamier demonstrated its use to colleagues in 1818.[27]

The pervasive climate of modesty in the United States, according to a report in the May 1850 issue of the *New York Journal of Medicine*, hindered acceptance of the speculum, and physicians themselves were hesitant about employing it. In 1844, Fleetwood Churchill, an English physician who had modified the speculum, said he considered the instrument highly overrated. He particularly objected to it because its use necessitated exposure of the patient, which digital examination did not, thus making it much more offensive to female delicacy. On the other hand, in the January 1851 issue of the *New York Journal of Medicine* Chandler Gilman charged with negligence those doctors who claimed never to have encountered a patient with a diseased cervix. He insisted that routine use of the speculum led to the discovery of previously undetected cases. Gilman strongly objected to the "anti-progress party" in the profession whose adherents opposed innovation in general, and chloroform and the speculum in particular. On June 15, 1851, the *New York Medical Gazette* reported that the recently organized American Medical Association had heatedly debated the "speculum mania." Thus, at mid-century, many doctors still took the position that a competent physician need not resort to visual examination for any reason whatsoever.

Given the acknowledged embarrassments of obstetrical and gynecological practice, it is not surprising that the profession remained sensitive to criticism. For years opponents had protested vehemently, if in-

26. *Report of the Trial, The People versus Dr. Horatio N. Loomis, for Libel,* reported by Frederick T. Parsons (Buffalo: Jewett, Thomas, 1850), p. 25.
27. James V. Ricci, *The Development of Gynaecological Surgery and Instruments* (Philadelphia: Blakiston, 1949), p. 294.

effectively, against man-midwifery, calling for the restoration of obstetrics to the women from whom it had been wrested. Only in this way, they argued, could the nation be set back upon its proper moral course, with each of the sexes functioning as it should, within its own special sphere. Despite the abortive nature of the crusade against man-midwifery, it did serve to reinforce the physicians' awareness of their vulnerability. Added to this was the movement to educate women as physicians, which emerged in the 1850s and drew its support from radical feminists concerned about sexual equality and wider professional opportunities for women. Several years before the debate surfaced over the place of women in medicine, however, an event occurred in western New York State which threatened (or promised) prompt restoration of all obstetrical practice to women. The ramifications of the incident, felt throughout the profession, vividly illustrate not only the concerns of physicians caught up in early Victorian prudishness, but the way in which doctors effectively met the challenge.

Early in January 1850, Dr. James Platt White, professor of obstetrics at Buffalo Medical College, introduced onto the American scene a highly controversial innovation that soon became known as "demonstrative midwifery." In order to give his students practical knowledge of the birth process itself, White arranged to have his entire class attend an actual delivery. Before acting, he shared his plan with colleagues on the faculty and received their unqualified approval, as the *Buffalo Medical Journal* reported in March 1850. A twenty-six-year-old Irish immigrant, Mary Watson, then an inmate of the Erie County Poor House, unwed and pregnant with her second child, agreed to serve as the professor's subject. Subsequently, she received ten dollars from White, although this had not been part of the original agreement.[28]

Shortly before her confinement, Mary Watson was housed in the basement of the college, adjacent to the janitor's apartment. In the days immediately prior to the onset of labor, Dr. White permitted students to make abdominal stethoscopic examinations of the fully clothed patient in order that they might hear intra-uterine sounds. During the labor, students also made tactile vaginal examinations under White's supervision. As the fetal head was about to emerge from under the pubic arch, the class of twenty students, plus several physicians, entered the room to observe. Dr. White then partially removed the patient's clothing in order to demonstrate the correct technique of applying support to the perineum. Students later testified that although the patient had been exposed

---

28. *Report of the Loomis Trial*, p. 21.

for two to five minutes, they were not aware of any exposure of the genital organs inasmuch as the professor had covered the perineum with napkins while applying support. Mary Watson's labor and delivery were natural, and at no time did she complain of her treatment.[29]

Following the delivery, White's students adopted three resolutions expressing gratitude to their professor and pride in the fact that the University of Buffalo had been the first American medical school to introduce clinical instruction in midwifery. On February 19, the *Buffalo Commercial Advertiser* carried an editorial supporting the innovation. On February 27, however, the *Buffalo Courier* published an anonymous article criticizing Dr. White for demonstrating the process of childbirth on a live subject. The author acknowledged that White had been present during the labor, but noted that "delicacy forbids me to touch upon the manner in which these [eight] hours were passed. Suffice it to say that the tedium was relieved by such methods, as a congregation of boys would know well how to employ." The experiment had permitted students "their salacious stare" to satisfy a "meretricious curiosity" at Mary Watson's expense. He pronounced the whole episode irregular and an outrage to public decency.

Horatio N. Loomis, a Buffalo physician, agreed so completely with this assessment that he paid for the printing of additional copies of the article, which he distributed to patients and friends. In response, White and his colleagues sued Loomis for libel. In April, the Buffalo Grand Jury handed down an indictment, and in June, the case of *The People* versus *Doctor Horatio N. Loomis* was tried before the Court of Oyer and Terminer. The jury eventually returned a verdict of not guilty.

The Buffalo experiment and the attendant notoriety provoked bitter controversy within the profession. In March 1850, John Hanenstein and sixteen other doctors from the Buffalo area had sent a letter to the editor of the *Buffalo Medical Journal* challenging the need for demonstrative midwifery. White's experiment merited severe rebuke, they contended, because it was "wholly unnecessary for the purpose of teaching, unprofessional in manner, and grossly offensive alike to morality and common

---

29. For relevant information on the demonstrative midwifery case in Buffalo see: *Report of the Loomis Trial; Buffalo Medical Journal* 5 (February and March 1850), and 6 (July 1850); *American Journal of the Medical Sciences* 20 (October 1850): 447–49, and 21 (January 1851):270; *Boston Medical and Surgical Journal* 42 (April 24, 1850):257; *New York Journal of Medicine and the Collateral Sciences* 4 (May 1850):395–96; *Louisville Medical Journal* (June 1850), in Herbert Thoms, *Our Obstetrical Heritage* (Hamden, Conn.: Shoe String Press, 1960), p. 133; and "Demonstrative Midwifery," *New York Medical Gazette* 1 (July 6, 1850):5–6. The description in the text of the case and the ensuing debate was drawn from these sources as well as the periodicals noted in the text.

decency." They hoped, for the sake of the medical profession, that such an "exhibition" would not be repeated in Buffalo, "or in any civilized community."

Reaction to such criticism was prompt. Austin Flint, professor of theory and practice of medicine at Buffalo, and editor of the *Buffalo Medical Journal*, replied that the demonstration "commend[ed] itself to the cordial approbation of the medical profession." The *Boston Medical and Surgical Journal* agreed, applauding the innovation and pointing out that clinical instruction in obstetrics, although new to American medical schools, was common in the lying-in hospitals of Europe. It was regretable, commented the editor, that some doctors had objected. Similar sentiments were expressed by the editor of the *New York Journal of Medicine,* who pronounced Dr. White's course of action "Honorable, high-minded, and judicious." In the past he recalled, physicians had opposed innovation. The use of the stethoscope and the speculum had been disputed, and there had been "more than bitter persecution" visited upon the early accoucheurs. "We regret to learn," he continued, "that among the members of our own profession there is even one who retains a mite of the semblance of by-gone days in this respect." The *Louisville Medical Journal* took a dim view of the "prudish Miss Nancies of Buffalo." Commented that publication: "We can easily imagine a childlike simplicity that would put pantelets upon the legs of a piano and that would screen with a veil every thing capable of exciting prurient ideas, but we do not like to see this excessive flirtation with modesty, introduced into medical teaching."

During the course of the Loomis libel trial, presiding Judge Mullett attempted to put the question in perspective. He acknowledged the propriety of all legitimate means employed by practitioners, even when their use might suggest an offense to modesty and moral delicacy. To safeguard her health and preserve the happiness of those dependent upon her, he observed, a woman must turn to her physician. In doing so, however, she did not surrender her claims to modesty, delicacy, or sensibility. "These guardians of female virtue may be compelled to step back for the occasion," he noted, "but they stand around her like Diana's Nymphs while she is bathing; let the practitioner make one significant manifestation of an unholy thought, and they rally around the insulted one." Surely the defendant, as an honorable member of the profession, must realize that those who stood at the bedside of a woman in the agonizing throes of parturition did not harbor libidinous thoughts. They could feel only pity and sympathy for those who faced danger and often death in childbirth. If the imputations of impure thought were in fact true, he pointed out, they would be as true of students the day after graduation as they were the day before.

The conclusion of the Loomis trial did not put an end to the debate. Chandler Gilman expressed alarm over the effects on the profession of the public controversy. Personally, he believed that demonstrative midwifery had merit and was as important to students as clinical instruction in surgery. The principal question was whether physicians could win acceptance of any innovation without offending public opinion. Recalling the charges of indelicacy and impropriety raised against physicians who introduced the vaginal speculum, and noting the continued criticism of men in the fields of obstetrics and gynecology, he insisted that every physician needed to prove to the public that his motives were above reproach. "It is the motive with which he acts that is to be his defence; and if this defence will not avail demonstrative midwifery, neither will it avail the use of the speculum, the attendance of a male obstetrician, or in fact any prescribing by a man for the sexual diseases of females. All must stand or fall together," he warned.

In the *New York Medical Gazette,* July 6, 1850, the editor noted his sympathy for Gilman's uneasiness. If any impropriety had been involved in the Buffalo situation, the writer said, the public spotlight would soon provide a remedy. "If not," he predicted, "it will be a Godsend to the project of transferring obstetric practice to the other sex." As expected, the critics of man-midwifery found support for their cause in the Buffalo experiment. William Hosmer, for example, editor of the *Northern Christian Advocate,* charged in the issue for August 14, 1850, that the incident was only one specific abuse in a long list of objectionable practices that ought to result in returning obstetrical practice to women. Both groups of physicians, those who favored demonstrative midwifery and those who argued vehemently against it, were agreed on one point: the glare of publicity growing out of the Buffalo episode threatened the continuance of man-midwifery.

There were physicians critical of the Buffalo experiment who admitted that some form of clinical instruction in obstetrics was desirable. The aspect of the White demonstration most damaging to the profession, according to the opinion of one doctor in the *American Journal of Medical Science* for October 1850, was that the so-called *"improvement . . .* consisted in subjecting the process of parturition to *ocular* inspection in one of its stages." Although he did not feel that the demonstration had incited "libidinous emotions" in White's students, this was really beside the point. Dr. White ought not to have exposed his patient at all. In practice, physicians almost never resorted to ocular assistance in parturient cases; when they conducted vaginal examinations, they "instinctively" closed their eyes, both out of feelings of delicacy, and to improve their powers of concentration. It was, therefore, very wrong to teach students to employ vision in such cases, for they would be likely to carry this over into their own practices. American women, he warned, would never tolerate this impropriety.

Equally distressing was Chandler Gilman's testimony at the Loomis trial, continued the critic. Gilman had admitted that when he was required to turn a fetus in utero, it was his custom "to expose the woman entirely." A practice such as this, particularly when performed in the presence of students, "might well result in a public reaction against accoucheurs." The *New York Medical Gazette* agreed that exposure of the patient was "*never* necessary," and could not be condoned. "Catheterism, vaginal exploration, manipulations . . . whether manual or instrumental, delivery by the forceps and embryotomy itself, can all be performed by a competent man as well without the eye as with it." If this were not so, remarked the editor, "then should we hail the new project of educating female accoucheurs, and transferring all such practice to the other sex, as the dictate of propriety and good sense."[30]

In view of the furor created by demonstrative midwifery and the dire predictions of practitioners regarding the future of obstetrical practice, it is not surprising that the American Medical Association addressed itself to the innovation. At its third annual meeting in Cincinnati in 1850, the Association adopted a resolution calling upon the Committee on Medical Education to investigate whether "any practicable scheme" might be devised "to render instruction in Midwifery more practical than it has hitherto been in the medical schools."[31]

The committee's report, presented in Charleston the following year, focused on the most sensitive question surrounding demonstrative midwifery: was any exposure of a woman patient necessary? The committee outlined the four major contentions of the advocates of demonstrative midwifery: (1) the student witnessed the child emerge from under the pubic arch; (2) he was visually impressed with the need to support the perineum; (3) he could have immediately demonstrated to him the exact manner in which this support was to be given; and (4) the student received visual verification of the professor's diagnosis relative to the posi-

30. "Observations in Clinical Obstetrics," *New York Medical Gazette*, reprinted in *Medical News and Library* 8 (October 1850):83–84.

31. *Minutes of the Third Annual Meeting of the American Medical Association, Transactions of the American Medical Association* (Philadelphia: Collins, 1850), III, 42.

tion in which the fetus presented. In essence, the committee rejected all of these. There was no need for students to use a live subject, for the manner in which the fetus emerged from the os externum could easily be demonstrated on mannikins, and was thoroughly pictured on plates. Any student who failed to be convinced by his preceptor of the importance of supporting the perineum was too dull and irresponsible to become a doctor. Inasmuch as this support was normally given without utilizing vision, there was no point in permitting the student to observe the procedure. And finally, verification of the professor's diagnosis of presentation could be accomplished by touch, or the student could take the professor's word for it. When one compared true clinical instruction under the supervision of a preceptor with demonstrative midwifery, continued the report, it was obvious that the former provided instruction which the latter could not. Demonstrative midwifery, pronounced the committee, was "unnecessary" and "incompetent."[32]

It was unfortunate, observed the committee, that there existed an erroneous but widespread belief that women were asked to sacrifice their modesty in order to be treated for gynecological ailments. It was woman's duty to submit to proper treatment when necessary, and no necessary treatment could be considered immodest. There had been cases, acknowledged the report, where doctors had employed the vaginal speculum without justification. Such instances had tended to embarrass honorable physicians and their patients, for unnecessary treatment was always immodest. Nor could the committee countenance the lecture-room practice of making "indecent allusions" about the relations between physicians and their female patients. This pandering to the "depraved taste" of students did serious injury to the profession. It was of the utmost importance, cautioned the committee, that the confidential relationship between patient and doctor remain unimpaired. "The object both of the individual practitioner and of the profession, should be to meet most fully the demands of science and humanity, and yet not offend a sensitive, but rational delicacy, nor give countenance to an unblushing shamelessness."

Unnecessary treatment, demonstrative midwifery, and failure on the part of physicians to observe the proprieties were all responsible for the prevailing public prejudice against employing men in obstetrics and gynecology, warned the committee. Indelicate practices had "given rise to the project for training female practitioners of medicine. The project will

32. "Report of the Committee on Medical Education in relation to 'Demonstrative Midwifery,'" submitted at the fourth annual meeting of the American Medical Association, *Transactions of the American Medical Association* (Philadelphia: Collins, 1851), IV, 436–37.

for obvious reasons, be unsuccessful . . . chiefly because the community generally will be convinced that, although some physicians are guilty of transgressing the rules of propriety and modesty in their intercourse with their patients, medical men, as a body are pure-minded men, and . . . their honour, as well as their skill, is worthy of the public."

Regrettably, it is not possible to learn what was said during the debate which followed presentation of the committee's report. The *New York Medical Gazette*, June 15, 1851, informed its readers that the committee's comments were "discussed with some degree of ardor and sensitiveness." In any case, the delegates to the Fourth Annual Meeting adopted unanimously a resolution approving the opinions expressed in the report.

Demonstrative midwifery had provoked a warfare in medical journals in newspaper style, and the profession's central body had rejected the innovation. In doing so, doctors had recognized that the controversy threatened the reputation of the entire profession at a time when its claim to the practice of obstetrics and gynecology was being publicly challenged. The position of the American Medical Association in 1851 served as a portent for the future. In the ensuing decade physicians, conscious of a fully mounted attack in the form of projects to educate women physicians, mustered their forces in a successful effort to preserve their domain. This need not imply that physicians acted solely out of selfish motives, although this undoubtedly played a part. Given the idealized picture of nineteenth-century woman, doctors could advance many acceptable arguments in support of their contention that women had no place in medical practice. Curiously, there was a marked similarity between the arguments employed by advocates of female midwifery and those of the doctors determined to keep women out of the profession. Both groups spoke in terms of women's place in society; to the one group, morality and modesty were best served with women practicing obstetrics, while to the other, these same qualities were violated when women went against their feminine nature and "unsexed" themselves by venturing beyond their sphere into a man's world.

By keeping its medical colleges closed to all but a few women, by closing the hospitals to them and barring them from medical societies, male physicians did all within their power to prevent the growth of a large body of qualified women practitioners. In the final analysis, however successful a few individual women practitioners may have been in post-Revolutionary America, it is clear that the men in the medical profession had emerged victorious in their struggle to control obstetrics and gynecology.

6

The Meaning of Harriet Tubman

OTEY SCRUGGS

*ℋ*ARRIET TUBMAN was born a slave and died a free person. Although not entirely, it was essentially in slavery that she learned the value of freedom and dedicated herself to the cause of freeing others at the hazard of losing her own freedom and even her life. In a profound way, Harriet Tubman's life speaks to the praxis of freedom. It addresses itself as much to those already free—but who have yet to realize the fullest life for themselves in furthering freedom for others—as it does to a past when the urgency was to deliver blacks from slavery. It is the quest for freedom through the process of obtaining it that is the continually emerging legend of Harriet Tubman.

Born in Dorchester County, Maryland, around 1820, Harriet Tubman spent almost the first third of her long life in slavery. From it she emerged "a strange compound of practical shrewdness and of a visionary enthusiasm."[1] Powerful formative influences on her life were her family and her religious background. Her parents, whose own parents were African-born, were hard-working people who provided their eleven children

1. Elizabeth R. Haynes, *Homespun Heroines and Other Women of Distinction* (Wilberforce, Ohio: Homewood Cottage, 1926), p. 55. Also, Sarah Bradford, *Harriet Tubman: The Moses of Her People*, introduction by Butler A. Jones (New York: Corinth, 1961), p. 69. In addition to Bradford, the primary source on Tubman, see Earl Conrad, *Harriet Tubman* (Washington, D.C.: Associated Publishers, 1943); Ann Petry, *Harriet Tubman: Conductor on the Underground Railroad* (New York: Crowell, 1955); Dorothy Sterling, *Freedom Train: The Story of Harriet Tubman* (Garden City, N.Y.: Doubleday, 1954); and Frances T. Humphreville, *Harriet Tubman: Flame of Freedom* (Boston: Houghton Mifflin, 1967).

(at least two of whom were sold South) with care and affection. For example, when the youthful Harriet was exposed to overwork and ill-treatment, her mother, though overworked herself and tired, always nursed her rebellious daughter back to health. Her father, a workman of stature in the slave community, taught her woods lore, including the medicinal value of roots, and contributed to her growing love of the outdoors. She became so skilled with plow, axe, and hoe, developing the endurance and sinewy strength of the experienced field hand, that she was able to follow her father's example and hire herself out. Like many another slave, she learned to take the measure of nature and of people in order to survive.

An equally decisive element in Harriet Tubman's character was her powerful religious faith. It served to support the other elements—the courage, the resourcefulness, the industry, and the concern for others. It provided the moral basis for her yearning to be free. Biblical selections, quoted endlessly in conversation, became a part of her consciousness, and served as the principal reference point for her conception of the just society. It was largely against that standard that she measured the realities of life about her and judged the need for change. Sarah Bradford, her first biographer and close friend, said that Tubman's religion was based on an awareness of God as an intensely personal reality. Harriet had inherited from her parents a strong faith in God and she regarded the Divine Presence as a close friend, talking with God "as a man talketh with his friend." Bradford noted that Tubman abjured the practice of keeping a set time for prayers, preferring instead to share her problems with God as they arose, confident that matters would be set right.[2]

Like many slaves whose religion was a syncretization of African and Euro-American beliefs, she was much given to dreams and omens, claiming on numerous occasions to have foreseen people, places, and events. In Tubman's case, belief in dreams and omens may have been reinforced by those frequent periods of catalepsy from which she suffered most of her life. Her condition had been created by a severe blow to the head, dealt by an angry overseer who had struck her with a two-pound weight while she was attempting to protect a runaway slave. But whatever else slave religion may have been, it was essentially an expression of a desire for freedom. In the religious experience of many slaves, freedom was other-worldly. But for slaves like Harriet Tubman, freedom was to be

2. For comments of a similar nature on slave religion, see John W. Blassingame, *The Slave Community* (New York: Oxford University Press, 1972), p. 74; and Gilbert Osofsky, ed., *Puttin' On Ole Massa* (New York: Harper and Row, 1969), pp. 36–39.

sought in this world.[3] In 1849, when she learned she was about to be sold South, she rebelled by walking away from slavery, alone, over the underground railroad to Philadelphia. As she later told Mrs. Bradford: "I had reasoned dis out in my mind; there was one of two things I had a *right* to, liberty or death; if I could not have one, I would have de oder; for no man should take me alive; I would fight for my liberty as my strength lasted, and when de time came for me to go, de Lord would let dem take me." Survival was not enough. The slave community had provided her with the values that enabled her to transcend the view that life was just existence.

Once free, she vowed to bring others in her family out of bondage on the underground railroad. Personal loneliness may have played a part in that decision, but basically, however, she had learned that to gain freedom for herself, she must help others to be free. The initial objective—assisting her family to escape—was later broadened to include other slaves, possibly with the hope that the institution of slavery on the whole of Maryland's Eastern Shore would thereby be weakened.

Her role as the most successful conductor on the underground railroad during its heyday in the 1850s has perhaps best been described by Mrs. Bradford. Recalling Tubman's daring and dramatic rescue efforts, Bradford noted that Harriet's strategy was to disappear from her northern home and then reappear mysteriously in the middle of the night at the door of a darkened slave cottage. Leading a band of waiting fugitives, who had been forewarned of her coming, she guided them North, traveling by night and hiding by day. Together they traversed difficult terrain, always alert to the pursuers who inevitably dogged their steps. She carried the babies herself, keeping them drugged with paregoric in a basket on her arm. Bradford counted nineteen such trips, which resulted in freedom for at least three hundred people previously regarded as "property," all of whom owed their successful flight to Tubman. Slavery had prepared her well for this new and dangerous calling. Not only was her knowledge of field and forest crucial, but the deception that was a key to survival in slavery was her basic training for the ruses, pretenses, and disguises employed by the successful underground railroad conductor.

When she embarked upon this aspect of her career, the times could hardly have been less propitious. The Fugitive Slave Act of 1850 had just been passed. Designed to make it easier for slaveholders to recover runaways, the law made her job more hazardous. It was no longer enough

3. On this double-direction in slave religion, see Vincent Harding, "Religion and Resistance Among Ante-Bellum Negroes, 1800–1860," in *The Making of Black America*, edited by August Meier and Elliott Rudwick, I, *The Origins of Black Americans* (New York: Atheneum, 1969), p. 194.

to get them to the North; now she would have to guide them all the way to Canada. Her many trips were accomplished without loss of life, while the reward for her capture rose to a total of $40,000. This was the very stuff of romance and legend. Indeed, it was an American epic. Albert Murray recognized this when he remarked: "The pioneer spirit of American womanhood is widely eulogized. But at no time in the history of the Republic has such womanhood ever attained a higher level of excellence than in the indomitable heroism of a runaway slave named Harriet Tubman."[4] While white pioneers went West, Harriet Tubman and her fellow runaways went North, the advance guard of the great black migration of our own time. In one significant respect, however, her feats of courage and daring outshone those of the westward-moving pioneers: the latter were seldom chased by anyone possessed of the full power of the law. Moreover, settlers went West impelled by the hope of new land over the next hill, while the fugitives could only content themselves with the thought that they were leaving behind an inhuman situation.

The Tubman legend was in the making as early as the 1850s. To the slaves of eastern Maryland to whom biblical analogy came easily enough, she became "Moses," the redeemer of her people from the Egypt-land of the South.[5] Abolitionists, who quickly recognized the political value of the fugitive slave controversy, most often compared her with Joan of Arc. But it was not anti-slavery politics alone that led them to embrace her. They were captivated by her daring and the nobility of her exploits. In an article in the *Boston Commonwealth* in July 1863, abolitionist Franklin B. Sanborn observed that the true romance of America was to be found not in Cooper's stories about Indians or Judd's delineations of New England character or Thackeray's accounts of social contrast among planters, but rather in the drama of the fugitive slaves, and one "poor black woman" who was central to that drama. This remarkable woman possessed the power "to shake the nation that so long was deaf to her cries." Tubman, in Sanborn's opinion, was "a woman whose career is as extraordinary as the most famous of her sex can show."[6] She became for most abolitionists the symbol of an anti-slavery crusade increasingly cen-

---

4. Albert Murray, *The Omni-Americans: New Perspectives on Black Experience and American Culture* (New York: Outerbridge and Dienstfrey, 1970), p. 19.

5. Petry, *Harriet Tubman*, phrases the "Moses" legend beautifully: "They said, voices muted, awed, that she talked with God every day, just like Moses. They said there was some strange power in her so that no one could die when she was with them. She enveloped the sick and the dying with her strength, sending it from her body to theirs, sustaining them" (p. 130). For a discussion of Tubman's use of folk songs like "Go Down, Moses," see Earl Conrad, " 'General' Tubman, Composer of Spirituals," *The Etude* (May 1942):305 ff.

6. Quoted in Bradford, *Harriet Tubman*, pp. 106–107.

tered around the fugitive. Harriet Tubman was the personification of their hopes for Negroes after their chains were removed.

By the eve of the Civil War, Tubman moved easily in humanitarian circles, numbering among her intimate acquaintances Ralph Waldo Emerson, Bronson Alcott, William H. Seward, Frederick Douglass, Wendell Phillips, Susan B. Anthony, Thomas Wentworth Higginson, Henry Highland Garnet, and John Brown. Short and plain-looking, given to sleeping spells because of the blow on the head acquired in slavery, she impressed those reformers and intellectuals as a woman of strong will. Gifted with a highly developed dramatic sense, a deep but attractive voice, and a speech that combined the rhythms and cadences of the slave quarter with the poetry of the Bible, she was frequently in demand to relate stories of her marvelous life and to sing songs of slavery and freedom at private gatherings and anti-slavery meetings. So stark was her contrast with her audience that its members could only react to her with wonderment. By her deeds and her presence she compelled respect and admiration for herself, and she staked out a claim for equal treatment of her race and her sex.

But life among reformers was too tame for her. She had to be able to attack slavery in more direct, concrete ways. It was therefore inevitable that she and John Brown should meet and that they should take to each other. Both possessed a messianic vision, and both preferred action to words in the war against slavery.[7] She had the leadership skills he was seeking. So highly did he regard her that he called her "General" Tubman. More important, he confided to her his plans for running off slaves from the South. She appears to have agreed to recruit volunteers for his project from the black community in Canada, where she was well known, and also to guide liberated slaves North once guerrilla activity got under way. It has been said that only illness prevented her from being at Harper's Ferry. It is possible, however, that her sense of the practical led her to have second thoughts about the success of the undertaking. In any event, her involvement with Brown enhanced her status among abolitionists. To the end of her life she regarded him as the great liberator.

More in keeping with her concentration on "individual liberation"— certainly more successful—was her role in the rescue of the runaway,

---

7. In the words of Helen Beal Woodward, *The Bold Woman* (New York: Farrar, Straus, 1953), "theirs was a fraternity, the brotherhood of doing. Words were cheap—action counted. Others might declare the necessity of liberating the slave. John Brown and Harriet Tubman went ahead and liberated any slave they could get their hands on, and, praying to God, packed a gun" (p. 244). Woodward writes with wit, sarcasm, and considerable insight.

Charles Nalle, in Troy, New York, in April 1860.[8] This episode, the last of the celebrated rescues in defiance of the unpopular Fugitive Slave Law, was another of the many steps in the prewar decade leading to Fort Sumter in 1861. At Troy, Harriet Tubman was at her best, quickly assuming the leadership of a crowd of blacks and whites bent on forestalling Nalle's return to slavery. Throughout that long afternoon, marked by violence and bloodshed, during which Harriet was repeatedly beaten over the head with policemen's clubs, the exhausted and bloodied Nalle was twice taken from the authorities before escaping to Canada. Such heroics added to Tubman's reputation among abolitionists as a warrior-humanitarian and provided further inspiration for anti-slavery orators.

This reputation—and the legend that accompanied it—assumed even greater proportions during the Civil War: the outcome of the war was, incidentally, reportedly foreseen by Tubman in a dream several years before Sumter. From the start, she was determined to play an active part in this war for liberation; it offered the opportunity for adventure, for release from the relatively inactive life she had been restlessly leading, and for direct action against the slave power, this time with government sanction. That she managed to become an actual combatant, however, was due not only to her own persistence, but also to the recognition by her influential abolitionist friends of her military and symbolic value. Those characteristics that had made her a highly successful conductor on the underground railroad would be useful in military intelligence, reconnaissance, and medical support. These activities were, in a sense, extensions of her more basic function, which was to serve as a link between northern whites and southern blacks. Even more significant, she and her friends understood that this was an important test for Negro people to prove (and improve) themselves. For humanitarians and for black people, she thus came to symbolize this larger meaning of the Civil War.

Harriet Tubman's understanding of freedom went beyond ending slavery and included recognition of the rights of full citizenship for black people. In May 1862, backed by abolitionist Governor John Andrew of Massachusetts, she went to Beaufort, on Port Royal, which was one of the South Carolina Sea Islands recently captured by Union forces, where she assisted the fugitive slaves in developing economic and educational skills. This work foreshadowed what has now come to be known as community development. By 1863, Beaufort had become the hub of the Port Royal "experiment," a Northern humanitarian enterprise made up largely

8. The phrase "individual liberation" belongs to Sidney Lens, *Radicalism in America* (New York: Crowell, 1969), p. 108. See Bradford, *Harriet Tubman,* pp. 119–24, 124–28; and Conrad, *Harriet Tubman,* Chapter 14.

of civilian volunteers who went South to help elevate the freed slaves. Tubman plunged into the work with characteristic vigor, organizing a variety of classes, including one in homemaking that was designed to provide marketable skills for women who had been field hands. She could point to herself as a model, for every night she made pies, ginger-bread and root beer, which she sold to help meet her own living expenses.[9]

She demonstrated her medical skills in the freedmen's hospital. She cared for people suffering from everything from malnutrition to the viru-lent diseases of the swampy lowlands. At repeated risks to her own life, she nursed soldiers and contrabands alike who had smallpox and "malig-nant fevers." She was frequently called upon to dispense her herbal rem-edy for dysentery, once being sent to Fernandina, Florida, where many men were dying of the disease.

But it was for her military work that Harriet Tubman became best known, for while her community development efforts were notable and exceptional, certainly few women could match her legendary military exploits. She consulted with military leaders on matters of strategy. She either knew or worked closely with those in the heavily abolitionist De-partment of the South. There was the radical Colonel Thomas Wentworth Higginson,[10] commander of the black 1st South Carolina Volunteers, whom she had already known well before the war in Boston and to whose education in the ways of black people she and other fugitives contributed extensively. There was Colonel James Montgomery of the black 2nd South Carolina Volunteers, with whom she collaborated on tactics of un-restricted guerrilla warfare. And there was the aristocratic Colonel Robert Gould Shaw, scion of a Boston anti-slavery family and commander of the black 54th Massachusetts Volunteers. Shaw, along with many of his black troops, died in the suicidal assault on Fort Wagner, the soldiers demon-strating with their lives the courage of Negroes under fire. Harriet Tub-man nursed the wounded and buried the dead from that costly action.

---

9. For the Port Royal "experiment," see Willie Lee Rose, *Rehearsal for Recon-struction* (New York: Vintage, 1967), p. 248. At the same time, Sojourner Truth was going through the freedmen's camps around Washington, D.C., with the cry, "Be clean." Tubman's concern with cleanliness was probably less for its own presumed values than as a means of training in a useful skill. It was more practical than ideological.

Charlotte Forten, who visited with her in early 1863, wrote: "She is living in [Beaufort] now; keeping an eating house." The *Journal of Charlotte Forton*, edited, and introduction by R. A. Billington (New York: Collier, 1961), p. 180.

10. For a dramatic account of Higginson's adventures in South Carolina, see his *Army Life in a Black Regiment*, introduction by Howard N. Meyer (New York: Collier, 1962).

But the episode that best epitomizes her military career was the guerrilla raid up the Combahee River.

Engaged in reconnaissance and military intelligence, she spent considerable time behind enemy lines coordinating an effective network of black informants. It was on information thus supplied that the Combahee expedition was based. In the early morning of June 2, 1863, three gunboats carrying Harriet Tubman, Colonel James Montgomery whom she had requested to be put in charge, and 150 black troops went up the river. Before the morning was over, they had removed torpedos placed there by the Confederates, set fire to the plantations bordering the river, and carried away 756 slaves, all without loss of life. The raid had about it a touch of the successful underground railroad conductor as well as that of the Kansas barnburner.[11] Small wonder Montgomery could laud her as "a most remarkable woman, and invaluable as a scout," and Hunter could praise her as "a valuable woman."[12] Earl Conrad, her most recent biographer, might be right when he refers to the Combahee raid as "probably the most celebrated achievement of her life, one that may well be the envy of any white American woman."[13] It was in keeping with her identification with the black rank and file as well as her awareness of the war's larger significance that, in a letter to Sanborn shortly afterwards, she should ask: "Don't you think we colored people are entitled to some of the credit for that exploit, under the lead of the brave Colonel Montgomery?"[14]

Harriet Tubman ended her wartime career—or, more appropriately, three or four war-related careers—in 1865 as a worker in a freedmen's hospital in Fortress Monroe, Virginia. In that situation she brought together the wide range of technical and human skills necessary for effective health care delivery. Ironically, it was after she had left Virginia and was traveling to her home in Auburn, New York, that this "greatest heroine of the age,"[15] who had managed to escape physical injury during all her hazardous experiences, received the most cruel blow of her life.

11. The analogy of the underground railroad conductor hardly seems appropriate where the activity is much more like that of the commandos in World War II. Conrad, *Harriet Tubman* (pp. 169–71), following a contemporary account, contends that Tubman "formulated" the strategy and "led" the raid. However, the campaign strategy of "thorough" has the Montgomery touch; on Montgomery's incendiary tactics, see Rose, *Rehearsal*, pp. 251–53.

12. Bradford, *Harriet Tubman*, pp. 138, 140.

13. Conrad, " 'General' Tubman, Composer of Spirituals," *The Etude* (May 1942):352.

14. Conrad, *Harriet Tubman*, p. 177.

15. The phrase was coined by Thomas Wentworth Higginson. Quoted in ibid, p. 107.

Rudely ejected from a "for whites only" train, she was wounded in body and soul. The incident revealed that while blacks were coming out from under slavery, whites were still held firmly in its grip.

With the end of slavery, the popular image of Harriet Tubman as the deliverer of her people tended to fade. But to appreciate the larger meaning of Harriet Tubman it is necessary to understand her continued quest for freedom during the balance of her long life. To begin with, the national mood changed after the war.[16] In 1868, for instance, in the preface to her biography, Mrs. Bradford anticipated public incredulity at the idea of a black heroine. On the surface, Tubman's subsequent career mirrored the declining fortunes of the Negro. For example, to her repeated attempts to secure some form of compensation for her wartime service, the government turned a deaf ear until 1899, when she was finally granted $20.00 a month—not as an American patriot, but as a war widow. What was "an activist obsessed with liberation" to do when reform was out of fashion?[17]

Her new struggle was in the North, on the much restricted stage of Auburn, New York. It was a struggle behind a different kind of "enemy line," attempting to overcome the handicap of class as well as caste. She and her aged parents had moved there in 1857, and with the help of Auburn resident, William H. Seward, Republican Party leader and abolitionist senator, they managed to acquire seven acres of land. There she returned in 1865. In 1869, at about age forty-nine, she married a young ex-soldier named Nelson Davis[18] (who reportedly was afflicted with tuberculosis), in the presence of the city's first families, and began a relationship that challenges the opinion of some modern theorists who claim that a slave background failed to provide a sound basis for an enduring family life. Together they eked out a living, working in the homes of the wealthy and raising produce for sale. And while it became neces-

---

16. Samuel Hopkins Adams, who as a young boy knew Harriet Tubman, alluded to the changed mood as follows: "The postwar ebb of patriotic fervor left her stranded. Nobody wanted to hear her exhortations, which, delivered with the fire and art of the born orator, had been such a popular lecture-platform feature of an earlier generation," *Grandfather Stories* (New York: Random House, 1947), p. 271. Even the white abolitionists seemed to be busy "puffing up" their own deeds on the underground railroad, hardly giving the blacks a play. See Larry Gara, *The Liberty Line* (Lexington: University of Kentucky Press, 1961), Chap. 8.

17. The quoted phrase is that of Marcy Galen, "Harriet Tubman: The Moses of Her People," *Ms.*, August 1973, p. 16. Petry, *Harriet Tubman*, said of the Tubman of the immediate postwar years: "She was simply a reformer without a cause, and therefore lost, and lonely, and exhausted" (p. 234).

18. Davis was her second husband. Her first was John Tubman, a free black man whom she married in 1844. He had refused to come North with her and had discouraged her efforts to be free. He was killed in Maryland in 1867.

sary, from time to time, to accept assistance from white friends—which she viewed as something due to each of God's children—they nevertheless found a way to accommodate a steady stream of needy blacks who passed through their home. Historians perhaps have missed the fact that Harriet Tubman (Davis), in effect, continued to facilitate the northward movement begun before the war, but this new "railroad," although now above ground, was to be maintained only with sacrifices equally as great as those which had confronted the old.

In return for assistance from the white community, she gave generously of her talent as a storyteller, delighting the small-town elite with accounts of her unusual life. While her friend Booker T. Washington was calling for Negro uplift through self-help and racial solidarity, Harriet Tubman gave practical expression to the idea. Having first-hand knowledge of the needs of Southern Negroes, she included among her projects raising money for black schools during the early postwar years.

It was also while in Auburn that she conceived the idea of establishing a home for the aged and indigent. The home was to be called the John Brown Home, after the man she regarded as the quintessential symbol of freedom. It was a practical experiment in self-help. Active in the African Methodist Episcopal Zion Church,[19] she urged its members to join her in this larger philanthropic effort. In 1896, she purchased at auction twenty-five acres adjoining her property, and in 1903 she deeded it to the AMEZ Church to establish the home. She was upset, however, when the church decided on charging a fee for admission rather than offering to support the work through an inter-racial executive board. Her opposition may have been based as much on ideological as on financial grounds.[20] This dream of her later life was finally realized in 1908 when the Harriet Tubman Home was opened—a remarkable tribute to the energy and efforts of an eighty-nine year old woman.[21]

19. Conrad states, with no documentary evidence, that Tubman "took an active part in the growth of the African Methodist Episcopal Church in Central and Western New York." It is probably the AMEZ and not the AME Church that he is referring to, since she was a member of the local AMEZ Church and later gave much of her property to that denomination. In what ways she contributed to the growth of the church Conrad does not say. Moreover, according to Mrs. Gladys Bryant, Harriet Tubman's great grand-niece, her ancestor also attended the local white churches. She was married in the white Congregational Church. Conversation between Mrs. Bryant and author, Skaneateles, New York, July 5, 1973.

20. Conrad, *Harriet Tubman*, pp. 221–22, stresses the ideological aspect. If her opposition was based largely on financial grounds, her talent for prophecy was nowhere better vindicated. For within several years after her death at the Harriet Tubman Home in 1913, the enterprise collapsed. However, the property is still in the possession of the church. The Harriet Tubman Museum stands on it today.

21. "Program of the Unveiling of Bronze Tablet in Memory of Harriet Tubman,

Her humanitarian concern also found expression in the woman's suffrage movement, a cause that had developed out of the anti-slavery efforts of women reformers like the Grimké sisters and Elizabeth Cady Stanton.[22] Though never as closely identified with the women's movement as Sojourner Truth, another bold black woman of catholic reform interests, Harriet Tubman spoke at women's rights conventions as early as 1860 and continued to attend them after the war, mainly in upstate New York. She went partly, no doubt, because she was an attraction. Like some old soldier at a GAR encampment, she delighted in reminiscing about old days in the anti-slavery fight. But it was more than a matter of ego gratification that motivated her. In relating the experiences of her adventure-packed life to Victorian women who were protesting the limitations placed on them by tradition and social pressures, she introduced them to another perspective on slavery and freedom. In her person and in reputation she symbolized the free independent woman; her reputation as a Negro leader continued to be utilized by the suffragists.

For her, the struggle for female emancipation did not have the same basic urgency as the struggle for black emancipation, possibly because in the post-Reconstruction era all reforms were more difficult to achieve. Certainly, the reformer's platform, in spite of its attractions, was tame by comparison with her hazardous anti-slavery labors. Nevertheless, her interest in woman suffrage was genuine and life long. As a woman for whom trousers were nothing new, she appreciated the symbolic value of the bloomers worn by feminist leaders, though it was not the sort of attire she herself wore on the platform. Her continued attendance at woman suffrage gatherings testified to her commitment to and recognition of the interrelatedness of the two freedom struggles. She knew that blacks could not be really free while the large female population remained less than full, participative citizens. As she said in 1911 in response to the question, "Do you really believe that women should vote?"—"I have suffered enough to believe it."[23]

Harriet Tubman's nearly century-long life consistently personified the quest for human dignity that has been so basic to the national self-image. The deepest meaning of her life is that freedom is a God-given

Auburn, New York, June 12, 1914." In possession of Mrs. Gladys Bryant, Skaneateles, New York.

22. Woodward expresses the relationship somewhat poetically: "the white woman found herself in self-forgetfulness, found her own rights in defending them for her enslaved sister, who had no rights at all; and their two causes grew entwined from the start. Both causes were wrapped up in Harriet Tubman and Sojourner Truth," *The Bold Woman*, p. 243.

23. Conrad, *Harriet Tubman*, p. 217.

right everyone should work for and enjoy. At the same time she was growing up in slavery, the defenders of "the peculiar institution" were perfecting the myth of the childlike, improvident Negro who required constant supervision. Whether consciously or not, she set out to demolish that myth. The result was the rise of a counter-myth: the Harriet Tubman legend. She became transformed into Moses, Joan of Arc, and John Henry—all rolled into one dark body. But how thin is the line between myth and reality. As William Breyfogle has written: "Harriet Tubman is one of those rare cases where the legend, so far from exaggerating, scarcely catches up with the known facts. One cannot exaggerate a story that, from beginning to end, is a tissue of improbabilities verging on the impossible."[24] The significant thing is that it is a story perfectly attuned to the national experience, itself a "tissue of improbabilities verging on the impossible."[25]

More than anything else, Tubman brought out of the slave community the will to resist all limitations on the rights of individuals to control their own destiny. To supporters of women's rights she became the symbol of woman freed from the restrictions of a male-dominated society. To black people she symbolized the strength, patience, and faith of the generations of unsung black women who in their less dramatic but equally dedicated way overcame the obstacles of color and sex. Harriet Tubman spoke for them—indeed, for all the powerless—by her deeds and in her determination to be dealt with as a moral individual.

24. William Breyfogle, *Make Free: The Story of the Underground Railroad* (Philadelphia: Lippincott, 1958), p. 180.
25. The theme of America as a place and as a civilization where the new continually emerges out of the "old," carrying the possibilities inherent in the old to some hitherto unrealized point, is provocatively suggested in Murray, *The Omni-Americans*, especially pp. 13–22.

SECTION III

The "New Woman" and Social Change

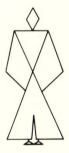

THE "NEW WOMAN" of the twentieth century owed a great debt to her nineteenth-century feminist ancestors who had brought the "woman question" to public attention. Not only had the woman's rights movement of the previous century heightened public awareness of the injustices that women experienced, but it also made noticeable progress in attempting to correct them. When the National American Woman Suffrage Association (NAWSA) was created in 1890, the campaign for women's rights entered a new, more exclusively political phase, producing social reverberations that left few women indifferent to its purposes. But it was a mistake—and one frequently made by social critics at the turn of the century—to assume that all who called themselves "new women" traced their transformation to the direct effects of suffragism. While many did, of course, there were others besides radical feminists who acknowledged a much greater debt to their nineteenth-century sisters and the legacy of the feminist intellectual tradition.

By the standards of the time, the "new woman" was a liberated woman. Her liberation was predicated on a new perception of herself and her role; she was an individual with valid needs to be met. She expressed her liberation in a variety of ways, the form depending on a variety of factors, including economic status, geographic location, personal ability, family response, and social contacts. "New women" demanded recognition of their individuality in ways both public and private. A minority demonstrated their liberation by working actively for the suffrage and related social reforms; the rest preferred to accept the gains achieved by the activists while affecting less public liberating changes in their personal and family lives. Historians and economists have documented some of the choices they made; for gainful employment, more education, association with women's clubs. But a literary character of the period, Mr. Dooley, an Irish bartender created by Finley Peter Dunne, expressed in more human terms one man's reaction to the "new woman":

> It's been a good thing f'r ol' man Donahue, though, Jawn. He shtud iverything that mortal man cud stand. He seen her appearin' in th' road wearin' clothes that no lady shud wear an' ridin' a bicycle; he was humiliated whin she demanded to vote; he put his pride under his ar-rm an' ma-arched out iv th' house whin she committed assault-an'-batthry on th' piannah. But he's got to th' end iv th' rope now. He was in here las' night, how-come-ye-so, with his hat cocked over his eye an' a look iv risolution on his face; an' whin he left me, he says, says he, "Dooley," he says, "I'll conquir, or I'll die," he says.

Other literary critics, as well as politicians and clergymen, described the "new woman" in different terms. A threat to social order, she was accused of attempting to destroy the family and collectivize the state. She was said to endorse sexual license rather than monogamy, career rather than motherhood. If she did have children, she would attempt to relegate their care to public institutions to free herself for radical political activism. Women who did, in fact, choose to live in ways conspicuously different from the traditional pattern were not surprised when they were singled out for notoriety.

The "new woman" was the product as well as the cause of social change. The growth of industrialization lowered some of the barriers in her way, and particularly during the period of military preparedness and war in the second decade of the century, she found new employment opportunities—although usually in low-paying and semi-skilled or unskilled jobs. The reforming spirit of progressivism not only eased her passage to the ballot box, it stimulated her interest in other social reforms. During the Progressive Era, too, as William O'Neill points out, a legitimizing ideology was developed on the issue of divorce, creating a potential for personal liberation that was overshadowed only by Margaret Sanger's sustained struggle to circulate birth control information.

For "new women," as for everyone else, divorce was a very private matter, but until quite recently, commentators insisted on describing it as a social "problem." Critics of divorce regarded it as another sign of the decline of the family and growing immorality. Feminists saw it in a very different light; drawing on Elizabeth Cady Stanton's defense of divorce as an individual right, they hailed it as a means for creating a wholly new view of marriage. If either partner had the opportunity to walk away from an unhappy marriage, they said, both might feel a new sense of responsibility to make it work. Furthermore, for women who in nineteenth-century terms were "civilly dead" after marriage, divorce offered the chance for a kind of resurrection. That some "new women" saw divorce-law reform in a less favorable light was unimportant to their critics; they were associated collectively with the rising divorce rate.

The Flapper of the 1920s, whose new womanhood was expressed in personal rather than political ways, was blamed not only for the increase in divorce but for all the other social challenges she presented to the conventional image of woman. Having acquired the ballot as an inheritance, the Flapper sought liberation by rejecting the social and cultural restrictions that had bound her mother. As Gerald Critoph notes, Flappers were chary of marriage and somewhat less than enthusiastic about involuntary motherhood. Critics found their behavior outrageous. Defying convention, Flappers shortened their skirts, cut their hair, smoked, drank, dated, and worked, to demonstrate their independence. While the Flapper's priorities seemed frivolous to male observers and some feminists, the Flapper herself recognized a correlation between her values and the role of the new woman.

At about the same time that the Flapper made her appearance in the United States, a decidedly different model of the new woman emerged in Japan. According to Noriko Shimada, Hiroko Takamura, Masako Iino, and Hisako Ito, the Japanese "new woman" patterned herself after nineteenth-century American women educators rather than after her contemporary American sisters. The "new women" of Japan owed much to the efforts of Ume Tsuda and Motoko Hani, two of their countrywomen who introduced educational innovations based on American practices. Tsuda and Hani were caught up in the nationalist spirit that was sweeping their country, which identified economic progress with Westernization. The Japanese educators believed that the American "new woman" was synonymous with Western progress; the liberated American woman was the key to Western economic and cultural prosperity. Believing so, the two women introduced forms of cultural feminism that adapted American examples to Japanese customs.

The American models chosen by the Japanese women were those of an earlier time; a political figure like Jeanette Rankin would have been out of context in Meiji Japan. When Rankin was elected to the United States Congress in 1917, she was the most public symbol of the American "new woman." She entered Congress three years before the woman's suffrage amendment was finally ratified, and her presence in the House of Representatives was a reflection of women's growing political involvement. Some women found their way into politics through the suffrage movement, others through participation in related social-reform efforts. The latter provided the background for the four women who helped create the federal Children's Bureau—Florence Kelley, Grace Abbott, Julia Lathrop, and Lillian Wald. Accused by their political foes of bolshevism, feminism, and communism, the women combined brashness and courage with newly developed skills in political maneuvering to secure the adoption of their legislation. And they were the first to acknowledge that their success was due largely to the efforts of women, as voters, feminist activists, and members of women's clubs. The feminism of the four reformers, says James Johnson, was an integral part of their social philosophy.

7

Divorce as a Moral Issue:
A Hundred Years of Controversy

WILLIAM L. O'NEILL

A striking feature regarding the history of divorce is not only that it aroused intense fears, but that they continued long after they should have died out. Another is that most public discussions of divorce bore little relation to the facts, regardless of how much or little was known about it. These points cannot be explained without briefly reviewing the American experience with divorce.

American divorce laws were always comparatively generous, and became even more so in the 1830s and 1840s when many state legislatures revised their statutes, but divorces were still infrequent before the Civil War.[1] There are no reliable figures on the divorce rate for this period, but it was probably low, judging by the lack of interest in it. A handful of feminists condemned various impediments to divorce such as the law in New York State which allowed divorce only in the cases of adultery. Horace Greeley debated the question in his *New York Tribune* twice in the decade before the war, but otherwise, little was said on the matter. However, during the 1860s divorce came increasingly to be seen as a threat to the common welfare. Thereafter, while the tide of public concern ebbed and flowed, divorce was always considered a problem.

According to a U. S. Census Bureau publication issued in 1909 entitled *Marriage and Divorce, 1867–1906*, from 1889, when the first govern-

1. For a full history see Nelson M. Blake, *The Road to Reno* (New York: Macmillan, 1962). See also William L. O'Neill, *Divorce in the Progressive Era* (New Haven: Yale University Press, 1967).

ment report on marriage and divorce was issued, until World War II the increase in divorce was remarkably constant. A projection of future growth made in 1891 by the statistician Walter F. Wilcox, in *The Divorce Problem*, held for more than forty years. The divorce rate reached its peak in 1946; then it fell sharply until 1958, after which it rose again.[2] From the 1870s until the 1920s repeated attempts were made to limit the number of divorces, usually by making them more difficult to obtain. Many states responded to this pressure by abolishing omnibus clauses (which in effect allowed judges to award divorces at their own discretion), extending residence requirements, and defining the grounds for divorce more closely. None of this had any appreciable effect on the divorce rate. Almost everyone except a few radicals, free lovers, free thinkers, liberal clergymen, and sociologists agreed that divorce was a bad thing, and yet people went on getting divorced by the tens and then hundreds of thousands. During the Progressive Era conservative resistance to what was a kind of folk movement collapsed, and thereafter, while appeals for more restrictions on divorce continued to be made, they were increasingly hopeless and always beside the point—except in New York. In 1966, however, even New York gave way and its divorce law now resembles those of other states.

Several points about divorce are often misunderstood. Migratory divorces—that is, divorces obtained outside the state of actual residence—have never been very numerous. The overwhelming majority of divorces are obtained in the couple's home state, and this seems to have always been the case. Anywhere from one-third to one-half of all divorces are obtained by childless couples. Although the evidence is incomplete on this point, it appears that the first year of marriage is the most hazardous and that most marriages which break up do so fairly soon. However, since it takes time to win a divorce, this early problem is not reflected in the figures, which show that most divorces are won in the third or fourth year of marriage. Most divorced people remarry, but the time lag between their marital breakup and their remarriage is long enough to suggest that at the time they decide on a divorce they have not usually selected their future mates. In other words, most people divorce to escape a failing union, not to immediately form a new one.[3]

2. Paul H. Jacobson, *American Marriage and Divorce* (New York: Rinehart, 1959), p. 90.
3. For evidence bearing on these disputed points see Donald Gilbert McKinley, *Social Class and Family Life* (Glencoe, Ill.: Free Press, 1964), p. 114; Thomas P. Monaghan, "When Married Couples Part: Statistical Trends and Relationships in Divorce," *American Sociological Review* 27 (October 1962):625–33; William M. Kephart, *The Family, Society, and the Individual* (Boston, 1961), pp. 614–28; and

The origins of mass divorce remain obscure. In 1850 no one divorces, by 1900 divorce has become commonplace, and by 1950 ubiquitous. We know very little about these great demographic changes. Even though divorces were frequent then, almost no one in the nineteenth century thought to find out who was divorcing and why. Even had they been interviewed they would surely have been no more helpful than divorced people today, who know only the specific and personal reasons behind their act. Why a marriage which is bearable in 1850 becomes unbearable a decade or two later is extraordinarily hard to determine. At first, the rising divorce rate was blamed variously on permissive legislation, moral decline, Western divorce colonies, feminism, and dirty books (loosely construed, the most obscene book of the nineteenth century according to many reviewers was *Jude the Obscure*).

By the turn of the century, however, the first generation of professionally trained sociologists had emerged, and they attributed divorces to the rise of libertarian propaganda and the industrial revolution. This last rapidly became the most intellectually respectable explanation, and from the turn of the century until very recently it dominated academic discussions of divorce. In part this came from obvious changes which the factory system inspired. The family as a productive unit on the farm or in a small shop was replaced by clusters of individual wage earners who produced separately and only consumed together. Women became capable of self-support. Lower-class children went off to work at an early age, and middle-class children left the home daily for school. Later many sociologists came to believe that these and related changes in the family took place because the factory system somehow demanded it.

The trouble with this explanation, as William J. Goode points out, is that "industrialization in this vague but enveloping sense does 'cause' the modern social and family patterns, but only because it is identical with them. Such a hypothesis is true but trivial."[4] Moreover, it is clear, now that industrialism has begun to affect a wide range of cultures, that a variety of family types are compatible with the factory system. In Japan, France, Canada, Brazil, and elsewhere, pre-industrial family systems have accommodated themselves to the modern factory. Thus, while the industrial revolution has affected family life in significant ways, there is no necessary connection between it and the rise of mass divorce. The English divorce rate was hardly affected by industrialization while pre-industrial countries like Egypt were often divorce-prone in the extreme.

---

especially William J. Goode, *The Family* (Englewood Cliffs, N.J.: Prentice-Hall, 1964).

4. Goode, *The Family*, p. 105.

There is, however, another way of viewing the history of the family. For a long time scholars believed that the modern family was a product of the nineteenth century; that it displaced the old extended, patriarchal, self-sufficient family in the very recent past, and that divorce was a consequence of this change. However, Philip Ariés, a French historian and demographer thinks otherwise.[5] He argues that the patriarchal family as historians and sociologists describe it never really existed. Instead, he sees the modern family beginning to emerge in the sixteenth century, displacing a far looser medieval family system. Life then was polymorphous, promiscuous, and collective to a high degree. Family, relatives, servants, and friends lived together, not only in the same house but usually in the same rooms. Children were unimportant so long as there were enough of them, and were apprenticed out or sent to other families for training at an early age. The upper-class family, at least, was essentially a public institution that made few demands upon its members, who lived primarily not in the family but in society.

But in the sixteenth century, Ariés continues, the child was discovered, and as his or her well-being and education became progressively more important the family drew in upon itself and away from society. The home assumed its modern characteristics of comfort, privacy, isolation, and domesticity. Beginning with the middle classes this transformation moved downward and upward until by the nineteenth century the bourgeois family had become dominant if not universal. Although this brief summary hardly does justice to Ariés' dense and sophisticated analysis, it ought to suggest why his argument helps us to understand the origins of mass divorce. As Christopher Lasch points out in the *New York Review of Books*, February 17, 1966, if we see the modern family, the success of which largely depends on women attending to the numerous details of a complex and demanding domestic life, as a fairly recent development, the function of divorce becomes more apparent. The family now takes up such a large part of life that those who marry badly, or cannot adjust to the requirements of marriage, must have some means of relief. Looked at in this manner, divorce becomes not a pathological response, but a safety valve essential to the system's continued vitality. It would appear, then, that the divorce rate started to rise after the middle of the nineteenth century because bad marriages came to be seen as so oppressive that people were determined to escape them. The rising divorce rate was a reaction either to higher marital expectations or a more oppressive domestic system or both. Far from jeopardizing the system, it

5. Philip Ariés, *Centuries of Childhood: A Social History of Family Life* (New York: Knopf, 1962).

guaranteed the survival even to our own time of a difficult set of marital and family customs. Divorce is, therefore, not a threat to the domestic status quo, but an essential complement to it.

The development of a rationale for mass divorce preceded its emergence. There seems to have been no great public force behind the liberalization of divorce laws in the 1830s and 1840s. Divorce reform in this sense was apparently a carryover from the libertarian and humanitarian spirit of those years. In 1860 only about 7,000 divorces were awarded in the entire country, but the case for divorce was already well established. This is consistent with our contemporary experience for, as Goode points out, in many developing countries the ideology of family change appears before the fact. Nelson M. Blake has demonstrated that the case for mass divorce in America and the legal facilities essential to it were clearly established by 1860, well in advance of need. The United States became the first country in the Western world to experience divorce on a large scale because only here did the two crucial requirements —ease of access and a legitimizing ideology—exist. In the post–Civil War era Americans in growing numbers took advantage of this.

This was a necessary condition for the survival of the modern family with its high demands and intense pressures. In an age marked by libertarian principles, personal mobility, declining religious authority, affluence, and self-indulgence, something like divorce was essential to the survival of marriage and the family as they had come to be understood in the nineteenth century. But the mere fact that mass divorce was necessary or, at the very least, inevitable was not of itself sufficient reason for middle-class Americans to accept it. By Victorian standards divorce was immoral, anti-social, and a threat to everything they held sacred. It made a mockery of those connubial ideals that were the glory of Christian civilization and, indeed, threatened its very existence. But as the divorce rate kept rising, society had either to suppress or accept divorce. This did not become clear for many years, though as early as 1860 the major positions on the issue were well established.

They were displayed in a famous exchange between Horace Greeley and Robert Dale Owen that year, which Greeley later reported in his *Recollections of a Busy Life*. Both men based their cases on moral and practical grounds. Greeley argued that divorce for any reason save adultery was immoral because Jesus had said so. It was also dangerous because children could be properly reared only by both parents. Owen considered divorce a moral act because it freed women from tyrannical and degrading domestic situations without forever denying them another chance at marital happiness. It was eminently practical and necessary because in the absence of divorce, as he knew full well from his experience in Italy, prostitution, desertion, and like evils prevailed. Both men claimed to have the highest opinion of marriage as an institution, Owen going so far as to say that he believed in divorce, "precisely because I regard the marriage relation as the holiest of earthly institutions. It is for that reason that I seek to preserve its purity, when other expedients fail, by the besom of divorce."

Religious arguments were most commonly used against divorce well into the twentieth century. Among Protestants, Episcopalians led the attack. High churchmen were against allowing divorces for any reason except adultery, and sometimes believed that only men had the right even then. As George Z. Gray, Dean of the Episcopal Theological School in Cambridge put it: "The woman, by marriage, becomes a member of the man. Therefore she cannot put him away, for a member cannot put away his head."[6] Episcopalians were obliged to allow divorce for adultery since their canon law permitted it, but they tried to have the rule qualified further by allowing only the man to secure a divorce, or by forbidding remarriage even to the innocent party in an adultery suit. In effect, this was to deny divorce for any reason, since the principal distinction between divorce and judicial separation was that remarriage was possible after the former.

A historical dimension was added to the case against divorce by President Theodore Dwight Woolsey of Yale whose "History and Doctrine of Divorce" was serialized in the *New Englander* in 1867 and 1868. Hebrew marriage was generally admirable, he discovered, although flawed by divorce and polygamy. The Greeks suffered from corrupt customs. The Romans started well but ended up poorly and their awful example should be a lesson to modern America which was in danger of taking the Roman road. Subsequently, conditions improved until the mid-nineteenth century when they began to deteriorate. His notion of an ideal divorce law was that passed by England in 1857 which allowed divorce only in the case of an adulterous wife, or to a wronged wife whose husband had committed another offense in addition to adultery.

Woolsey's account became standard, and thereafter both scholarly and popular discussions invariably praised Hebrew marriage while glossing over its more awkward features, such as polygamy, dwelt at great length on the Roman path to ruin which America was in danger of taking, and admired the early Christians. Few later accounts were as un-

6. George Z. Gray, *Husband and Wife, or the Theory of Marriage and Its Consequences* (Boston, 1885). His main purpose was to demonstrate the wisdom of continuing to forbid a man from remarrying.

abashedly aristocratic as Woolsey's though. He did not think that divorce threatened Christian homes, but rather the lower classes who unrestrainedly demanded "free rum, free Sundays, free suffrage, free divorce, and the like." If the country was to escape a tidal wave of proletarian license the divorce laws would have to be tightened and the country's extraordinary facilities for sensual gratification curtailed. In the same manner society as a whole would be purified through redemption of its lower orders.

Few postwar critics of divorce were as reactionary in this sense as Woolsey (or Gray). Most took popular democracy as a settled question, and most believed that divorce was an upper-class luxury. But Woolsey's account, and the later histories based on it, fortified their conviction that history proved divorce to be a menace. It was also thought that divorce was only a more refined form of polygamy. The association of divorce with polygamy was especially favored because it enabled the user to link denunciations of divorce with attacks on Mormonism, thereby enlisting the passions of one cause in support of another. Divorce was also understood to be the product of unrestrained individualism. George Washington Gladden, humane and liberal clergyman that he was, made this charge in a widely circulated article attributing divorce to the tendency of lawmakers to legislate for individuals rather than families, the woman movement, and other factors. "The individualism of the present is not much better than the tyranny of the past," he wrote in the *Century*, January 1882. Few attacks on divorce between the 1860s and the 1920s omitted this point. Whatever their political or social views, almost all enemies of divorce agreed that the common good was being steadily ignored for the sake of individual well-being. The family was the foundation of the state, and its interests superseded those of the individual. To arrest the decline of morals and the decay of society better education and stricter and (usually) more uniform laws were required.

While no one could be certain as to exactly how fast divorce was increasing, by 1880 the rate was much higher than generally supposed. Nathan Allen, a writer in the *North American Review* of June 1880, pointed out in that year that random soundings had persuaded him that among the non-Catholic population of New England the ratio of divorces to marriages in 1878 ranged from a low of 14.8 marriages to 1 divorce in Massachusetts to a high of 8.1 to 1 in Connecticut. The following year Samuel Dike, a Vermont minister who had been collecting material on divorce for several years, President Woolsey, and other concerned citizens founded the New England Divorce Reform League. Agreement with its intent to halt the spread of divorce was so general that soon a critic warned, somewhat prematurely, that divorce reform had reached the stage every reform movement encountered on the brink of success when its friends were more to be feared than its enemies.

In general, then, conservatives opposed divorce first on theological and moral grounds, and second because it harmed society. Liberals defended divorce on humanitarian grounds, arguing that it strengthened the social fabric and that it was essential to the emancipation of women. Elizabeth Cady Stanton maintained in the October 22, 1868, edition of *Revolution* that marriage was a mere contract that should be as easily dissolved as other contracts if its terms were not met. Love and happiness were the purposes of marriage: "There can be no heaven without love; and nothing is sacred in the family and homes, but just so far as it is built up and anchored in purity and peace." Her short-lived journal, the *Revolution*, declared on October 29, 1868, that all such questions should be settled on the basis of the "highest good of the individual. It is the inalienable right of all to be happy."

Until the 1880s public interest in divorces was limited since they were still comparatively infrequent. But thereafter divorce rapidly became an important object of concern. From 1854 to 1881, only about one divorce article a year appeared in major periodicals. Between 1887 and 1891 the rate increased to about five articles a year, and thereafter interest rose to a peak of about fifteen articles a year from 1905 to 1909.[7] Almost a third of all the books published on marriage and divorce between 1889 and 1919 appeared in the years 1909 to 1912. One of the chief reasons for this flood of literature was the steadily increasing divorce rate which by the Progressive Era had attained imposing dimensions.

On the conservative side attitudes hardened and a variety of steps were taken to arrest the spread of divorce. Some people, of whom Felix Adler, the founder of Ethical Culture, was most important, exchanged liberal views for conservative ones. Many states tightened up their divorce laws. Most of the major Protestant denominations added their voices to the chorus of condemnation, and in 1904 the Episcopal Triennial Convention narrowly defeated a resolution that would have denied all sacraments to divorced persons. Many efforts were made to secure

---

7. James Harwood Barnett, *Divorce and the American Divorce Novel 1858–1937* (Philadelphia: University of Pennsylvania Press, 1939), p. 35. As a subject of periodical attention compared with related topics—prostitution, birth control, sex morals, family-home-marriage—divorce was second only to family-home-marriage in this period, but declined to fifth place from 1915 to 1918. Its usual position in the period 1900–30 was third. From 1910 to 1914, the years of the White Slave Panic, it trailed prostitution, from 1922 to 1924 sex morals were of greater interest, and from 1930 to 1931 birth control led it. Hornell Hart, "Changing Social Attitudes and Interests," *Recent Social Trends in the United States* (New York: McGraw Hill, 1933), p. 414.

uniform divorce laws throughout this period in hopes that uniformity would reduce the divorce rate. Clergymen were usually in the van of such campaigns, but as America entered the twentieth century the case against divorce came more and more to rest on practical rather than moral and theological grounds. The argument that the family was the foundation of civilized life and must not be destroyed by divorce became the most potent argument of moral reformers.

The liberal position, as articulated by Elizabeth Cady Stanton and Robert Dale Owen, did not change much. The notion that marital happiness was a basic right, and the absence of it a legitimate reason for divorce became more common. The doctrines of prophets like Havelock Ellis and Edward Carpenter did not directly influence the divorce controversy, but by advocating sexual freedom these new moralists made divorce seem less shocking while at the same time infusing the moral atmosphere with a certain degree of permissiveness. The religious opposition was undermined by the efforts of a small but crucial band of ministers and higher critics. Equally important was the effect of sociology as a maturing discipline. The first Americans with some scholarly if not scientific, credentials to study divorce opposed it as a threat to the family order. But, as early as 1869, the scientific sanctions for Victorian family norms were shaken by W. E. H. Lecky's superb *History of European Morals,* which boldly condemned not only the Christian opposition to divorce, but endorsed a type of free love as well.

Divorce was partially endorsed by Herbert Spencer, and then by the first great American sociologist, Lester Ward. At the turn of the century most professionally trained sociologists had adopted a liberal view. The third annual meeting of the American Sociological Society, in 1908, was devoted to the family, and its proceedings, published in Chicago in 1909, showed that of the leading sociologists concerned at all with family matters only a few were actively hostile to divorce. The principal paper on divorce endorsed it, and the resulting discussion was profoundly demoralizing to conservatives. By this time not only was the weight of scientific testimony on the side of divorce, but some important religious figures had declared themselves in its favor. While the great majority of clergymen continued to oppose divorce, the religious sanctions against it were crumbling.

Judging by the periodical press and the numerous efforts to restrict its spread, most middle-class Americans continued to oppose divorce throughout the Progressive Era, but the ideological groundwork had been laid that made possible the substantial shift in public opinion which seems to have taken place in the 1920s. As early as 1914, Walter George

Smith, the leading lay opponent of divorce, was forced to concede that the public was not interested in uniform legislation on marriage and divorce, regardless of the methods used to secure it.[8] The great flood of divorces which came in the wake of World War I completed the ruin of conservative hopes. They had not been able to restrict divorces at a time when the public was with them, and it was not to be expected that they could do so after 1920 when there was no longer a consensus on the question. By the twenties divorce was no longer a valid issue, for society as a whole had, in effect, given up any serious hopes of reducing the divorce rate.

The change from a generally conservative to a generally liberal view of divorce came very quickly, and with it the modern attitude that divorce, if unpleasant, is a natural right.

An analysis of periodical literature on sex and the family published in 1933 concluded that "attitudes toward birth control, divorce, and sex freedom . . . became more liberal, or radical, from about 1918 until about 1925 and then became more conservative again, particularly with respect to divorce and sex freedom."[9] But they never again became so conservative as they had been before 1918. This more relaxed view of divorce was part of the new pattern of sexual behavior, often, although perhaps wrongly, called the Revolution in Morals.

But if divorce cannot be separated from the broad patterns which embraced it, it had a life of its own as well. During the Progressive Era a legitimizing ideology was worked out specifically for divorce—an ideology which was ready for popular consumption when the public came to accept divorce on a massive scale as unavoidable. It only remained for the rationale which had been developed in a period of denial to be turned up and adjusted for a period of acceptance.

The characteristic divorce article of the Progressive Era denounced the practice as immoral and especially anti-social. The typical liberal article of the period very nearly reversed this formula by bearing down so hard on the necessity of divorce as to make it seem almost attractive. In the 1920s, liberals, having won their point by default, no longer found it necessary to exaggerate. Charlotte Perkins Gilman noted in *Outlook*, January 25, 1928, that divorce was like a surgical operation, painful but in the long run therapeutic. In Bertrand Russell's collection of statements on the issue *Divorce*, which appeared at the decade's end, H. G. Wells declared that "Divorce is Inhuman"; Fannie Hurst exclaimed "Divorce is

8. Walter George Smith, "Ethics of Divorce," in Julia E. Johnson, ed., *Selected Articles on Marriage and Divorce* (New York: Wilson, 1925).

9. Hart, *Recent Social Trends*, p. 415.

Sordid and Ugly"; and Rebecca West solemnly observed that "the divorce of married people with children is nearly always an unspeakable calamity."[10] But they, and most of the other contributors, agreed that, however painful and destructive it might be, divorce was nonetheless essential.

The earlier generation of professional social scientists played down the human cost of divorce so as not to give ammunition to moral conservatives. By the 1920s it was possible for them either to be neutral or actually pessimistic about divorce without fearing that they would thereby assist reactionaries. Willard Waller, who in 1930 published one of the first studies on the consequences of divorce, concluded after examining thirty-three cases in depth that "there are so many things to avoid, if one is to assimilate a divorce in a healthy manner, and it is so difficult to avoid some of them, that one who succeeds in working out a thoroughly sane adjustment finds himself in select company."[11]

The sociological contention that divorce was the product of industrialization, not human depravity or seductive radicalism, enjoyed wide support, even among moral conservatives like G. K. Chesterton, although Chesterton turned the argument to his own uses. It was clear to him that the plutocratic state was out to destroy the family for the sake of the factory: "This indeed is the only sense in which it is true that capitalism is connected with individualism. Capitalism believes in collectivism for itself and individualism for its enemies."[12]

But Chesterton's belief that divorce should be abolished because the family was a bulwark against plutocracy made few converts. Actually, marriage and the family as institutions were in no danger. Earlier social scientists had generally accepted this on faith, but before long statistical evidence supported them. In the November 1928 issue of *Current History,* I. M. Rubinow noted that while it was constantly asserted that divorce was destroying marriage, the marriage rate had increased enough since 1892 to largely offset the rising number of divorces. The continuing popularity of marriage showed the institution itself to be in no danger. Although very few people seemed aware of this fact, common sense and

10. Bertrand Russell, ed., *Divorce* (New York, 1930), pp. 29, 21, 62.
11. Willard W. Waller, *The Old Love and the New; Divorce Readjustment* (Carbondale: Southern Illinois University Press, 1930), p. 297. Even at their most enthusiastic, social scientists since then have rarely gone further than Joseph K. Folsom, who admitted that some legal restrictions on divorce would always be necessary while believing that "the main progress comes through giving greater freedom and educating people in the use of it." *The Family and Democratic Society* (New York: Wiley, 1943), p. 524.
12. Gilbert Keith Chesterton, *The Superstition of Divorce* (New York: John Lane, 1920), p. 37.

personal experience demonstrated to the majority of Americans that, whatever the divorce rate, most people were still marrying and having children.

Until recent years mass divorce was always linked with feminism. There were two principal reasons for this association. In the late nineteenth century two-thirds of all divorces were secured by women, and those who advocated easy divorces were invariably feminists or sympathizers. Thus, as late as 1920 people took it for granted that feminism was the prime cause of the divorce rate. Preston Slosson, in his authoritative history of the era, made the point in this manner: "American feminism meant freedom from custom and tradition more than from positive legal restriction. Many European nations, for example, had enacted divorce laws as liberal as those of most American states, but in none of them . . . were divorces so frequently obtained by discontented wives."[13] But the association was always more apparent than real. While most divorce advocates were feminist sympathizers, most feminists, especially in the nineteenth century, did not support free divorce. Moreover, those advocating divorce and those securing them were quite different people. The defenders of divorce were members of the middle class, while the majority of divorcees were from the lower classes. What the women's movement wanted was social purity and the single standard of morals. In the Victorian age most women failed to see how easy divorce would advance these cherished causes. As a defense against masculine beastliness divorce was clearly a good thing, but it was also, in the minds of Christian women, immoral. And it threatened to undermine the defenses which women in the nineteenth century believed essential to marriage's survival.

It took a long time for feminists to appreciate the ways in which divorce supported the single standard of morals. That it did was made clear by Rebecca West when she pointed out that in countries where no divorce was possible male sexuality lost all meaning and female sexuality became immensely significant. At no risk to themselves men might coerce or seduce women into sexual acts which, when exposed, invariably brought women into disrepute: "That a woman should be held in contempt for submitting to the same physical relationship that is the core of marriage degrades marriage, and all women, and all men; and the greater contempt she is held in the more she becomes genuinely contemptible."[14] Thus, while divorces were bad, the right to divorce was necessary if women were to be truly free and a single standard of morals upheld.

13. Preston W. Slosson, *The Great Crusade and After, 1914–28* (New York: Macmillan, 1930), p. 131.

14. In Russell, *Divorce*, p. 69.

By the end of the twenties the progressive accommodation with divorce was more solidly grounded than ever before. What it amounted to was the acceptance of a few basic propositions. Almost everyone agreed that divorce was intrinsically undesirable. Most conservatives admitted, although rarely in so many words, that nothing could be done about it. Liberals and social scientists insisted that, bad as it was, the alternatives to divorce were worse still, and that, in any event, it was part of the emancipation of women and consequently a progressive though distasteful act. Underlying this relative complacency was the simple fact, almost never acknowledged but crucial to the entire debate, that divorce had been on the rise for generations and yet the institutions which it presumably threatened—marriage, the family, the home—seemed almost as secure as they had ever been.

Moreover, in a peculiar way divorce was comfortingly well-regulated at a time of growing moral confusion. It was still more difficult to get divorced than to get married. While slackness and moral relativity seemed everywhere on the increase, the divorce court was one of the few places where the old beliefs still obtained. There was a guilty party and an innocent party. The innocent party was rewarded, the guilty punished, right prevailed over wrong, and the American verities were reaffirmed. Society at large might wink at adultery and assorted other breaches of law, custom, and good taste, but the divorce court did not. In this sense, divorce, though offensive to traditional values, reinforced them all the same.

In the 1930s both the divorce rate and interest in it declined. During the period 1939 to 1941 the *Readers' Guide* listed only three periodical references to divorce. But in the postwar era the divorce question, which had been effectively answered in the Progressive Era and ratified in the 1920s, was reopened again. In 1946, there were 40 divorces for every 100 marriages and a cry of alarm was raised—so much like earlier outbursts that it almost parodied them. On October 7, 1949, *Newsweek* magazine approvingly quoted a Chicago judge as follows: "No community can remain law abiding if the very foundation and structure of society are shattered by the destruction of the family and home through the curse of divorce." This was a perfect Victorian statement—thanks especially to the use of *curse* as against the more modern and neutral word *problem.*

On March 10, 1947, *Newsweek* was gratified by the appearance of Carle Zimmerman's *The Family and Civilization,* a study in the worst tradition of nineteenth-century family historiography, filled with the usual ominous references to Rome's fall, and the customary extravagant prophecies of imminent ruin and decay. Similarly, the *Christian Century,* June

13, 1945, called for a constitutional amendment to permit uniform national divorce laws in order to preserve "the institution of the family, on which the stability of the national life so largely depends." In 1948, the National Conference on Family Life demanded the reform of divorce legislation and an end to adversary proceedings. The American Bar Association sponsored an Interprofessional Commission on Marriage and Divorce which reached the same conclusion.

But as early as 1950 it was clear that this latest reform movement was following the path of its predecessors. In the Progressive Era it required roughly twenty-five years for conservative reformers to raise the alarm, study the issue, call for changes, and finally concede defeat. In the post–World War II period it took barely five years to reach the same conclusion. The first reason for the decline of interest in divorce reform was that after 1946 the divorce rate fell sharply. Moreover, as America entered the fifties it became clear that family life, far from being in peril, was actually more popular than ever. The postwar orgy of domesticity— marked by early marriages, large families, and the retreat of women from competition and responsibility—was now in full swing. The age of "togetherness" had dawned, bringing with it assurances that the family as an institution was alive and well.

Surprisingly enough, however, despite the anxiety that divorce produced in the late forties, the scientific study of it advanced but little. For the most part, social scientists continued to repeat the clichés of thirty or forty or even fifty years ago, and when William J. Goode undertook what was to become the best study of the problem ever made, the usual sources of academic research funds failed him and he was forced to turn to the *Saturday Evening Post* for support.

When Goode's complete work, *After Divorce*, finally appeared in 1956, public alarm had diminished and his findings received less notice than they deserved. Among other useful things, his study of divorces showed that husbands usually take the initiative, either by first asking for a divorce or by adopting a strategy which forces the wife to do so, but when questioned most wives stated that they brought up the matter. Thus, the traditional view that divorce was a result of liberating women was proven false. A handful of vocal feminists considered free divorce to be in the best interests of women. However, the majority of divorcees seem to have been forced or manipulated into taking a step they did not necessarily want, but which law and custom made easier if they were the plaintiffs. Goode also pointed out that the great emphasis on education for marriage, on marital counseling and the like was aimed at the wrong target. The beneficiaries of the family-uplift industry were mainly middle class, while most divorces were secured by lower-class men and women.

In the same way, the correlation between divorce and crime, insanity, and other pathological characteristics was probably false in that poverty, not divorce, was the common element in each case. Moreover, divorce is for the individuals involved an expensive business, since it is those who are least able to bear the cost of divorce who usually secure them. What little property the family has usually goes to the wife, but husbands contribute little to the support of their children, and that often late or irregularly. This fact, plus the ambiguous social role of divorcees, led most of them to remarry as soon as possible.

To a historian the most interesting effect of Goode's study was its demonstration that one cannot change public opinion with mere evidence. The discussion of divorce continued, at a lower level of intensity to be sure, as if it were principally a middle-class experience. Thus, shortly after Goode's book appeared, Albert Q. Maisel, in the August 1957 issue of the *Reader's Digest*, declared that the divorce rate was half what it had been in 1946 because people were getting married earlier, were better educated on marriage and family matters, were living in suburbs that produced happiness and stability, and because "the battle of the sexes has all but ended in total victory for the feminine contingent." Maisel was, of course, wrong on every count. The correlation between early marriage (itself especially pronounced among the lower classes), was well established, the middle classes who were the objects of most marriage and family education programs had a comparatively low divorce rate anyway, suburban divorce rates were lower than urban rates by reason of the class difference, and the battle of the sexes had ended with feminism in temporary retreat.

But soon Americans were once more defying the conventional wisdom in large numbers. During the 1960s divorces increased again, and in the 1970s boomed upward. In some respects this new rise in the divorce rate followed predictable lines. As always the incidence of divorce decreased as incomes increased.[15] Divorces continued to be most frequent among those who had married young and least common among those who were mature when married. And, despite the accelerating divorce rate, as of 1967 most marriages were still intact. At that time only 15 percent of all men and 17 percent of all women under the age of seventy had ever been divorced.[16]

15. In fact one study found that divorces increased as income decreased regardless of such variables as race, education, and prestige of occupation. Phillip Cutright, "Income and Family Events: Marital Stability," *Journal of Marriage and the Family* (May 1971): 291–306.

16. Paul C. Glick and Arthur S. Norton, "Frequency, Duration, and Probability of Marriage and Divorce," *Journal of Marriage and the Family* (May 1971): 307–17.

Figures like this were not reliable guides to the immediate future. The divorce rate continued to rise so that in 1972, thirty out of every 1,000 women obtained divorces compared with twenty in the mid-sixties and fifteen in the mid-fifties. Nonetheless, it was far from clear that this rate of increase would continue. For one thing, the age of marriage was rising too. *Newsweek,* October 30, 1972, reported that in 1960 only 28 percent of all women between the ages of twenty and twenty-four were single, whereas in 1972 this had risen to 37 percent. As age at first marriage has always been inversely related to divorce the tendency to marry later should eventually retard the divorce rate. Further, a temporary factor influencing it may have been the widespread liberalization of divorce laws that took place in the 1960s and 1970s. On March 12, 1973, *Newsweek* stated that by 1973 fourteen states had enacted what were called "no fault" divorce laws making it easy for people to divorce through mutual agreement. Twenty more states granted divorces automatically after a specified period of separation. Making divorce easier might well have led to a burst of divorces, but if so the rate ought to taper off once those who had been blocked by difficult laws were processed.

Still, one would be very foolish indeed to try to predict future divorce rates. They have always been volatile, influenced by law, the economy, and intangible states of mind such as the emphasis on togetherness in the 1950s, and the rage for personal fulfillment and gratification in the 1960s and 1970s. Whatever may happen in the future, the most remarkable aspect of this latest increase in the divorce rate has been the relative calm with which it is being received. Previous waves had been met with cries and lamentations, but this one seems to be arousing fewer fears. Although the *Guide to Periodical Literature* has thirteen entries on divorce in its volume covering the period March 1973–February 1974, the volumes preceding it indicate that much less was being written on the subject. More important than numbers probably is the tone of recent publications. Conservatives continue to moralize, but a large part of the literature is surprisingly matter of fact. Joseph Epstein in his *Divorced in America* looks back nostalgically to the good old days when no one divorced and women knew their place. More typical, however, is the book *Uncoupling: The Art of Coming Apart,* a "how-to" work that concentrates on such basic questions as what to ask for and what to expect.[17]

It would seem, then, that at long last Americans have grown accustomed to divorce. This is not to say that many are enthusiastic about it,

---

17. Joseph Epstein, *Divorced in America: Marriage in an Age of Possibility* (New York: Dutton, 1974). Marya Mannes and Norman Sheresky, *Uncoupling: The Art of Coming Apart* (New York: Viking, 1972).

or are even willing to admit that easy divorce is a necessary accompaniment to easy marriage. But the old tradition of seeing divorce as a threat to marriage and the family, if not to American civilization itself, seems on the wane—and high time, too. If the history of divorce tells us nothing else it is that enormous amounts of time and money have been wasted denouncing what could not be prevented. All along what has been needed is more understanding of why people divorce, when they need to, and when they do not, and how to make divorce not only an easy but a socially responsible act as well. For all that has been written about it divorce remains something about which we need much more solid information. Perhaps now the way is open to acquiring it.

8

The Flapper and Her Critics

GERALD E. CRITOPH

*O*HEN hostilities ended in Europe in 1918, most Americans apparently yearned to restore their lives to what they remembered them to be before the Great War started. Senator Warren G. Harding of Ohio expressed this wish in a speech he delivered in Boston in May 1920. He called for "not heroism but healing, not nostrums but normalcy." The Republican Party nominated Harding as its candidate for president later that year, and based its appeal on a return to "normalcy." The voters, including the newly enfranchised women, responded overwhelmingly to the call. However, Americans under the voting age of twenty-one had already begun to show that they preferred change to a return to the status quo. And the most noticeable members of this latter group were the young women termed Flappers.

A Flapper was commonly understood to be a girl or young woman who demonstrated a rebellious, or at least unconventional, attitude through her appearance, behavior, and speech. In 1936, *Webster's Collegiate Dictionary* defined a Flapper as "A young girl, esp. one somewhat daring in conduct, speech and dress." Details changed from time to time —the impression was that she was someone who wanted to keep ahead of the pack. As one eighteen-year-old commented in 1922: "Of all the things that flappers don't like, it is the commonplace. When it was the style to wear dresses eight inches from the ground, she put hers at sixteen. When styles followed her to sixteen, she put hers to her knee, regardless of how far the knee was from the ground. And all to be different! When people wore long hair she bobbed hers. Now it looks as if she's going to have to shave it to get a real effect."[1]

The Flapper and her male counterparts were in rebellion against the Victorian code of manners and morals which had developed over several generations in Great Britain and the United States. One of the essential elements of this code, as it applied to middle- and upper-class Americans, was based on the widespread assumption that women were morally superior to men. Therefore, they were to be "guardians of morality" and were expected to act accordingly. "Proper" young ladies refrained from all physical contact with men before they married. They were supposed to wait until the "right man" came along, then marry, and presumably "live happily ever after." Most Americans felt that it was wrong for respectable women to smoke or drink, although among some families, it was acceptable to sip an occasional glass of wine.[2]

The so-called Victorian code also drew upon the almost universal conviction that women were weaker than men physically, emotionally, and perhaps intellectually, and were dependent on male relatives for social position, security, and direction. Therefore, women's greatest aspiration should be to be dutiful daughters, sisters, wives, and mothers. As Rheta Childe Dorr described the role of women in 1910, "women . . . have been engaged in the rearing, as well as the bearing of children. They have made the home, they have cared for the sick, ministered to the aged, and given to the poor. . . . They lived lives of constant service, within the narrow confines of a home. Their labor was given to those they loved, and the reward they looked for was purely a spiritual reward."[3] Because they were supposed to be dependent upon men, proper young ladies restrained any temptations to be aggressive or authoritative. Men must make the decisions and women must accommodate themselves obediently to those decisions.

This code had been under strain before World War I. Forces generated by the industrial developments of the late nineteenth century had opened up new job opportunities for women and had increased middle-class affluence sufficiently to encourage some women to go beyond the well-established patterns of behavior. One contemporary observer, Duncan Aiken, described the groundwork laid for the emergence of the

1. "The Flapper's Side of It," by One, New York *Times Book Review and Magazine,* March 26, 1922, p. 4.

2. Frederick Lewis Allen, *Only Yesterday* (New York: Bantam, 1959; originally published in 1931), p. 62.

3. Rheta Childe Dorr, "The Role of Women," from *What Eight Million Women Want* (Boston, 1910), in *The Progressive Movement, 1900–1915,* edited by Richard Hofstadter (Englewood Cliffs, N.J.: Prentice-Hall, 1963), p. 86.

Flapper in June 1926, by calling the early years of the twentieth century "the age of the 'good pal' in American sex relationships." According to him, "during that era the young virgin had put off the coyness, the simpering reserves, the sniffy innocence of the Victorian era. She prided herself on sharing in all male sports that were physiologically attainable, slapped us on the back and 'rough-housed' with us in ostentatiously sexless camaraderie, talked pertly of her equal powers and the equal rights coming to her, and almost wept that she could not be a man and play football and Rooseveltian politics. Yet, under these symbols of equality, the old inferiority sense of woman persisted—and controlled!" If Aiken intended to suggest that he approved of the changes, the note of nostalgia which crept into the last sentence betrayed his true sentiments.

But a more socially significant commentator on the prewar changes that affected young women was F. Scott Fitzgerald. In his first novel, *This Side of Paradise* (1920), he casually revealed that many debutantes coming out before the war had been kissed quite often before their families presented them to society. Many, it seemed, had indulged in "that great current American phenomenon, the 'petting party.'" Their Victorian mothers had no idea "how casually their daughters were accustomed to be kissed." Amory Blaine, the novel's young protagonist, reacted uneasily to the changes he saw, considering them symptoms of "a real moral letdown."

While recognizing that the code had been under pressure to change, most commentators attributed the postwar revolution in manners and morals to the war. John F. Carter, Jr., writing in *The Atlantic Monthly* in September 1920—the year of his graduation from Yale—responded to the description of his generation as "wild young people" by saying: "the older generation had certainly pretty well ruined this world before passing it on to us. . . . We may be fire, but it was they who made us play with gunpowder. And now they are surprised that a great many of us, because they have taken away our apple-cheeked ideals, are seriously considering whether or no *their* game be worth *our candle.*"

Frederick Lewis Allen asserted that the pressures of wartime conditions had provided millions of young Americans "with an emotional stimulant from which it was not easy to taper off. Their torn nerves craved the anodynes of speed, excitement, and passion."[4] Ruth Hooper declared in a *New York Times* feature article on July 16, 1922, that "the war with its sundry excuses for self-sacrifice, bravery and courage, . . . came upon us and surrounded us all about." Then, came the "Peace." "'Yes,' say we

4. Allen, *Only Yesterday*, p. 66.

who won our freedom in the slippery paths of war. 'Peace.' And the outcome of it all is the Flapper."

F. Scott Fitzgerald further defined the Flapper for many Americans in several short stories which were published in the *Saturday Evening Post* during 1920. In "The Offshore Pirate," for example, Ardita is a woman "about nineteen, slender and supple, with a spoiled alluring mouth and quick grey eyes full of radiant curiosity." She is first seen reading *The Revolt of the Angels* by Anatole France. Just when she was beginning to think that life "was scarcely worth living," she says, she discovered "courage as a rule of life." Optimistic about the future, she asserted "my courage is faith—faith in the eternal resilience of me—that joy'll come back, and hope and spontaneity." Nineteen-year-old Sally, in "The Ice Palace," bored with life in her sleepy little south Georgia hometown, told a young male friend, "I want to go places and see people. I want my mind to grow. I want to live where things happen on a big scale." Fitzgerald's Flappers were all anxious to break out of the dull routine of what one of them called "the womanly woman." Most were eighteen or nineteen when Fitzgerald's stories opened. They wore rouge and lipstick and bobbed their hair. They smoked, they drank, and some acted as though they were indulging in premarital sex relations. They refused to follow the traditional code, insisting that life could be more exciting if they were free to pursue new opportunities.

As Flapperism became more and more in vogue among young women and girls, its characteristics were more specifically identified. In looking back on her recent Flapper experiences, Ruth Hooper explained: "Of course a flapper is proud of her nerve . . . She is shameless, selfish and honest, but at the same time she considers these three attributes virtues. Why not? She takes a man's point of view as her mother never could, and when she loses she is not afraid to admit defeat, whether it be a prime lover or $20 at auction. . . . She can take a man—the man of the hour—at his face value, with no foolish promises that will need a disturbing and disagreeable breaking." Except for the heavy application of bright cosmetics, the Flapper was acquiring traits and behavioral practices hitherto belonging exclusively to men, and this ex-Flapper did not repent of her actions one bit.[5]

Attitudes of this sort were bound to cause controversy between the generations, and they did. They drew special attention from clergymen, educators, and other arbiters of manners and morals. The *Literary Digest* inquired in its issue for May 14, 1921: "Is the Younger Generation in

5. New York *Times Book Review and Magazine*, July 16, 1922, p. 13.

Peril? Is the 'old-fashioned girl,' with all that she stands for in sweetness, modesty, and innocence, in danger of becoming extinct? Or was she really no better nor worse than the 'up-to-date' girl—who, in turn, will become 'the old-fashioned girl' to a later generation? Is it even possible, as a small but impressive minority would have us believe, that the girl of today has certain new virtues of 'frankness, sincerity, seriousness of purpose,' lives on 'a higher level of morality,' and is on the whole 'more-clean-minded and clean-lived' than her predecessors?" The *Digest* asked the opinions of church newspaper editors, presidents of colleges and universities, and editors of college newspapers, and in so doing laid the groundwork for a literary debate on the Flapper that was to continue throughout the decade. The responses to the *Digest* inquiry showed a surprisingly even division of opinion between those who believed that conditions were unusually bad and those who believed that they were not.

Slightly more of the college editors criticized the new modes of dress and behavior than defended them. A typical criticism came from the Hobart College *Herald* which objected to the modern dance, because "it is immodest and lacking in grace" and because it was based "on a craving for abnormal excitement." In the editor's opinion, "The dance in its process of degradation has passed from slight impropriety to indecency, and now threatens to become brazenly shameless." He thought that "American morals have undoubtedly degenerated with the dance." The New York University *News* saw a moral decline in the way many young women dressed when attending these dances. They wore fewer petticoats than their elders, if they wore any at all, and a great many left their corsets at home or in the powder room at the dance. Because of "this laxity of dress, . . . every dancing step discloses the entire contour of the dancer." Too many of the girls wore "a minimum of clothes and a maximum of cosmetics, head-decorations, fans, and jewelry," so that they resembled "a South Sea Island savage." *The Round Up* of the New Mexico College of Agriculture and Mechanic Arts, the *Digest* reported, asserted that "to jig and hop around like a chicken on a red-hot stove, at the same time shaking the body until it quivers like a disturbed glass of jell-o, is not only tremendously suggestive but it is an offense against common decency that would not be permitted in a semi-respectable roadhouse." Several other college editors expressed similar attitudes toward the new dances, agreeing with the Mercer University *Cluster* that "the young people who take part in them cannot fail to lose their fine sense of decency and propriety."

Hundreds of recommendations were made in response to the *Digest's* inquiry. About half of them were summed up in a letter from President

Frank H. Gaines of Agnes Scott College. He suggested that "the home, the press, the church, and the college . . . could do much toward creating a healthy public sentiment which would counteract the evils of which you speak." Replies from "scores of institutions" indicated that a great many students were joining the movement to restrain Flapper behavior. In fact, "various student governing associations· [were] able to do away with suggestive dancing and clothing." Women students at Oberlin College, Nebraska University, and Smith College campaigned against "immodest clothing." In 1921, Flappers by no means constituted a majority of the young women.

The clergymen who answered the *Digest's* inquiry were "more nearly unanimous in agreeing that there is a peril." Reactions tended to be influenced by regional and denominational differences. Northeastern clergymen were less severe than those from other areas of the country. Much of the denunciation came from those "denominations opposed to dancing and worldly amusement on general principles," like the Baptists and Methodists.

Dr. Francis E. Clark, founder and president of the Christian Endeavor Society, "the largest and most important interdenominational Protestant young people's organization," thought the modern dances were "indecent" and "an offense against womanly purity, the very fountainhead of our family and civil life." He was shocked "that many girls who call themselves respectable so dress or undress themselves as to be more acceptable to the amorous embraces of the men." *The Mission Herald* of Plymouth, N.C., an Episcopal diocesan organ, summed up "a very general opinion among church editors" by declaring that "there is an ugly, sinister wave of immorality sweeping over the country." The editor of a similar Episcopal diocesan organ for Chicago asserted that "a common question heard when a young girl is asked to dance in . . . better circles is, 'With or without?' meaning with or without corsets!"[6]

The Southern Churchman reported that in New York some churchwomen had sent an appeal to church officials urging efforts "to discourage fashions involving an 'excess of nudity' and 'improper ways of dancing.' " Among the signers were women identified as Mrs. Pierpont Morgan, Mrs. Borden Harriman, Mrs. Henry Phipps, Mrs. James Roosevelt, Mrs. William Sloan, and Mrs. E. H. Harriman. These women were convinced they saw a "breakdown of high moral standards" which was revealed "in insidious conversation, profane language, indecent dress, improper dancing, excessive drinking, gambling, and a general indifference to reasonable

6. "The Religious Press on Youthful Morals," *Literary Digest* 69 (May 21, 1921):28.

safeguards of proper conduct" among women of all ages. They recommended that women's groups develop strong social sanctions against such objectionable activities.

The *Digest* reported that Catholics were joining Protestants in decrying Flapperism. In an encyclical letter, Pope Benedict admonished the many women, "who, infatuated with the ambition of charming others," wore dresses that "not only excite the disapproval of honest people, but, what is worse, offend Our Lord." He also reprimanded those who indulged in the "barbarous and exotic dances which . . . tear away the shreds of modesty." Reactions from many Catholic publications expanded on the Pope's theme.

Pictures accompanying the *Digest* articles on May 14 illustrated lines of modesty and morality in dress and dance. A photograph made by the YWCA depicted a modest, "moral" dress length that reached just to the ankle, as compared to an immodest, immoral dress that came to the middle of the woman's calf. Drawings made up from the reactions of Philadelphia area clergymen from fifteen denominations to the question of proper dress length agreed with the YWCA limits. In the examples of proper dresses, necklines were high, exposing no more than the throat. In the improper dress examples, necklines revealed some chest area, though not even a hint of uncovered breast. The dance which shocked many commentators was the fox-trot. Additional illustrations described various positions of the body during the dance. They showed men holding women close in body-to-body contact, gliding across the floor in what appeared to be rapture. The women wore dresses that could not have passed the tests designed by the YWCA and the Philadelphia clergymen. A number of state legislators were sufficiently concerned that they introduced bills regulating women's dress. The New York *American* reported that legislatures in Utah, Virginia, Ohio, New Jersey, South Carolina, Kansas, Iowa, and Pennsylvania were debating bills that would limit skirts to three or four inches above the ankle and outlaw transparent material in blouses. The Flapper was obviously causing quite a stir among those who considered themselves the arbiters of manners and morals.

While the critics of Flapperism outnumbered its defenders in 1921, there was a substantial group that felt compelled to point out its positive qualities. Supporters suggested that Flapper dress fashions were more sensible and even more healthful than those worn by previous generations of women. President Ray Lyman Wilbur of Stanford University, who thought the new style afforded women "greater freedom of action and better health," was seconded by the mother of a growing girl who said, "the short, not too narrow skirt, and the throat freed from the stiff, uncomfortable collar are a decided improvement in women's dress." Mrs. H. Fletcher Brown, a forty-year-old matron from Wilmington, Delaware, approved the Flapper dress style for older women. She wrote in the *Literary Digest,* July 9, 1921: "Skirts can't be too short for me, now that at this age I am climbing in and out of automobiles, and gardening in the mud, and playing golf in all weather." She also complained about corsets, "with bones digging in and garters pulling at every move. No wonder the modern athletic girl wants them off."

Other defenders of the Flapper in 1921 denied that the morals of the young women, or their male companions, had degenerated. President Kenneth C. M. Sills of Bowdoin College suggested that the new dances and dress styles represented changes in manners rather than morals, and President Henry Lewis Smith of Washington and Lee University concurred. In Smith's opinion "the level of sexual morality is higher today than formerly" among college students, and the Dean of Women at Northwestern University supported these views by declaring in the *Literary Digest,* May 14, 1921: "There is nothing wrong with the girl of to-day."

The editor of the student newspaper at Carnegie Institute of Technology condemned "the custom for every college paper to take a slam at the girls," and disputed the charge that "all the young women are going from bad to worse." He insisted that "wholesome, clean-minded men" should prefer to "see a woman in a sane, short skirt, with plenty of freedom to move as nature intended she should," instead of a sheath dress "which emphasized her every contour while hobbling her movements, . . . sweeping the ground in an attempt to trip her at every step." The Columbia University *Spectator* agreed, suggesting that the dress and behavior of college students were reflections of changes in society at large.

Although the Flapper's defenders were in a much smaller minority among the clergy than those on the college scene, there were a few who expressed their faith in the young people of 1921. The Reverend Dr. Thomas F. Gailor, presiding bishop of the Episcopal Church, contended that "the girls of to-day are as fine and as high-minded as any girls ever were. . . . I have yet to meet one who seems tainted in the least degree by what they tell me is the tendency of the age, which is toward too much freedom with their male friends." In fact, he saw a great improvement, because "people do openly to-day things that they used to do in secret." The Unitarian *Christian Register* of Boston admitted that there were "a few gilded youths," but they hardly compared with the many "young people in our communities who are courteous, studious, orderly, and in their attitudes idealists." Making a similar point, the editor of *The American Israelite* of Cincinnati, declared in the May 21 issue of *Literary Di-*

gest: "The present generation of women are perhaps more sophisticated than were their grandmothers, but that they are less virtuous or less clean-minded, I do not for a moment believe."

The Flapper's defenders were likely to agree with the editorial writer of *The Nation* who was less concerned with her increased frankness and casualness in her social relationships than he was with her critics' tendencies toward "insipid, smug propriety." As Gertrude Atherton, the novelist, said, "if the United States of America is conquered by internal or external enemies, it will not be from bad morals but smug stupidity." The New York *Tribune* summed up the Flapper's defense by praising her "candor, frankness, sincerity [and] seriousness of purpose."

The crucial issue in the Flapper controversy centered on whether her actions and attire constituted a basic change in the moral code or simply a shift in style. Those who believed that she was threatening the moral code condemned her. Most of those who considered her a pace-setter in style cheered her on. The debate in 1921 set the tone of the arguments for the rest of the decade.

The following year Flappers and their boy friends continued to cause consternation among members of the older generation. According to newspaper stories, Flapperism seemed to be on the increase. One claimed that sixteen-year-old boys and girls in a small city near New York were slipping out of their high school dance to drink liquor which they had left in their cars. In Chicago a newspaperman reported that high school girls and boys were going the "round of cabarets, jazz resorts, tea shops and roadhouses." He blamed "Too much spending money and the free use of automobiles." Mrs. Julia H. Kennedy, Educational Supervisor in the Social Hygiene Division of the Illinois Department of Health, asserted in the *New York Times,* January 18, 1922, that small-town girls from the St. Louis and Chicago areas were behaving more shamefully than those in the big cities. She said that some girls were known to carry flasks tied around their necks which hung inside the bosom of their dresses. She claimed they were drinking white mule and lemon extract. The stories revealed the degree to which the older generation, keeper of the Victorian code, was outraged by the behavior of high school and college students. The implication that the girls often initiated the action intensified the condemnation.

Critical reactions came from a variety of sources, including parents, school administrators, and students themselves. Four hundred members of the high school Girls League in Albuquerque, New Mexico, voted to ban from their activities "jazz dancing, 'petting parties' and cigarette smoking"—behavior which they identified as causes of girls getting into "trouble." The Parents' League of Brooklyn set up a code defining activities of fifteen to eighteen-year-old boys and girls. It limited parties to a midnight curfew on Fridays and Saturdays, mandated chaperones, refined clothing, and simple refreshments, and prohibited improper dancing. According to the statement issued by the parents, the rules were set up "to counteract the flapper invasion into the life of the young girls." The Kearney, New Jersey, school board banned dances in the high school, because "spooning" was reported in dark cloakrooms, and cigarette butts and empty liquor bottles were discovered in the vicinity. In addition, the *New York Times* reported on February 18, 1922, that the principal objected to what he called "jowl to jowl" dancing in the popular steps. The forces of respectability and propriety were rising up in righteous indignation to "protect" the high school girls against what they considered to be the insidious influence of the college-age Flappers.

Critics predictably began to question the Flapper's qualifications to be a proper wife. According to the *New York Times* on March 16, 1922, the editor of the school paper at Colorado College had observed: "This is the age of jazz, the flapper and the snake. All play their parts and how degrading that part is sometimes. . . . To look at some of the modern girls on the campus today with their short skirts, often showing bare knees; with their bobbed hair, certainly violating God's greatest gift to woman, her hair, and all their vanity and frivolity, man thinks a second time as to whether that type of woman would make him a helpful mate through life." Some young men in Las Vegas, New Mexico, even formed a Men's Mutual Matrimonial Protective Association "to eliminate the flapper from the matrimonial race." It apparently never occurred to these self-appointed guardians of traditional womanhood that the Flapper was not interested in becoming "desirable in the eyes of serious-minded men," in order to be "a helpful mate."

John Walker Harrington, attempting to poke fun at Flappers in a *New York Times* feature article on April 2, 1922, revealed his own personal bias. He argued that Flappers appeared as they did because some young women thought that Flapperish antics would get them more male attention. Men, therefore, were at fault. Man, said Harrington, has paid too little attention to "his own reforms," and because of his frivolity and preoccupation, has made it possible for woman to "go sailing over the sea of life." But things will return to normal once men recognize the problem. "Man, as the pilot of her destiny and the Captain of her fate, is due to take the helm," he predicted.

A man who appeared to act vigorously against the invasion of Flapperism into his office was the newly appointed Chief of the Division of

Parole for New Jersey. According to a *Times* report on April 8, when a new secretary came to work "in bobbed hair, red glass earrings, short skirt and sheer silk stockings," the chief responded by issuing severe orders regarding dress for office wear. The women met with him and reportedly cried, but to no avail. The result was that "they are now on good terms, the girls are dressing decorously and business is going on as usual."

Despite the criticism that Flappers were attracting in 1922, more defenders were showing up in print. An eighteen-year-old Flapper declared that she was bored by most of the young men she knew, preferring instead older men whose conversation she regarded as more mature and worldly. Flappers, she said, disliked the commonplace and looked for the exceptional in life. She wanted excitement, both emotional and intellectual.[7] In many ways, she resembled Fitzgerald's heroines. She believed she was any man's intellectual and social equal, capable of making her own decisions for her life.

In a *Times* feature article on the controversy on April 16, 1922, Margaret O'Leary observed that the Flapper had become a popular topic of conversation because "she disports herself flagrantly in the public eye," and if any man tried to assume the posture of mental superiority, "it is her game to spoil his high attitude." She quoted Virginia Potter, for years president of the New York League of Girls Clubs, as saying, "I think the modern young girl is a delight. She dresses simply and sensibly, and she looks life right straight in the eye; she knows just what she wants and goes after it, whether it is a man, a career, a job or a new hat." Miss O'Leary identified three types of reactions to the Flapper, "those who delight in her, those who fear her and those who try pathetically to take her as a matter of course." This description of the Flapper's place in society was to hold true, generally, for the entire decade. Her freshness and directness made her exciting for some and unsettling for others.

Several clergymen once again offered moral support to the Flapper in 1922. For example, the pastor of the First Presbyterian Church of Michigan City, Indiana, told his congregation that the Flapper's unbuckled galoshes were no less attractive than men's bulging shirts hanging over the tops of their pants. He thought their bobbed hair was far more attractive than a man's shaved head. The minister of the Covenant Church of Evanston, Illinois, labeling Flapperism "a diversion," said "bobbed hair, short skirts and knickerbockers are not signs of sin, but a declaration of independence." He was convinced that Flappers "will give

7. "The Flapper's Side of It," by One, New York *Times Book Review and Magazine*, March 26, 1922.

us the finest generation of women the world has ever known." Other
clerical supporters concurred. Episcopal Bishop Gailor reiterated a position he had taken in 1921, and Dr. W. A. Harris, corresponding secretary
of the Board of Education of the Methodist Episcopal Church, observed
that American culture was absorbing the innovations made by the Flappers.[8] As a former president of Northwestern University and chairman of
the Chicago Vice Commission, Harris drew on his wide experience in his
statement carried in the New York *Times*, May 21, 1922: "the short
dresses of the young girls commonly called Flappers have almost become
the usual thing now, and have lost much of their suggestiveness they were
said to have at first." This held true for reactions to bobbing the hair and
painting the face. If a major trait of the Flapper was her cynicism, she
was "only reflecting the spirit of the times."

This point of view received reinforcement in a provocative analysis
of the Flapper phenomenon by G. Stanley Hall, president-emeritus of
Clark University and founder of the *American Journal of Psychology*. In
an article in *The Atlantic Monthly*, June 1922, he agreed with those commentators who saw the Flapper as "more or less a product of movies, the
auto, woman suffrage, and especially, of the war." The movies offered
women unconventional role models; the auto provided new opportunities
for dating; the woman's suffrage amendment suggested the prospect for
greater equality with men; and the war, by disrupting normal social
processes, made demands on women to act in roles previously limited to
men. Through these influences, "her manners have grown a bit free-and-
easy, and every vestige of certain old restraints is gone." She treated her
male companions "as if sex differences did not exist . . . she may sometimes even seem almost aggressive." As a result, Hall saw the Flapper as
something special in social history: "Never since civilization began has
the girl in the early teens seemed so self-sufficient and sure of herself, or
made such a break with the rigid traditions of propriety and convention
which have hedged her in." He concluded that the Flapper was making
an important contribution to American social progress—"individuality is
being developed, and the new and ostensive assertiveness has in it the
promise and potency of a new and truer womanhood." He criticized the
feminists of the early twentieth century for being too masculine in com-
peting "with man along his own lines." However, he observed, "these girls
not only accept, but glory in, their sex as such, and are giving free course
to its native impulses. They may be the leaders in the complete emancipation of woman from the standards man has made for her."

8. New York *Times*, April 10, 1922, p. 1; May 23, 1922, p. 3; May 29, 1922,
p. 11.

The realization that the Flapper was more than just a collection of faddish behavior patterns was expressed by other thoughtful observers, who saw her as a force which would have a lasting impact on American culture. In an *Outlook* article on teachers, June 7, 1922, Angela M. Keyes commented that training schools were "receiving the flapper cordially," despite "the wild bob, the short skirt, even the ugly flesh-colored stockings." "The flapper," she concluded, "has brought into the serious, often over-weary, sometimes all but discouraged, training schools of our crowded cities vigor, daring, directness, and withall unmistakable braininess, fine practical ability. She has brought back hope." *Forum,* November 1922, carried the opinion of another observer, Gilbert Frankau, who said that the Flapper was "less mock-modest than her predecessors," and had shown herself to be a woman capable of "adapting herself to this phase of present-day existence." He advocated full partnership rights for women in marriage, because modern girls were capable of equal responsibility.

As more and more young women appeared to be breaking out of conventional ways, more and more of the older generation approved of their behavior, especially its seemingly liberating effects. Some applauded the "pretty, practical and comfortable frocks" they insisted on wearing, instead of the "long skirts and other abominations" decreed by fashion designers. One commentator cheered that the corsetmaker was "doomed to the scrap heap, where the makers of skirt linings and of hoopskirts have long lain dejected." Others welcomed the appearance of "The Middle-Aged Flapper," an obvious manifestation of the changes by the young.[9] The Flapper was winning acceptance, reluctantly in some quarters, happily in others.

The Flapper controversy continued throughout the decade along the lines developed in its early years. Newspapers continued to report incidents involving teenagers who were smoking, drinking, and petting during and after dances. Critics persisted in seeing Flapper behavior and dress as a threat to national morals, while defenders contended that the young were more sensible than the previous generations.

The argument that Flappers would not make good wives and mothers did not die. In 1923, a teacher at Hill School, Pottstown, Pennsylvania, told the Germantown Women's Club: "The modern flapper may be a success as a companion, but as an ideal she fails to impress." Mrs. Mina Van Winkle, chief of the women's division of the Washington, D.C., police department, blamed cabaret life and cheap literature for making the majority of American girls unfit to become wives and mothers. Dr.

9. Editorial, New York *Times,* August 22, 1922, p. 16; editorial, April 16, 1922, section II, p. 6.

Abraham A. Roback, a Harvard psychologist, asserted that, on the basis of hundreds of tests given college coeds, "the modern 'flapper' possesses the lowest degree of intelligence." He said Flappers "are undependable," and "they chafe under discipline and enforced tasks."[10] He did not make clear what kind of tests were taken to measure these traits, but from his comments they seem to have been based on the assumption that women need to be predictably docile to be considered intelligent.

The influential New York *Times* became persuaded that the Flapper was having a significant impact on American attitudes. It had been supporting her campaign for the same freedom of choice that her brothers had, and in feature articles and editorials, the paper expressed a strongly favorable view of the Flapper. In its overall approach, it demonstrated its agreement with the Reverend Dr. Gardner that the Flapper was "a symbol of the time."

By the middle years of the decade, the Flapper had become a well-established female type. Certainly not all American women were Flappers in 1924, 1925, and 1926, but a great many were. The fashion pages of the magazines and newspapers for these years revealed a general acceptance of the Flapper style of appearance. Stories, both fact and fiction, revealed a fascination with Flapper behavior.

Bruce Bliven offered a middle-of-the-decade summary of "Flapper Jane" in the *New Republic* on September 9, 1925. She was nineteen, just as she had been for Fitzgerald in 1920. She was pretty, but "heavily made up, not to imitate nature, but for an altogether artificial effect—pallor mortis, poisonously scarlet lips, richly ringed eyes." She wore "one dress, one step-in, two stockings, two shoes." The corset and petticoat were "defunct." "The brassiere has been abandoned since 1924." Her hair is "the very newest thing in bobs. . . . It leaves her just about no hair at all in the back, and 20 percent more than that in the front." Her clothes were "The Style" for 1925, at least on the eastern seaboard. "They are being worn by ladies who are three times Jane's age, and look ten years older; by those twice her age who look a hundred years older." Bliven commented that styles had taken "a long step toward genuine nudity. . . . Next year's styles, from all one hears, will be, as they already are on the continent, even More So."

On the subject of marriage, Bliven had Flapper Jane say: "Of course, not so many girls are looking for a life meal-ticket nowadays. Lots of them prefer to earn their own living and omit the home-and-baby act. Well, anyhow, postpone it years and years. They think a bachelor girl

can and should do everything a bachelor man does." Despite her statement, Bliven saw "a good deal more smoke than fire" on the moral question. He believed that the United States was maintaining its traditional
monogamous structure. However, he insisted, "women today are shaking
off the shreds and patches of their age-old servitude." He concluded,
"Women have highly resolved that they are just as good as men, and intend to be treated so. They don't mean to have any more unwanted children. They don't intend to be debarred from any profession or occupation
which they choose to enter. They clearly mean (even though not all of
them yet realize it) that in the great game of sexual selection, they shall
no longer be forced to play the role, simulated or real, of helpless quarry."
To which he made a final comment—"Hurrah!" That women are still
struggling to realize those objectives suggests that the wheels of social
change turn exceedingly slow.

Toward the end of the decade, the Flapper slipped out of fashion.
It happened even before the stock market crash wiped out much of the
affluence that made her possible. While there were premature notices of
the Flapper's demise, it was not until 1928 that signs of disloyalty to the
image came out in strength. A significant expression of the change was an
article written by four Junior Leaguers from different parts of the nation,
drawn from a nationwide survey of Junior League chapters in thirty-five
cities. Their description of the Flapper was purposefully unflattering.
"The flapper," they said, "was a postwar creation. Her hair overnight
resembled a Hotentot's; her skirt ended about her knees; she sneaked
her brother's cigarettes and swore like a trooper. She chewed gum—
great wads of it—vigorously and incessantly. Her make-up was as crude
as a clown's. She was supposed to be a 'neck artist,' 'booze hound' and
'human smoke-stack.'" They compared her with their version of the new
ideal American girl: "Young 1928 uses more subtle methods, that is all.
. . . She is more refined and veils her frankness with artful politeness,
takes life for granted and lives frankly and calmly, if not wisely." While
the Junior Leaguers announced the Flapper's demise, their new ideal retained the frank and cool appraisal of life that had marked the earlier
girl.[11] They did not seem ready to give up any of the freedoms that the
Flapper had won, just what they regarded as her brassy ways.

In a New York *Times* feature article on January 20, 1929, Mildred
Adams recognized the change by declaring: "This year the flapper is as
out of date as last year's dance tunes." She noted that the new ideal girl
was wearing her hair and her skirts longer. While Miss Adams was saying

11. New York *Times*, February 15, 1928, p. 12, quoted from *The Junior League
Magazine* for February 1928.

"farewell to the Flapper," she recognized that she had been a pacesetter in manners and morals. The Flapper "had set her mother and her grand-mother at reducing their matronly proportions to approximate her straight young figure," and she had freed them from the hobbling dress styles of the previous century.

Even though the outward appearance identified with the Flapper was no longer in vogue, her spirit of independence was not lost. While this change in attitude did not elicit approval from all Americans, it was supported by sufficiently large numbers of persons in responsible posi-tions to make it unlikely that the American woman would return to the completely subservient role imposed upon her before World War I.

The Flapper gave the women who followed her an important legacy. She created a breach in the wall of tradition and convention that was never quite closed, despite continuing efforts to keep women in "their place"—the home. She reduced the bulk of clothing that the traditional code had insisted was necessary for modesty. She established woman's equal claim to such previously male-only privileges as drinking, smoking, swearing, sexual aggressiveness, and even disturbing the peace. As each crop of Flappers came of age, they helped to undercut the strength of the old social values, but this would not have been possible if those values had been constructively relevant to the times.

9

Ume Tsuda and Motoko Hani:
Echoes of American Cultural Feminism in Japan

NORIKO SHIMADA, HIROKO TAKAMURA,
MASAKO IINO, and HISAKO ITO

*O*NE result of the rebirth of the women's movement has been the incentive it has given to scholars—more traditional historians as well as feminists—to re-examine past events and issues that involved women. The suffrage campaign, for example, until recently regarded as a "woman's issue" to be treated in a nonanalytical narrative fashion, has been investigated in terms of its wider philosophical implications. By fixing their gaze steadily on the franchise, it has been asked, did American suffragists ignore other potentially liberating prospects on the horizon? It raises the basic question of the relative value of sharply focused political action as opposed to fundamental social change. Some historians tell us today that the majority of suffragists were conditioned by their bourgeois bias to pursue a very limited objective, while simultaneously adhering to anti-black, anti-immigrant, anti-labor principles. Small wonder, then, they remind us, that the woman's vote has "made so little difference."

While the dust of the ideological battle on this controversial issue has not yet settled—indeed, it is probably just rising—we would like to suggest the value of employing another approach to the problem, one used successfully in the study of slavery, and that is comparative, or cross-cultural, investigation. Toward that end, we have studied two Japanese women, Ume Tsuda (1864–1929) and Motoko Hani (1873–1957), "new women" and "cultural feminists" active during the period 1900–30. Unlike slavery, comparisons between women in different cultures are not limited to particular geographic areas: women are found in all societies; captive

161

slavery is not. Thus, while we have singled out Japanese women for our study, it can be argued convincingly that women from other countries could offer equally useful models.

Tsuda and Hani were most active in promoting their "cultural feminism" during the first three decades of the twentieth century, a period when Japan was experiencing basic social and political changes. This period also corresponded not only with the suffrage campaign in America, but with an era that witnessed war, depression, and prohibition along with racial and class antagonisms. At the time, Japan was a society reawakened, motivated by nascent nationalism to achieve the level of industrial development found in more advanced Western nations. Westernization—the introduction and adaptation of Western practices—was an important tool in the process of modernization, and one that women activists like Tsuda and Hani employed with telling results. With industrialism in its early stages and nation-building on the rise, Japan during this period resembled more Jacksonian America than Progressive America. Tsuda and Hani certainly had more in common with nineteenth-century American women educators than with twentieth-century suffragists.

Tsuda and Hani can be described as both "new women" and "cultural feminists," although there were significant personal and philosophical differences that separated the two women. We refer to them as "cultural feminists" because their plans to liberate Japanese women from discriminatory practices were based on education rather than political action, and to that extent they resemble the pioneer women educators in America. Of the two, Tsuda was more Westernized and culturally American than Hani, the result, in part, of several years' residence in the United States. Hani, fully Japanese but with a high regard for Western culture, attempted Westernization in the practical sphere. Class differences also distinguished the two women: destined to be a member of the elite, Ume Tsuda established a women's college designed to develop elites and prepare Japanese women for responsible positions in society; Motoko Hani, from a more modest background, was concerned with liberating middle- and lower-class women from ignorance and conventional restrictions. One might claim Ume Tsuda as the Japanese equivalent of Mary Lyon while Motoko Hani could be regarded as the Eastern counterpart of Catharine Beecher. They were active during a period when traditional patterns still dominated people's lives, although old practices coexisted alongside political modernization and industrial development. Women's legal status, for example, though somewhat improved, was still restricted by conventional morality and feudalistic customs. As in antebellum America, however, political and industrial changes began to encourage women to consider their own civil rights. In both countries, teaching was the first of the professional jobs open to women, while the expansion and upgrading of women's education became one of the first targets for modern feminists.

Women's education in Japan in the late nineteenth century lagged far behind that of men. Though the Meiji government encouraged elementary education for girls, the girls' rate of entering elementary school was about half the boys' rate until 1890. On the secondary school level, male students further outnumbered female students: the enrollment of girls was only 2.6 percent of the boys' in 1882, 22.1 percent in 1890, 12.6 percent in 1900, and 34.5 percent in 1910.[1] In higher education, the number of female students entering normal schools was quite low until the end of the nineteenth century, because professional education for women was not yet socially acceptable, and because women themselves did not seek "professional" employment. Moreover, universities and colleges were not open to women. Under these semi-feudal social conditions, Ume Tsuda and Motoko Hani pioneered a "new womanhood," opening up a new phase in women's education in Japan.

The Meiji government pursued a vigorous modernization policy best expressed in the slogan "civilization and enlightenment," and it set up a special educational program which came to determine the course of Ume Tsuda's life. Aware of the importance of education as a major tool of modernization, the Meiji government sent Japanese students, including five women, to technologically advanced Western nations to develop future leaders for the new state. Ume Tsuda, seven years old in 1871, was the youngest of the five girls sent to the United States. By this unique experience, which she later referred to as a "strange destiny," she became one of the most modernized women in Japan. Sending young girls abroad represented a dramatic departure from the traditional pattern of women's education, and it required great courage for parents to agree to let their daughters study in an unknown land. Tsuda's father, Sen Tsuda, a farsighted and ambitious man who had served as official interpreter of English for the Tokugawa government, had felt keenly the need to learn about situations outside Japan, and he decided to let his young daughter go to the United States.

Ume Tsuda was transplanted from still half-feudal Japan to comparatively advanced America at a time when the liberalization of women's education was in full bloom. Tsuda received her elementary education at Stephenson Seminary, a private girls' school in Washington, D.C., and then continued her secondary education at the Archer Institute in the

1. Japan Statistics Research Center, *Nihon Keizai Tokei-shu* (Japanese Economic Statistical Tables) (Tokyo: Hyoron Sha, 1958), p. 312.

same city. At nine, upon her own request, she was baptized as a Christian. She was quickly learning American ways and forgetting Japanese, although her writings reveal that she was still conscious of being Japanese.[2] Furthermore, she already understood—though only vaguely—that the Japanese government had had a particular purpose in mind when it gave her such a rare opportunity to study in the United States, and that concerned her future responsibility to Japan. She returned to Japan in 1882 after an absence of eleven years.

Ume Tsuda's residence in the United States during the most formative years of her life proved decisive; it determined her way of thinking, her feelings and habits. When she returned to Japan in 1882, she was like a foreigner, "an American with a Japanese body."[3] Aside from the habitual inconveniences of daily life which she had forgotten but which time would solve, she was virtually outside the mainstream of Japanese culture. Having received an exceptionally high education for a Japanese woman of the time, she found herself far apart from the majority of tradition-bound Japanese women, a then extreme example of the "new woman." On her return she was most struck by "the great difference between men and women, and the absolute power which the men held." She compared it with her experiences in the United States between 1871 and 1882 and noted that the thing she found most striking was "the position American women hold, the great influence that they exercise for good, the power given them by education and training, the congenial intercourse between men and women, and the sympathy existing in the homes, between brothers and sisters, husbands and wives.[4]

There were three alternatives for this eighteen-year-old girl. She could, first of all, return to the United States, where she might have felt at home. Secondly, if she adjusted her values to fit Japanese social standards, she could marry a peer in high society, who would recognize the value of her knowledge of Western languages and manners. As a matter of fact, two girls sent to the United States with Ume Tsuda followed this course. Tsuda chose a third alternative: she committed herself to the struggle to become a new woman despite conservative opposition. A woman with courage, energy, and a strong will, she could not accept the

2. Toshikazu Yoshikawa, *Tsuda Umeko Den* (Biography of Ume Tsuda) (Tokyo: Tsuda College Alumnae Association, 1961), pp. 110–14.

3. Masunori Hiratsuka, *Joshi Kyoiku Shi* (History of Women's Education) (Tokyo: Teikoku Chiho Gyosei Gakkai, 1965), p. 215.

4. Ume Tsuda, "The Education of Japanese Women," an address made in Philadelphia (newspaper not named, no date, but presumably 1892), Ume Tsuda Collection at Tsuda College.

inferior place assigned to Japanese women in general, nor could she ignore her personal responsibility to enlighten her fellow Japanese women.

During the period following her return to Japan in 1882 until the opening of her own school in 1900, Ume Tsuda worked at a variety of what might be called preparatory tasks, since they served later as a background for her cultural feminism. In 1885 she was employed by the Peeresses' School, founded by the Imperial Court in that year for the girls of noble families. Teaching was one of the few professions open to women, and the connection with the most prestigious school in Japan was an honor highly regarded by the general public. Tsuda, however, was not satisfied, for the educational philosophy of the school was so different from her experience in America and from her own ideals. Japanese women's education in the 1880s was more than a half-century behind that of American, and, as in the girls' schools of America during the early nineteenth century, "ladylike" character and traits were emphasized, the primary aim of education being the training of women to be obedient wives. Surrounded by women of the nobility whom she critically observed as living in monotonous quiet, knowing nothing of the great changes outside, she felt a need to explore more fully her own potentialities.

In 1889, the twenty-four-year-old Ume Tsuda left Japan once again, this time to receive in the United States the higher academic training still unavailable to women in Japan. She entered Bryn Mawr, which had been founded only four years before, and studied biology under T. H. Morgan. At the end of her study in 1892 she received an offer to remain in the United States to collaborate with her professor on special research, an opportunity that would have made her one of the first Japanese woman scientists. But she declined this "overwhelming temptation to her intellect and ambition,"[5] because she felt obliged to go back to the Peeresses' School.

Her decision to forego a career as a scientist is best understood in the light of her increased interest in the education of Japanese women. Her stay at Bryn Mawr had been marked by several moves which advanced her thinking regarding the need for a college for women in Japan. In the summer of 1890 she stayed in Hampton, Virginia, with Alice Bacon, a woman whose father had accepted one of the five girls sent by the Meiji government, and who was herself Tsuda's colleague at the Peeresses' School. Alice Bacon was at that time writing a book about Japanese

5. Anna Hartshorne, "The Years of Preparation: A Memory of Miss Tsuda," *Alumnae Bulletin*, edited by Tsuda College Alumnae Association, no. 35 (Tokyo: Tsuda College, July 1931), p. 2.

women, and her comments and insight excited Tsuda's concern about the condition of Japanese women. That concern matured into a wish to establish a higher educational institution. Tsuda decided to enroll in a six-months' training program in education and teaching at Oswego Teacher's College in New York.

Her next move, regarded as "her first independent scheme for education," called for creating an American Scholarship for Japanese Women. Like such American feminists as Emma Willard and Mary Lyon, Tsuda recognized the need to increase the numbers of educated women teachers, and appealed to the women of Philadelphia to support her plan for the American Scholarship. She herself raised money, as Mary Lyon had done, giving lectures on Japan, for the first time showing her practical ability to turn wishes into facts. If Japanese women could be properly trained, Tsuda believed, they would make far better teachers than foreigners, because they would be better able to understand and reach their own countrywomen. And her idea of bringing them to the United States for training underscored her commitment to American culture. The American scholarship program would help other Japanese women to share what she had so enjoyed and benefited by. She said: "I regard the intimate association with American girls and women and the glimpses obtained of woman's position in American homes and woman's work in the world, as one of the most important points of this [Scholarship program]."[6]

This was the first sign of what was to become her characteristic strategy of feminism: she promoted cultural feminism derived from her American experiences and pursued through intellectual Westernization.

In 1892 Tsuda once again returned to Japan to resume her teaching at the Peeresses' School. Eight years later, she resigned from the school and announced her plan to found Joshi Eigaku Juku (School of English Studies for Women). The letter she sent to her close friends in the United States indicated her determination to live a free but difficult life:

No one would believe me when I asked to resign and I had some fights to go thro' and some yet before me. But I am now *free* and have burned so to speak all my ships [*sic*] behind me. . . . I broke off a 15 years [*sic*] connection with the highest rank[ing] school in Japan, and gave up my official rank and title worthless to me, but valued so among our people. Most of my acquaintances were surprised . . . but I was glad to say that I wanted to get away from all the Conservatism and Connection of my old life, and now I am only a commoner, free to do what I like, and free also from my salary, which however small, still in Japanese eyes was ample![7]

6. Tsuda, "The Education of Japanese Women," Philadelphia address.
7. Letter from Ume Tsuda to Abby and Emily Kirk, August 6, 1900.

When Tsuda started her new school in September 1900, she fulfilled her obligation to the country to contribute to its nation-building. She had a strong sense of mission to produce the new kind of Japanese woman—many other "Ume Tsudas"—that she thought Japan badly needed. She observed that while much progress had been made for men, no corresponding advantages had been given to women. She wished that good women could arise at that critical period in Japan's history, to be helpers and co-workers with the men. A modernized Japan needed "new women" —able, intelligent, responsible and independent—who fitted the new life.

While Tsuda had a distinctive Japanese purpose in mind, she adopted many educational ideas and methods from American colleges, particularly Bryn Mawr. For example, she set the educational standard very high, "as high a standard as possible, in the kind of work done, rather than in quantity."[8] As a consequence, the entrance examination was strict and in the first year she admitted only ten students. In twenty years the total number of graduates was only 236, showing the school's policy of educating elites. Also like Bryn Mawr, Tsuda's school stressed the importance of language instruction and liberal arts education. At the opening ceremony she said that the main purpose of the school would be to offer advanced courses in English and to make her students well-rounded women through English studies. At a time when other women's schools were stressing domestic science education, the introduction of liberal arts education for women was a remarkable development. It was necessary, she believed, to make women "intellectual and spiritual co-operators" with men. Expressing an optimistic belief in her strategy of cultural feminism, she said: "When women through a more liberal education have proved themselves capable of greater things, there will come the day when they can take a higher place in society, as they certainly will in the home."[9]

Her stress on English was a characteristic of her program. A great admirer of American culture and American women, Ume Tsuda naturally tried to use English and English literature as a means for liberation and enlightenment. "The thorough mastery of a Western language, especially a close study of the literature, [could] give us of the East the key to Western thought, ideals and point of view," she said, and it would be of great help in bringing the nations closer together. She also believed that "the reading of the good and noble thoughts of great English writers was the best help possible in moral training."[10]

8. Ume Tsuda, "Introductory," *Alumnae Bulletin*, no. 1 (1905), quoted in Yoshikawa, *Tsuda Umeko Den*, p. 358.
9. Ume Tsuda, "The Future of Japanese Women," *The Far East* (January 1897).
10. Ume Tsuda, "Teaching in Japan," *The Bryn Mawr Alumnae Quarterly* (August 1907).

At the same time, she recognized certain utilitarian values also involved in learning English. She regarded vocational training, particularly teacher training, as another important basis for women's liberation. The graduates of Joshi Eigaku Juku (now known as Tsuda College) were encouraged to acquire enough ability to pass the government examination for a teacher's certificate in English, thereby opening up a place for women in the field of education. Women, Tsuda believed, should have training of commercial value that would enable them to be self-supporting. She pointed out the fact that "even a thorough knowledge of English [would place] a girl on a separate plane, giving her a 'weapon to defend herself in the fight for independence.'" At the time, this was a pioneering approach to women's education in Japan. Using the image of American woman as her ideal, she urged Japanese women to acquire reason, judgment, and will. Her observation of the girls of the period was critical: "Japanese girls are timid, lack self-confidence and independence. They dislike taking responsibility beyond all things, especially for fear they may be blamed for what they do. They have never been taught to think and act for themselves. Emotion and not reason is their guide, so they are impulsive and over-sensitive."[11]

From this grew the characteristic feature of her teaching, to teach the students to form their own opinions on various matters, an approach unique in women's education. By letting students arrange social entertainments and perform dramas, she tried to teach them to take initiative and to lead, which was difficult for them since they were accustomed to respond obediently to the guidance of a superior.

The early stage of women's education in Japan was closely related to and largely influenced by the relatively recent introduction of Christianity. In Tsuda's school, too, Christianity exerted a strong influence. Christened at age nine and educated at Quaker Bryn Mawr, she could not think of higher education apart from Christianity. Spiritual growth came through Christian education. Christianity, she believed, was one of the influences that would bring about changes in women's status; in her speeches she observed repeatedly that education and a Christian background would give Japanese women the power to assert themselves and assist in nation-building.

In analyzing Ume Tsuda's ideas and beliefs as a cultural feminist, it becomes clear that American influence was pervasive and profound. Im-

11. "Talks on Position of the Japanese Women: Miss Tsuda Believes They Will Gain a Higher Place," an article on Tsuda's speech, "Women's Movement in Japan," at Karuizawa (newspaper not named, no date, but presumably August 1914), Ume Tsuda Collection.

pressed with the position and influence American women held in society
—though she admitted that "the woman question" had not "entirely
ceased to be agitated in progressive America"—she thought there was no
reason why it should not be the same in Japan. Nevertheless, she did not
promote sweeping Americanization or Westernization. American influence
was essential in every sphere of her life, her teaching, and her belief, but
she was not blind to the values of traditional Japanese virtues. She felt
that if "gentle ways, loveliness or sweetness," the traditional training for
Japanese women, were combined with the strength of character and
knowledge of Western women, Japanese women would be "an example
for the world."[12]

At the same time she was careful not to invite petty and unnecessary criticism by abandoning traditional appearance. She might have
taken a lesson from Amelia Bloomer and her feminist friends. When her
school was established she warned her students not to abandon the traditional Japanese way of life because of their training in English: "This
school will be the first that will give a professional education for women.
I think that this school will be conspicuous and criticized, and that most
criticisms will center on such trifling matters as speaking expressions,
social manners, style of dress, etc. People will tend to evaluate the school
in terms of one or more of these. I hope that you will be reserved, modest,
and polite in all matters. Such an attitude will not be contradictory to the
best interest of study."[13]

To teach girls Japanese manners and etiquette, Tsuda chose as a
dormitory mother her own aunt, who had served at the court of a feudal
lord for a long time. Her discipline was strict. Although Tsuda was a new
woman, she did not live the "free" life style associated with American
flappers, who seemed careless of social reputations. She had a mission
and she had to be socially accepted.

Like many of the educational reformers in antebellum America,
Tsuda used essentially conservative methods to enlighten and modernize
Japanese women. She adapted her techniques to Japanese society and
tried to improve the situation of women from within the existing social
framework. From her perspective, it would have been too radical to advocate women's inroads into men's professional fields, and for the same
reason she did not support the political feminism which was beginning to
develop in Japan in the late 1910s. She claimed that the role of educated

12. Tsuda, "The Future of Japanese Women," *The Far East* (January 1897).
13. Tsuda's opening address at Joshi Eigaku Juku (1900), *Tsuda Juku Rokuju-Nen Shi* (Sixty Years of Tsuda College), edited by Tsuda College (Tokyo: Tsuda College, 1960), p. 66.

women was not to compete with men but to understand and help men build a new Japan. This attitude was both her strength and weakness. On the one hand her moderate approach was successful in producing "new women" with intellectual and vocational training without inviting too much criticism. On the other hand, it bound her and her followers to traditional Japanese customs.

It may be that her strong patriotic love for the nation made her think that radical reform or Westernization would be neither accepted nor effective in Japan. Tsuda was always aware of her debt to the Japanese government for sending her to the United States. She was likewise always committed to the established national policy of modernizing women, and she attempted to educate elites who could contribute to the Japanese establishment as leaders. Her realization of the uniqueness of her experiences and the prevailing national "Meiji spirit" moved her in this direction. Although she recognized the importance of the non-elite housewife, her own life (and she remained single throughout her life), her educational principles, and the graduates of her school clearly proved that her education was designed for the elites. Not only the English-language education offered, but also the adherence to a strict training in Japanese manners and customs express how Ume Tsuda, conscious of being one of the elite, committed herself to upper-class ethics and upper-class necessities. She could easily find her counterpart among her American sisters, particularly in the nineteenth century.

The task of liberating the Japanese housewife fell to Tsuda's contemporary, Motoko Hani (1873–1957). Unlike Ume Tsuda, who enjoyed a bright beginning in the United States, Motoko Hani spent her youth in Hachinohe, a small rural town in the northern part of Japan. She was a plain country girl. Her grandfather, however, had a liberal concept of what a woman could be, and gave her some preparatory education to help overcome the traditional attitude of subservience and dependence. Under his influence, she cultivated such traits of the "new woman" as rational thinking, activism, and a spirit of self-reliance. Opposed to the prevailing custom of discriminating against women in education, her grandfather encouraged her intellectual growth and allowed her to have the highest education available. In the secondary school in Hachinohe, Motoko Hani was the only female student in the class.

At the age of sixteen and at her repeated request, Hani was sent by her grandfather to Tokyo for higher education. After the six-day trip from Hachinohe to Tokyo, she entered the recently opened First Tokyo Public Girls' High School. The excitement of life in Tokyo stimulated her growth as a "new woman." She absorbed new ideas, including Christianity which seemed to impress her most of all. Christian teachings were surprising to her, and yet they seemed clear, sensible, and attractive, and she was soon baptized. It is probable that she was impressed by her understanding of the Christian doctrine of human equality, suggesting that men and women were equal before God, because she wrote about women's active participation in the church, a situation very new to her. And, like Ume Tsuda, in later years she found strong support in her Christian faith for her venture in educating and liberating Japanese women.

In 1893 she advanced to Meiji Jogakko (Meiji Women's School), which was regarded as the most liberal girl's school of the day. The school's president, Zenji Iwamoto, had been publishing a magazine for girls which advocated women's liberation based on Christian principles, and Meiji Jogakko was regarded as the embodiment of the magazine's ideals. While at the school, Motoko Hani also learned to become economically independent of her family. Since her family could not afford to pay for her school expenses, she pleaded with Iwamoto repeatedly for the chance to work for his magazine in exchange for her tuition and dormitory expenses. He agreed to the unprecedented arrangement, and her new work acquainted her with the world of journalism, giving her the opportunity to meet leading public figures of the day and to come in contact with a much wider view of the world.[14]

Although she enjoyed life in Tokyo, she withdrew from school in 1894 for unknown reasons and became an elementary school teacher in Hachinohe. There she fell in love with one of her colleagues and married him in his home town of Kyoto. Six months later she divorced him on the grounds of personality disagreements. At the time, a love-match was uncommon, and it was still less common for a wife to divorce her husband, especially for such a reason. Furthermore, when Hani left her husband, she decided not to return to Hachinohe, hid the fact of the divorce from her family and friends, and secretly returned to Tokyo alone.

This was apparently her declaration of independence, because from this point, refusing any familial assistance, she began the life of an independent career woman. To sustain herself, she worked as a housemaid, an elementary school teacher, and then a proofreader of the *Hochi*, a leading newspaper. When she applied for the position of proofreader, the fact that she was a woman caused a sensation in the company. She insisted, however, "I should not be discriminated against simply because

14. Motoko Hani, "Story of Half My Life" (1928), *The Writings of Motoko Hani*, vol. 14 (Tokyo: Fujin no Tomo Sha, 1969), pp. 51–52, 56–59.

I am a woman,"[15] and became the first female proofreader ever employed by a newspaper company. She was soon able to contribute an interview article on her own initiative, winning the recognition of her editor. In 1897 she was promoted to become the first female journalist in Japan. She enjoyed her new career and succeeded in opening this new field to women, affirming that "woman's thinking and woman's pen could in many cases provide better expression than men's."

It is interesting to note that in both America and Japan, the pioneer professional women were successful in similar fields. Literature and education had been accepted as respectable fields for woman for some time. And then subsequently, in both countries, women achieved a breakthrough in medicine and journalism. Few women succeeded in business, law, or politics either in the United States or in Japan.

While writing for the *Hochi*, Motoko Hani met Yoshikazu Hani, a man who also worked for the paper, and they married in late 1901. The marriage marked the end of one period of her life, a time of preparation, and now, with her husband, she began a new phase, publishing a home magazine for the cause of the new womanhood. Yoshikazu Hani understood her completely, and advised and assisted her in her work until his death in 1955.

In April 1903 the first issue of *Katei no Tomo* (Family Friend, succeeded by *Fujin no Tomo*, Women's Friend, 1908) was published, despite poor prospects for success. Like Catharine Beecher, Motoko Hani was much concerned with unsound and impractical housekeeping and made the reform of the home her primary mission. And what Catharine Beecher had done in her series of books, Hani did through her magazine, namely promote reform of housekeeping through scientific principles. The three purposes of the magazine, stated in the April 1904 issue, were: (1) to reform unsound homelife and build happy homes, (2) to introduce new devices for better housekeeping, and (3) to publish easy, interesting and enlightening articles for housewives. Motoko Hani's magazine was idealistic, educational and anti-commercial. It introduced new ideas on etiquette and morals, as well as cooking, sewing, and housekeeping. Refusing to exploit the readers commercially, she attempted to apply her Christian faith with readers and treated them not as customers but as friends. She formed them into "readers-unions" in 1923, a network which grew to be the Zenkoku Tomo-no-Kai, or the National Friends Association in 1930.[16] Indeed, for many housewives, Motoko Hani was at once a teacher, friend, and model.

15. Setsuko Hani, *Watashi no Uketa Katei Kyoiku* (My Home Education) (Tokyo: Fujin no Tomo Sha, 1963), p. 18.

16. *Soritsusha no Ayunda Michi* (Road of Our Founder, or Short History of Fujin no Tomo) (Tokyo: Fujin no Tomo Sha, 1969), pp. 15–28.

In contrast to Ume Tsuda, Motoko Hani was a social educator with charismatic leadership qualities who tried to educate not elites, but masses of middle- and lower-class housewives and their daughters. Like Catharine Beecher, she stressed the importance of a "home" and the role it could play in social progress. It was her basic and characteristic philosophy that a home was the most influential unit acting upon society, and its improvement would eventually result in social reform and progress. Therefore, unlike more radical feminists such as Charlotte Perkins Gilman, Motoko Hani regarded the role of a housewife as extremely important to society. She constantly taught readers of her magazine that they could best contribute to society by fulfilling their responsibilities as housewives and by improving their homes. She observed, for example: "In order to create sound democratic spirit and foster its noble emotion in our society, by all means our homes must first become democratic. And this cannot be done by men. If a woman can learn the free spirit of democracy and its noble emotions, and if she can demonstrate them in her attitude to her husband . . . then, I think, Japan can be reformed by means of women's actions alone."[17]

Hani believed that young people had the best potential for modernizing Japanese women and home life. If the younger generation created new styles of married life, eventually the whole society would be changed. Convinced from her own experience that, contrary to the prevailing custom, a love-marriage was the basis on which to build modern home life, she stressed the importance of young peoples' experiencing love before getting married, and encouraged social interchange between young men and women.[18] And like Catharine Beecher, Hani placed great emphasis on training girls for an occupation, insisting that those young women who had received a high school education should neither stay at home nor marry quickly, but rather contribute their talents to society through employment. Women could, thereby, become economically independent. Curiously, in this last respect she can be compared with her contemporary feminist in America, Charlotte Perkins Gilman, who was also concerned with women's economic position in society. Less radical than Gilman, who thought that "only as women worked outside homes, they could become humanly developed and civilized,"[19] Motoko Hani never recommended sacrificing home life for outside employment. Once women married she advised them to concentrate on being good house-

17. Motoko Hani, "My Recent Thoughts" (May 1919), *Writings*, vol. 11, pp. 132–33.

18. Motoko Hani, "Social Interchange Between Men and Women as a Premise for Marriage Reform" (November 1921), *Writings*, vol. 13, pp. 340–52: passim.

19. Charlotte Perkins Gilman, *Women and Economics* (Boston, 1898), quoted in William L. O'Neill, *Everyone Was Brave* (Chicago: Quadrangle, 1969), p. 40.

wives, while still retaining their social awareness and concern. Women might continue their jobs after marriage, she said, if they could make the work harmonize with good housekeeping and home building.

There are other ways in which Hani compares favorably with Catharine Beecher. Like Beecher, she was a gradualist. She firmly believed that gradual changes in the level of home life would eventually result in social reform and progress. She once said, "I do not like unnatural revolutions."[20] This approach was at once the strength and weakness of both Beecher and Hani. In Hani's case, it encouraged her to be optimistic about the future and to maintain great faith in progress, but it led her to rely on individual moral changes rather than structural changes in society. Because her feminism was not political but cultural, she was indifferent to the efforts of political feminists, just as Beecher had dissociated herself from the abolitionists and suffragists. In the traditional society of Japan between 1900 and 1930, Motoko Hani's moderate approach was fruitful. If her magazine had advocated political feminism in the 1900s, it is doubtful whether she could have attracted such a large number of followers. And perhaps, as with Beecher, her optimistic faith in Divine Providence and the Christian attitude of obeying existing authorities undergird her moderate and non-revolutionary progressivism. The philosophical basis for her life and work was undoubtedly Christianity. To her followers she said: "The Friends Association is neither fascism, nor communism, nor liberalism, but solely Christian and God-center-ism."[21]

Because she had a deep concern for middle- and lower-class women in general, Hani initiated various social service activities through her magazine. Coming from the backward country of the North-East District, she made the modernization of that area her special interest, much as Catharine Beecher had worked to end "irreligion, ignorance, abject poverty, filth, and wretched vice" in the backwoods of Western America.[22] While Beecher tried to remedy the situation by training and sending teachers to the area, Hani used a more contemporary method of settlement. When a great drought brought hunger to the whole district in 1934, she made an appeal in the magazine, collected unused household articles from readers' homes, raised money, and began six agricultural settlements for the "Movement to Modernize Farm Life in the North-East District." Aware of the submarginal existence of the lowest-class tenant farmers,

20. Hani, "Beauty of Trees and Beauty of Animals" (June 1925), *Writings*, vol. 14, p. 304.
21. Hani, "What Is the Friends Association?" (May 1933), *Writings*, vol. 20, p. 20.
22. Catharine Beecher, quoted in Andrew Sinclair, *The Emancipation of the American Woman* (New York: Harper & Row, 1965), p. 96.

tion in class. For example, she taught the Japanese classes herself, incorporating such new methods as oral reports, speeches, dramas, and compositions based on students' own experiences. The girls were forbidden to take notes in class, except on very vital points, so that they might be free to participate actively in discussions. When they went home they composed daily summaries of what they had learned at school, which they then submitted weekly to the teachers for comment.

Under Motoko Hani's influence, Jiyu Gakuen was social, experimental, and progressive. Hani stressed the relationship between school and society, and, responding to her teachings, graduates of Jiyu Gakuen every year organized themselves to extend the "new society" of Jiyu Gakuen into the outer "old society." Volunteers among the first graduates began the consumer union movement in 1928; the second group of graduates organized an agricultural settlement in a village near the school; the third class formed a research group for productive handicrafts and arts; and the fourth cooperated with *Fujin no Tomo* in efforts to promote the "Modernized Home-Life Exhibition."

Although Motoko Hani was a Japanese-bred new woman, her activities all revealed the influence of Western culture—her magazine, the school, her social service projects. Her example lends support to the assertion that women's liberation and home modernization in Japan were, to a great degree, aspects of the introduction of Western ideas and practices. Significantly, Motoko Hani was even freer than Ume Tsuda in adopting a Western style of living. She introduced readers of her magazine to Western foods, clothes, manners, home and family life, as well as childrearing practices. Education at Jiyu Gakuen was more or less influenced by the "New Education" identified with such Western educators as Paul Natrop, Maria Montessori, John Dewey, and Helen Parkhurst. But Motoko Hani's Westernization was characterized by skillful adaptation. She utilized Western customs and ideas only when necessary, and integrated them into the Japanese situation before recommending them to other women. For example, when she promoted Western clothes for children, she invented a method of reshaping the old Japanese kimono into Western clothes, which made it easier for readers to adopt.

How then did Western women influence Hani in her new womanhood? She made friends with many Westerners and generally had a favorable opinion of Western women, especially Americans. She was particularly impressed with the voluntary social activities of Western women, probably because she was herself a social activist and regarded this as the primary lesson Japanese women needed to learn from their Western sisters. She noted, for example, the efforts of American women

Hani began her efforts by teaching housewives such basic tasks as
wash their faces and comb their hair. She sent her followers to p
stricken villages where they remained as social workers. They "cult
the hearts" of the housewives reading stories, introducing new disc
for better home life, and teaching women how to enrich their diet, re
old clothes, and even how to build safe, healthy little houses (some
tages lacked windows and toilets).[23]

But Hani's fame rests largely on her establishment in 1921 of J
Gakuen (Freedom School). Her Christian faith played an important pa
in its development. Believing that school education had been crippled b
the lack of religious teachings, she decided to teach the girls "real free
dom" and so named her new school Jiyu Gakuen with the text of John
8:32 in mind, "The truth shall set you free." The basic purpose of her
school was to develop the total personality, creating a woman of free
spirit who could "entrust God with her life under His education."[24]

At the same time, the feminist spirit of Jiyu Gakuen represented an
extension of *Fujin no Tomo*. Stress was put on home life. Since Hani
regarded the home as the most influential unit in society, she wanted the
graduates of her school, "first of all, to become good housewives." For
this purpose she organized girls into small groups called "families." Because of this system of "family" organization Jiyu Gakuen was able to
dispense with a working staff, relying on the girls themselves to prepare
the daily meals. Rotating chores, the girls took charge of the school bud
get to learn home economics, and they tended the school garden to stud
biology. It was assumed that in such ways the girls would learn the valu
of labor and self-reliance. While children of the newly rising and pro
perous middle classes "were required to rely on servants, even if the
wanted to take care of themselves,"[25] Hani encouraged self-support ar
self-government.

To prepare women for participation in public life, Hani complete
abolished the cramming system which, she thought, had made studer
passive and dependent. She replaced it with a more creative educati
which emphasized the cultivation of self-expression and active particip

23. Motoko Hani, "Let's Build a Family Japan; Helping the Rebirth of
North-East District" (February 1935) and "Reclamation of Waste Land; Hope
the Farms in the North-East District in the Near Future" (September 1935), V
ings, vol. 20, pp. 94–126.
24. Motoko Hani, "The Purpose of Education and Its Method" (August 19
Writings, vol. 18, pp. 7–16.
25. Keiko Hani, *Jiyu Gakuen no Kyoiku* (Jiyu Gakuen Education) (T
Jiyu Gakuen, 1970), pp. 44–45; and Motoko Hani, "A School Living, Growing
Working as a Society for Itself," *Writings*, vol. 18, pp. 28–29, 32, 34–36.

at the time of the Great Kanto Earthquake in 1923, their speedy, cooperative, and unselfish service to help the needy, and observed, "those American women understood the situation so quickly, and immediately did
whatever they could! . . . How enviable!"[26] Unlike Ume Tsuda, however, Motoko Hani did not regard Western woman as the ideal model. It
seems fair to say that, while she learned much from Western women, her
behavior pattern and feminist philosophy were largely "self-made" and
"home-grown" which clearly distinguished her from Tsuda. Her sympathy
for Western women was based essentially on pragmatic considerations.

But while Hani and Tsuda differed in their approaches, as well as
their personal backgrounds, they were committed to a common objective:
the modernization of Japanese women. In different, though not opposing,
ways they worked toward that end during the period 1900–30. They
shared a strong faith not only in Christianity but in the current national
policy which directed Japan's resources toward modernization and parity
with the advanced Western countries. And they both used Westernization as an important tool for modernizing Japanese women and home life.
Consequently, both of them were major contributors of Western ideas
and customs for women in Japan.

It is interesting to observe some of the characteristics these two
women shared with pioneer American feminists such as Emma Willard,
Mary Lyon, and Catharine Beecher, who were more like them than their
contemporary, twentieth-century American sisters. Religious, moderate
in approach, they were all concerned about educational improvement.
Like their American counterparts, Tsuda and Hani regarded education
as the means for raising the status of women in society and at home. All
of them believed that their respective countries could not be considered
modernized or advanced unless women were enlightened. Therefore, their
primary aim was not to attempt legal or political changes, but to reshape
society by educating women for new roles in the family and the wider
world. Characteristically, although all struggled to make inroads into
society for the benefit of women, none encouraged women to participate
in political feminism. They all failed to attribute discrimination against
women to legal, economic, and political systems. Rather, they considered
that it was women's educational disadvantages and customs that were
largely responsible for their unequal status in society and the home. This
was a common limitation of their feminist perspective. In the mid-nineteenth century in America and in the early decades of the twentieth

26. Motoko Hani, "At the Time of the Great Kanto Earthquake" (September
1923) and "Flowers Blooming in the Ruins" (October, 1923), both in *Writings*, vol.
14, pp. 192–95, 221.

century in Japan, however, cultural feminism was sufficiently revolutionary to effect meaningful social change.

Tsuda and Hani, therefore, had little in common with the exclusively political suffragists in Progressive America. While they admired the independence of American women, they shied away from political activism, which they believed would be inappropriate and untimely in still semi-feudal Japan. In a country in which national resources were being directed toward the early stages of industrial development, these two women found it more useful, and perhaps expedient, to direct their efforts toward education. One can find a similar trend in nineteenth-century America. It is to be hoped that other students of cross-cultural analysis will be interested in pursuing comparative investigations of the correlation between women's status and industrial development.

10

The Role of Women
in the Founding of the United States Children's Bureau

JAMES JOHNSON

*F*OUR women, once referred to as "A Wonderful Galaxy of Women"
by Justice Felix Frankfurter,[1] had a profound effect on the lives of children of the United States during the early part of the twentieth century.
Florence Kelley, Grace Abbott, and Julia Lathrop, originally mid-West-
erners, along with Lillian Wald, who came from New York City, were
active social reformers who demonstrated their concern for the particular
needs of children in a variety of ways. Kelley, Abbott and Lathrop, after
spending some time at Hull House, joined forces with Wald to help create
the Children's Bureau in 1912, a federal organization over which Lathrop
and Abbott eventually presided. Lillian Wald had also been the founder
of the Henry Street Settlement House in New York.

Early in their own lives the four women had developed a sensitivity
to the needs of children, and each had somehow managed to acquire the
resources—in terms of education and experience—that enabled them to
attempt to respond to those needs. Julia Lathrop, who had helped care
for four brothers and sisters, was instrumental in establishing the first
juvenile court in the country; Florence Kelley, herself a sickly child, was
chief factory inspector for Illinois; Grace Abbott headed the Immigrants'
Protective League; and Lillian Wald set up a neighborhood nursing program for immigrant families. These activities provided a useful back-

1. Edward T. James, Janet Wilson James, and Paul S. Boyer, eds., *Notable
American Women 1607–1950, A Biographical Dictionary* (Cambridge, Mass.: Harvard University Press, 1971), II, 319.

ground for the women as they combined skills, compassion, and experience to work for children's rights. That three of them chose to remain single throughout their lives resulted in their being continually subjected to personal criticism by members of congressional committees when they appeared before those bodies.

The primary objective of all four was to obtain minimal standards of decency in the field of child welfare, and they worked tirelessly, against formidable opposition, to help see that objective accomplished. When the New Deal was inaugurated, Grace Abbott hoped that the time had finally arrived when the children of America would benefit from congressional legislation; she worked to help realize that promise by serving as a member of the President's Council on Economic Security, 1934–35, and by assisting with the drafting of the Social Security Act. The women proved to be the most concerned friends that the children of America had, and their combined efforts in the years from 1900 to 1935 helped to ease the burden of child labor, provide for public school health examinations, reduce the infant and maternal mortality rate, and publicize and advance the cause of child welfare on all fronts.

Initially, the group focused its attention on the problems relating to child labor. Although Julia Lathrop and Grace Abbott had witnessed child labor in Illinois, it was Lillian Wald and Florence Kelley who sparked the early national movement to abolish the evil. Lillian Wald had joined the Child Labor Committee in the Neighborhood Workers' Association in 1902, an organization directed by Robert Hunter, the author of a book on poverty. She had herself chaired a committee that tried to keep children out of the dangerous street trades. In 1903, she joined with Kelley and others to form the National Child Labor Committee (NCLC) and the first formal session of the group was convened at Carnegie Hall on April 15, 1904. The NCLC introduced legislation in 1906 which was aimed at abolishing child labor, and it continued to agitate for the passage of a law creating a federal children's bureau, a goal not finally achieved until 1912. They gained additional support in 1916 from a measure President Wilson recommended and Congress passed; the law prohibited the interstate shipment of the products of factories that employed children under fourteen, or that permitted those from fourteen to sixteen to work more than eight hours a day. The Children's Bureau, whose founding is discussed below, was designated to administer the act, and Grace Abbott was selected to head the new child labor division of the Bureau. She realized that successful enforcement of the law depended on federal-state cooperation.

Florence Kelley felt that this was the first meaningful reform made in the area of child labor. Lathrop, who served as chief of the Bureau, and Abbott, who administered the new child labor law, compiled statistics and set up the machinery to ensure federal-state cooperation in enforcing the act. Then, in 1918, the Supreme Court declared the law unconstitutional. That decision, rendered in *Hammer* v. *Dagenhart,* came as a personal blow to Kelley and to all those who had worked for the child labor bill.

Meanwhile, Congress acted by passing a new law that placed a tax on goods made in certain industries which employed child labor. In 1922, the Supreme Court declared this law unconstitutional as well. "Why," asked Florence Kelley, "are seals, bears, reindeer, fish, wild game in the national parks, buffalo, migratory birds, all found suitable for federal protection; but not the children of our race and their mothers?"[2] The advocates of child labor reform concluded that the only effective course was to secure an amendment to the Constitution. During this time, Abbott replaced Lathrop as chief of the Children's Bureau, and Kelley threw herself into the campaign to get the amendment ratified, but at the time of the latter's death in 1932, only six states had done so.

Opponents of the child labor amendment responded vigorously and emotionally to the women's campaign. "This proposed amendment," said one industry paper, "is fathered by Socialists, Communists, and Bolsheviks."[3] The amendment, in the paper's opinion, would make millions of young people idlers in brain and body and thus provide "the devil's best workshop." The Woman Patriot Publishing Company singled out Florence Kelley and Grace Abbott for attack. "This benign looking Amendment," it said, "drawn and promoted chiefly by an American Socialist leader (Mrs. Florence Kelley, translator of Karl Marx and friend of Frederick Engels, who instructed her how to introduce Socialism into the flesh and blood of America) is a straight Socialist measure. It is also promoted under the direct orders from Moscow."[4] The criticisms leveled at Abbott were also aimed at the Children's Bureau. According to the Publishing Company, the youth of the country could not be "placed under the guardianship of the pacifist, internationalist, Federal Children's Bureau without

2. *Ibid.,* p. 318. Information regarding the role of these women in the child labor movement can be found in R. Duffus, *Lillian Wald, Neighbor and Crusader* (New York: Macmillan, 1939), p. 94; and William L. Chenery, "A Good Citizen," *The Child* 4(August 1939):35; Clarke Chambers, *Seedtime of Reform* (Ann Arbor: University of Michigan Press, 1967), pp. 27–58; Josephine Goldmark, *Florence Kelley, Impatient Crusader* (Urbana: The University of Illinois Press, 1953), pp. 115–16.

3. *The Survey* 43(October 15, 1924):76–77. This is a quote from the *Manufacturer's Record,* a newspaper published in Baltimore, September 4, 1924.

4. William Chenery, "Child Labor, The New Alignment," *The Survey* 53(January 1, 1925):379–82.

endangering America's future means of national defense." It also took note of the lobbying efforts of the social workers: "In the teeth of this decision by the highest court that the Constitution reserves control of child labor to the States, the chief of the Children's Bureau, Miss Abbott, who had been administrator of the first federal Child labor law, again hastened to rally her feminist machine for another drive against the Constitution and the Supreme Court. This time it was for a Federal child labor amendment."[5] The *American Child* observed that if a cause is known by the enemies it makes, "the proposed Amendment is to be congratulated."[6]

The child labor amendment also ran into the legacy of the Red Scare. Its opponents deliberately aroused anti-Communist fears and speculated that the children of the land were about to be nationalized just as they were alleged to be in Russia. They compiled a list of red herrings, claiming that parental control would be surrendered to the federal government, federal bureaucracy would be ominously increased, and states' rights would be endangered by expanded federal power. As one legislator, the father of five, stated the issue: "They have taken our women away from us by Constitutional amendment; they have taken our liquor away from us; and now they want to take our children." And one of his allies concluded, "We shall rue the day when woman suffrage was allowed to become a law of our land."[7]

Undoubtedly many women recognized the political power potential they received with the Nineteenth Amendment, and the women reformers repeatedly turned to these new voters to enlist their support. Grace Abbott relied on a group she referred to as "our crowd" when developing strategy to get the Amendment passed. She, Kelley, and the others appeared before the Congressional committees, spoke to women's groups, and wrote articles in relevant journals in order to acquaint the public with the problems. They consistently championed the cause of the nation's children. "I cannot see why any state wants to ask to be able to exploit its children," said Grace Abbott in the August 1939 issue of *The Child*, "or why it would claim that its rights have been infringed if that is denied them." They lost this battle for the amendment, but in a sense they won the larger war when the Fair Labor Standards Act was passed in 1938 which prohibited most child labor.

5. Edith Abbott, "Grace Abbott, A Sister's Memories," *The Social Service Review* 13(September 1939):387.
6. Walter Trattner, *Crusade for the Children* (Chicago: Quadrangle Books, 1970), p. 167. This is the most extensive treatment in print on the National Child Labor Committee.
7. *Ibid.*, p. 171. Abbott Papers, Box 36, Folder 3, University of Chicago Library.

Even without the Amendment, the women were able to advance their interests in child welfare through the Children's Bureau, the founding of which was perhaps the most significant achievement of their public careers. The history of their efforts to create such a federal agency forms a crucial chapter in an analysis of their work.

Both Kelley and Wald were interested in such a bureau for children, although it has been claimed that "the idea of the Children's Bureau, so far as the record goes, was mothered by Florence Kelley."[8] As early as April 1905, the Board of Trustees of the NCLC had recommended the idea of creating a children's bureau as a federal government agency, the motion being introduced by Robert de Forest and seconded by Wald.[9] In Kelley's book, *Some Ethical Gains Through Legislation*, published in 1905, she suggested creating a commission for children whose function would be to correlate and interpret the facts concerning the physical, mental, and moral conditions of the youth of the United States. In it she suggested that if lobsters or young salmon should become scarce or were in danger of perishing, the United States Fish Commission would take immediate steps. Infant mortality, moreover, was a serious problem, and yet no one agency of the United States government was charged with the responsibility of doing something about it. Julia Lathrop, the Children's Bureau's first chief, noted that Kelley's book had a plan for a government agency for children which was implemented by the act passed in 1912.[10] Indeed, Kelley was suggesting that the commission for children could do what the Department of Agriculture was doing for the farmers, which was to make accessible the latest accounts of scientific investigation and methods of application.

The idea of a government agency for children persisted, mainly because of the efforts of the group of women involved. Wald had apparently considered the idea for a children's bureau as early as 1903. The evidence suggests that the origin of the proposal can be traced back to an incident that occurred one morning during breakfast at the Henry Street Settlement House. Wald reportedly read in the paper that Mr. Wilson, the Secretary of Agriculture, was going South to investigate a boll weevil invasion. Almost simultaneously, she noticed a letter from a woman in Boston who was concerned about the infant death rate during the summer months.

8. "Contribution of Settlement Workers to the Development of the Idea of a National Department to be Concerned with the Needs of Children," *National Federation of Settlements Papers*, #583, p. 1, Social Welfare Archives, University of Minnesota Library.

9. "Minutes of the Board of Trustees," April 27, 1905, *National Child Labor Committee Papers*, Library of Congress.

10. Goldmark, *Impatient Crusader*, p. 96.

The paradox seemed clear: if a boll weevil, or rather a cotton boll, was a matter for federal solicitude, then why shouldn't a child be also? Kelley passed on the idea to Edward Devine, who, in turn, opened the prospect to President Roosevelt. The Rooseveltian response was allegedly: "Bully! Bring her down and talk to me about it." Wald and Devine went to Washington, laid the plan before the president, and secured his promise to support the appropriate legislation. Even though the actual legislation was not passed until the Taft administration in 1912, at least the idea had been introduced into the needed reform circles. Social workers now had a goal, inspired by Kelley and Wald.[11]

The National Child Labor Committee devoted the next two years (1904–1906) to drafting a bill for the proposed bureau, while also gathering support for it among important individuals and the many agencies that worked with children throughout the nation. The Bureaus of Education, Labor and the Census were consulted, and lobbying efforts became intense. At the second annual meeting of the NCLC in Washington, D.C. in 1905, Florence Kelley gave a speech on the subject and made such an impression on Felix Adler, chairman of the organization, that he was reported to have said: "I felt that Mrs. Kelley must be our spokesman the country over."[12]

Kelley wrote numerous articles on the subject, claiming that a new era had dawned for children because of the NCLC demand on the federal government to establish a program for child welfare. She also cited the information published by the Department of Education and indicated that it was so inconclusive and so belated that it made our educational institutions the laughing stock of interested Europeans.[13] The matter was delayed and quietly killed in Congressional committees without any real arguments being presented against it. The opposition groups were, undoubtedly, opposed to any child labor legislation. "Not one dissenting voice," said Lillian Wald in 1906, "has it been possible to discover."[14] But impressive forces supported the measure. Twenty-five clergymen, along with women's clubs, consumers' leagues, child labor committees in the states, and others, raised their voices in favor of the measure, but each year it failed to gain the floor of either the House or the Senate for a vote. Impatient, Florence Kelley announced that since the National Child Labor Committee had been able to accomplish nothing, she would lead

11. Duffus, *Lillian Wald*, p. 95.
12. Goldmark, *Impatient Crusader*, p. 97.
13. Florence Kelley, "The Federal Government and the Working Children," *The Annals of the American Academy of Political and Social Sciences* 27(1906):289–92.
14. Duffus, *Lillian Wald*, p. 96.

the Consumers' League in an active campaign for the creation of a children's bureau.[15]

In January 1909, hearings were held before the House of Representatives Committee on Expenditures in the Interior Department. Many individuals and groups testified in favor of a bill creating a Children's Bureau, including Wald, Kelley, Jane Addams, and a representative from the General Federation of Women's Clubs. Florence Kelley pointed out the extent of public ignorance on the questions being raised, while Addams illustrated the ways in which the bureau could help social workers. "It is proposed that there should be devoted to the children one bureau of our government," said Kelley, "by means of which the people should be able to obtain from month to month, recent trustworthy information concerning everything that enters into the lives of children; everything that makes for or against their vital efficiency, their educational opportunity, their future industrial and civic value."[16]

Both the National Child Labor Committee and various individuals continued the pressure—Lillian Wald, "the woman behind the bureau"; President Roosevelt, who sent a special message to Congress urging passage of the act; individual senators like Cummins, Borah, Bourne, and La Follette; and Owen Lovejoy, whose recommendations resulted in a flurry of letters to President Taft urging him to recommend passage of the Children's Bureau bill.[17]

The women increased the pressure early in 1912. They sent telegrams in record numbers. One woman reminded Senator Root of his per-

15. Florence Kelley to Owen R. Lovejoy, April 29, 1908, Minutes of Board of Trustees Meeting, National Child Labor Committee Papers, Library of Congress.

16. Dorothy Bradbury, Five Decades of Action for Children: A History of the Children's Bureau (Washington, D.C.: 1962), p. 3.

17. Information about the lobbying activity by the women can be found in: "Contributions of Settlement Workers to the Development of the Idea of a National Department to be Concerned with the Needs of Children," p. 45, NFS Papers, #583, Social Welfare Archives, University of Minnesota Library; Goldmark, Impatient Crusader, p. 79; L. D. Wald to Mr. Crane, n.d. (December 1910?), Abbott Papers, Box 38, Folder #1, University of Chicago Library; A. J. McKelway to L. D. Wald, December 17, 1910; L. D. Wald to Senator Frank P. Flint, December 19, 1910; Senator Bourne to L. D. Wald, December 19, 1910; Lillian Wald to Senator Bourne, December 16, 1910; Elihu Root to L. D. Wald, January 2, 1911; Abbott Papers, Box 38, Folder #1, University of Chicago Library; Owen Lovejoy to L. D. Wald, February 15, 1911, Abbott Papers, Box 38, Folder #1, University of Chicago Library; Jane Addams to W. H. Taft, November 20, 1911, and Lillian Wald to Taft, November 22, 1911, William Howard Taft Papers, Library of Congress; L. D. Wald to Secretary of Interior Fisher, February 10, 1912, and L. D. Wald to Dr. P. P. Claxton, February 10, 1912, Abbott Papers, Box 38, Folder #2, University of Chicago Library; L. D. Wald to New York Times, February 1, 1912.

sonal promise to her. "I am sure," said Lillian Wald, "that must have sent Senator Root to the floor."[18]

The final act creating the Federal Children's Bureau, which passed the House of Representatives on April 2, 1912, was signed by President Taft on April 8, 1912. The years of hard work had finally paid off, and the social workers realized that they now had a government bureau dedicated to the proposition that information gathering was a proper and necessary function in the field of child welfare. The passage of this bill, partially accomplished by an intricate network of women reformers, was perhaps the first successful piece of lobbying by social workers and interested friends throughout the country.[19]

With adoption of the measure secured, the women set their sights on getting the right person appointed to head the bureau and direct its program. President Taft, acknowledging the power of the feminist lobby, consulted some of them regarding their preference. Jane Addams told Wald that the "Chicago Group" were united on the choice of Julia Lathrop. When Owen Lovejoy asked the NCLC its preference, the members also named Lathrop.[20] Grace Abbott's sister Edith said that Lathrop had long been the acknowledged guardian of Illinois children. "The President of the United States," said Edith, "has now asked her to be the guardian of the children of the nation and the whole country has rejoiced to hear that the interests of these children have been given into her hands."[21] The feminist movement realized that her appointment was due, at least in part, to its vigorous efforts. "It is with a feeling of pride," said one member, "that not only I, but women generally, note a woman has been ap-

18. L. D. Wald, to Owen Lovejoy, February 1, 1912, Abbott Papers, Box 38, Folder #2, University of Chicago Library. There is an addenda to this letter which tells more about the incident. A luncheon was held at the Gotham Hotel in New York City and Wald was speaking about the Children's Bureau bill. Mrs. Anderson asked her what was holding up the bill and she said Senator Root had doubts as to its constitutionality. Mrs. Anderson had made one million dollars available for a cause in which Senator Root was interested. Thus the telegrams, and within two hours Lovejoy telephoned from Washington that Root had changed positions. That was what sent the senator to the floor!

19. Carmen R. Delle Donne, "Two-Handed Engine at the Door; Social Workers and the Agitation for a National Children's Bureau," MA thesis, Catholic University of America, Washington, D.C., 1967.

20. Jane Addams and Julius Rosenwald to Lillian Wald, April 12, 1912, and Owen Lovejoy to L. Wald, March 27, 1912, Abbott Papers, Box 38, Folder #2, University of Chicago Library. W. H. Taft to Jane Addams, April 15, 1912, and Julia Lathrop to W. H. Taft, May 7, 1912, William Howard Taft Papers, Library of Congress.

21. Edith Abbott, "The First Chief of the Children's Bureau," *Life and Labor* 2(February 1912):301.

pointed at the head of the Children's Bureau, thus conferring a new honor upon women."[22]

The initial $25,000 appropriation for the Children's Bureau provided for a staff of fifteen persons to carry out the Congressional mandate to do research and compile statistics on child welfare. The problem was which field to tackle first. Julia Lathrop consulted those responsible for the creation of the bureau, in particular Florence Kelley, and arrived at the decision to begin a study of infant mortality. Field investigators began, covering the economic, social, and geographic factors that affected the lives of all children born within a given year. In each area studied, the history of every baby was traced from birth through the first twelve months of life, or as long as the baby lived in that first year. The results of these reports produced a profound national shock. Americans, who had taken their superiority in sanitation and health for granted, and who had assumed that American plumbing represented our national pre-eminence in health care, found that this was more fiction than fact. The house-to-house canvass by the Children's Bureau disclosed that nearly a quarter of a million babies were dying each year and that our infant mortality rate exceeded that of many other countries.

Although the Bureau's staff was accumulating information important to the nation's welfare, Congress was unwilling to increase Bureau funds when the time came to renew its appropriations. The NCLC and the feminist lobby went to work once again, this time to secure an increased budget for the Bureau. Kelley and Wald, working closely with Owen Lovejoy of the NCLC, organized a movement aimed at increasing the budget with such effectiveness that Kelley was able to assure Julia Lathrop that "Mr. Lovejoy's machinery is at work and protest letters ought to be pouring in by now." And Lillian Wald informed Lathrop that Mary McDowell, president of the National Federation of Settlements, "will probably get the machinery of the settlements going." She also asked the Bureau chief for her estimate of the amount needed to advance the work. Wald pointed out to Jane Addams that the "same week that the Appropriation Committee allowed $25,000 for the Bureau below which even they could not go according to law, $165,000 was appropriated for free seeds and $400,000 for hog cholera."[23]

22. L. K. Echman to Julia Lathrop, May 7, 1912, Taft Papers, Library of Congress. Since Julia Lathrop was the first woman to occupy the position as head of a federal government bureau, and since the salutation for a bureau chief had always been "Dear Mr. Chief," the story in official Washington was that there was no escaping the fact that she would have to be addressed as "Dear Miss Chief."

23. Owen Lovejoy to Julia Lathrop, April 10, 1914, and Florence Kelley to

Kelley next turned her attention to the task of securing hundreds of volunteer club women to get them to help with the registration of births. She was so successful that by 1921 twenty-seven states had established the machinery to register all births. She believed that the process by which the Bureau gathered its facts served as a means of stimulating people to act on them. While inquiring into infant mortality in one city, for example, she felt that the Bureau had, simply by its questioning techniques, encouraged the people of the city to do something about the problem.[24] Bureau publications were designed for average readers and for mothers located in out-of-the-way places.

When Grace Abbott left her work in Chicago to join the child labor division of the Bureau, she teamed well with Julia Lathrop. Both were determined to fight the spoils system of machine politics and insisted that staff members should be chosen on the basis of skills rather than political connections. According to one observer, "both had generous, discerning minds and the constructive imagination of true stateswomen."[25] They worked hard to make 1919, termed the "Children's Year," a year of achievement. They had ambitious objectives: to save the lives of 100,000 babies, to find an economic standard that permitted mothers to remain at home to care for their children, to abolish child labor and keep children in school, and to present uncommercialized recreation for all youngsters.

Julia Lathrop decided to resign from the Bureau in 1920, and she played politics to get Grace Abbott appointed as her replacement, promoting a letter-writing campaign to the Senators involved in the decision. The politicking apparently worked, for President Harding named Abbott to the post in August 1921. "Strength to your elbow in your new job. I need not tell you," said Paul Kellogg, editor of *Survey* magazine, "that you can count on us at any time."[26] Once in office, Abbott was charged with the task of administering the Sheppard-Towner Act, a bill designed

---

Julia Lathrop, April 8, 1914, Abbott Papers, Box 59, University of Chicago Library. L. D. Wald to J. Lathrop, April 3, 1914, Box 59, Abbott Papers, University of Chicago Library. L. Wald to Jane Addams, April 3, 1914, quoted in Alice Padgett, "The History of the Establishment of the United States Children's Bureau," MA thesis, University of Chicago, 1936, p. 93.

24. Florence Kelley, "Starving the Children's Bureau," *The Survey* 37, (December 23, 1916).

25. William L. Chenery, "A Good Citizen," *The Child* 4(August 1939):35.

26. Julia Lathrop to Senator La Follette, July 20, 1920; Julia Lathrop to Mrs. McCormick, September 7, 1920; and Ruth McCormick to Senator Lodge, September 27, 1920, Julia Lathrop Papers, Rockford College. Harriet Taylor Upton to Warren G. Harding, August 8, 1921, Harding Papers, Ohio Historical Society. Paul U. Kellogg to Grace Abbott, September 8, 1921, Folder #326, Survey Associates Papers, Social Welfare Archives, University of Minnesota Library.

to protect infant and maternal health. "If a declaration of independence were to be written today," she said, "American women would ask that in the enumeration of the objects for which governments are instituted the welfare of children should head the list; and the American man would agree."[27]

The Sheppard-Towner Act had become law only after years of hard work by the women reformers and their friends, whose efforts met with relentless opposition. The first outline of the act had appeared in 1917 in Julia Lathrop's annual report. It proposed a program of public protection for the needs of maternity and infancy, following the precedent set by federal aid projects to the states in the areas of agriculture, vocational training, and road building. In essence, Lathrop's measure was designed to extend local maternal and child health services through grants of federal funds administered by state health agencies. The Children's Bureau would establish the standards for such services, and the program, which eventually became the Sheppard-Towner Act, would include more adequate confinement care for pregnant women, more public health nurses, and more medical examinations and advice for well children. The women's organizations that helped to create the Children's Bureau turned their efforts toward securing the enactment of the Sheppard-Towner bill, and later, protecting it from repeal.

The passage of the Nineteenth Amendment had given Lathrop, Abbott, Kelley and Wald new allies. Congressmen feared the unknown power represented by the women's vote. For years the suffragists had promised to clean up government when they were enfranchised, and politicians were not sure whether or not women would cast a bloc vote. The Sheppard-Towner bill appeared for debate just when the women's vote became a reality, and President Harding relied on Harriet Taylor Upton, vice-chairman of the Republican National Committee, to interpret it for him. In addition, in 1920, the League of Women Voters helped to create the Women's Joint Congressional Committee (WJCC) which coordinated lobbying activities in Washington for nearly two dozen national women's organizations. The "Lathrop crowd" was not unaware of the power potential this represented, and they moved to bring the WJCC to its side in the debate over the Sheppard-Towner bill. Feelings ran high during the contest over adoption. According to the *Journal* of the American Medical Association, the women's lobby supporting it was one of the strongest ever seen in Washington. Senator William Kenyon, an advocate of the bill, said that it could not have passed if the vote had been

27. *Eleventh Annual Report*, Children's Bureau, p. 38.

secret. But the Joint Congressional Committee of Women exerted enough pressure to force the Congressmen to declare themselves publicly. Florence Kelley stated dramatically that while Congress was delaying the issue, 20,000 children were dying each month. Suppose, she said, that Congress was wiped out by some fearful catastrophe. The whole world would send its condolences. Yet each day six times as many children died as there were members of the Senate. "What answer can be given to the women," she said, "who are marveling and asking 'why does Congress wish women and children to die?' "[28]

The Children's Bureau had prepared the ground for the introduction of the Sheppard-Towner bill. Its early studies on infant mortality had shocked many people, and even in 1918 the United States ranked seventeenth and eleventh in maternal and infant mortality, respectively, among the countries of the world. Bureau studies revealed an absolute correlation between poverty and high infant and maternal mortality rates. In addition, the Children's Bureau had compiled statistical evidence which revealed that most expectant mothers received little or no advice or trained health care. Its pamphlet, *Infant Care*, became a best-selling government periodical, and Bureau influence on the local level was growing; by 1922 it was able to point to state child hygiene and child welfare divisions in forty-six states. The plan Julia Lathrop outlined in 1917 was eventually introduced in Congress by Jeanette Rankin, the first woman to serve in that body. The measure was reintroduced in the Sixty-sixth Congress; it depended on the enfranchisement of women to secure its passage because of the intense opposition lined up against it.

The critics of Sheppard-Towner resorted to personal attacks on the women who inspired it and worked for its adoption. Conspicuous among those groups who opposed the passage of the bill were the National Association Opposed to Woman Suffrage, the Woman Patriots and the Sentinels of the Republic (anti-Bolshevik groups), and the American Medical Association. Since Florence Kelley had been married to a man from Eastern Europe and had previously translated some of the works of Marx and Engels, she became the focal point of attack by the anti-Bolshevik groups. The Children's Bureau was accused of attempting to "nationalize" the children of America, and the unmarried women in the Children's Bureau were ridiculed by certain Congressmen, who were perhaps still rankled by the successful passage of the Nineteenth Amendment. The American Medical Association had sympathized with some of the objectives of the Progressive movement insofar as they related to the passage

28. Goldmark, *Impatient Crusader*, p. 107.

of the Pure Food and Drug Act, and the desire to protect the public from medical quacks and other hucksters. The AMA, however, which had remained silent on the problems of slums, tenement housing, child labor, sweatshop conditions, and other factory hazards, spoke out bitterly against the Sheppard-Towner Act.[29] The National Association Opposed to Woman Suffrage and a kindred organization, the Woman Patriots, claimed that feminism and woman suffrage were aspects of, if not identical with, communism. A member of one of the groups, Mary Kilbreth, upbraided President Harding for eventually signing the Sheppard-Towner bill. "It is not brought forward by the combined wisdom of all Americans," she said, "but by the propaganda of a self-interested bureau associated with the Feminist Bloc."[30] Indeed, she saw the whole issue as a threat to American civilization itself.

Senator Reed of Missouri, one of the most vocal opponents of the Sheppard-Towner bill, resorted to verbal barbs against the single women in the Children's Bureau, the agency that would administer the program outlined in the measure. "I care not how estimable the officeholding spinster may be, nor how her heart may throb for the dream children she does not possess," he said, "her yearnings cannot be substituted for a mother's experience. Official meddling cannot take the place of mother love." The Senator gave a roll call of the unmarried women in the Children's Bureau, beginning with Julia Lathrop, and emphasizing that almost the entire staff was composed of single women. He evoked laughter from his peers several times with such statements as, "it seems to be the established doctrine of this bureau that the only people capable of caring for babies and mothers of babies are ladies who have never had babies." He observed that Congress was involved in a rare bit of irony when it considered using "female celibates" to instruct mothers on how to raise babies. "I repeat," he said, "I cast no reflection on unmarried ladies. . . . But any woman who is too refined to have a husband should not undertake the care of another woman's baby when that other woman wants to take care of it herself." Senator Reed then launched one of his most caustic attacks on the employees of the Children's Bureau, as well as against the "galaxy" of single women who had carried on the fight for the rights of children: "We would better reverse the proposition and provide

29. J. Stanley Lemons, "The Sheppard-Towner Act: Progressivism in the 1920's," *Journal of American History* 55(1968–69):780; Goldmark, *Impatient Crusader*, pp. 108–109; Alice Padgett, "The History of the Establishment of the U.S. Children's Bureau," p. 68.

30. Mary G. Kilbreth to Harding, November 25, 1921, Box 157, Folder 117–1, Harding Papers, quoted in Lemons, "The Sheppard-Towner Act," *Journal of American History* 55(1968–69):779–80.

for a committee of mothers to take charge of the old maids and teach them how to acquire a husband and have babies of their own." In summing up his objections he said: "Mr. President, give a bill an attractive and appealing title, back it by well-organized propaganda, abundantly financed, and an active lobby of persuasive ladies who solicit and pledge votes, and the bill, whether good or bad, wise or foolish, is almost certain to pass."[31]

Senator Thomas A. Bayard of Delaware read into the *Congressional Record* a lengthy petition and letter from the anti-Bolshevik organization, the Woman Patriots. Bolshevist origins were attributed to the Children's Bureau, child labor laws, and the Sheppard-Towner Act. He, too, referred to Florence Kelley's marriage and writings, and described her as "the ablest legislative general Communism has produced." The whole coterie of social reform feminist organizations was cited as undesirable, and that included not only individuals like Jane Addams and Julia Lathrop, but also the constituent organizations of the WJCC (including the Parent-Teachers Association, the League of Women Voters, and the Women's Christian Temperance Union), as well as the Women's Bureau, the Children's Bureau, and the U.S. Department of Labor. Senator Bayard mailed copies of his document to all state officers of the DAR, who responded through their president-general to urge defeat of Sheppard-Towner.[32]

Some two years and seven months after the bill had been first introduced, Florence Kelley pointed out that while opposition forces continued to attack the measure, about 625,000 babies had died from causes (chiefly preventable) prenatal or connected with childbirth. "Our standing among the nations, measured by maternal mortality," she said, "has fallen so that we now rank number seventeen."[33]

The charges of Socialism, feminism, and Bolshevism notwithstanding, the Sheppard-Towner bill finally passed the Senate in August 1921, by a vote of 63–7. The Children's Bureau was designated to administer the law, and by 1922 Grace Abbott was able to report that five general lines of work had been undertaken. They were: (1) the promotion of birth registration; (2) the development of cooperation between health authorities and physicians, nurses, dentists, nutrition workers, and others; (3) the establishment of infant welfare centers; (4) the creation of maternity centers; and (5) the promotion of educational classes for mothers, mid-

31. *Congressional Record*, 67 Cong. 1 Sess. (1921), LXI, Part 9, pp. 8759–60.
32. Lemons, "The Sheppard-Towner Act," *Journal of American History* 55 (1968–69):784–85.
33. Florence Kelley, "Congress and the Babies," *The Survey* 46 (May 14, 1921): 200.

wives, and household assistants.[34] Federal funds would be made available if the states matched them. The social reformers had at last secured a bill and a program designed to protect infant and maternal health.

In New York State, Governor Nathan Miller, who had defeated Alfred Smith in the 1920 election, told the opening session of the 1922 legislature that he would veto any bill which would make Sheppard-Towner effective in the state. He cited as his reason the great financial strain from which the state was suffering. Despite this, he signed a bill which appropriated $125,000 for a hog barn on the state fair grounds. Florence Kelley observed that it did not improve the outlook for the governor to have "28 organizations of women experienced in working together know that swine shelters appeal to him more strongly than dying mothers and babies."[35] It should be noted that Miller approved an appropriation for a twin hog barn in 1923 and lost the election that year to Alfred Smith who pushed the cause of the Sheppard-Towner bill. Smith credited the New York League of Women Voters for the successful enactment of the bill. In Illinois the situation was similar. Julia Lathrop informed Grace Abbott that in that state the bill was "having a very fierce and relentless attack" from the forces representing local medical interests. Mrs. John Sherman, president of the General Federation of Women's Clubs, came to the defense of the bill, dismissing the familiar charges of socialism and bolshevism.[36]

When the original Sheppard-Towner Act was due to expire in 1927, Congress enacted a two-year extension. The same forces which had opposed the original bill tried to prevent its renewal. The *Woman Patriot* once again voiced the sentiments of its followers: "Children are now the best political graft in America. They furnish the best possible screen behind which to hide cold-blooded, calculated Socialist feminist political schemes to raid the United Treasury to supply . . . 'new fat jobs,' plus publicity, prominence and power, to childless bureaucrats and women politicians."[37] The old clichés about "socializing medicine" or "nationalizing the children" were renewed, and the opposition, fresh from having

34. Grace Abbott, "Administration of the Sheppard-Towner Act: Plans for Maternal Care," *Transactions of the American Child Hygiene Association* 13 (1922): 194–201.

35. Florence Kelley, "The Children's Amendment," *Good Housekeeping* 74 (February 1923):170; quoted in Lemons, "The Sheppard-Towner Act," *Journal of American History* 55(1968–69):782.

36. Julia Lathrop to Grace Abbott, April 28, 1923, Abbott Papers, Box 57, University of Chicago Library and Address by Mrs. John Sherman, Federation of Women's Clubs, 1927, *ibid.*, Box 36, Folder #19.

37. *The Woman Patriot* 12(1928):185–86, quoted in Robert Bremner, ed., *Children and Youth in America, A Documentary History* (Cambridge, Mass.: Harvard University Press, 1971), II, 1024.

defeated the child labor amendment, were determined to do away completely with the Sheppard-Towner bill. The politicians were by now less worried about the women's vote: President Hoover, refusing to press the matter, issued only perfunctory statements on behalf of renewal, thus allowing Sheppard-Towner to lapse in 1929.

During the next few Congressional sessions, sporadic suggestions were made to resume the Sheppard-Towner programs, but none was accepted until the passage of the Social Security Act of 1935. Infant and maternal health issues became entwined with proposals to reorganize the Children's Bureau itself. When the White House Conference of 1930 convened, it had a committee on Public Health Service and Administration, chaired by Dr. Hugh Cummings, the Surgeon General of the Public Health Service. A subcommittee of the Conference recommended that all federal health work for children should now be transferred to the U.S. Public Health Service, a recommendation with which Grace Abbott could not concur. Hence, Abbott, Florence Kelley and Lillian Wald divided their efforts between trying to get the Sheppard-Towner program reinstated and attempting to keep the Children's Bureau intact. The Children's Bureau issued a convincing report of the effectiveness of the Sheppard-Towner program throughout the 1920s, but that failed to reactivate the program. All was not lost, however, since the Children's Bureau did not go through the projected reorganization.[38]

Thus another battle had been lost and another war had been won. Since the Children's Bureau remained intact, its effectiveness was enhanced, and its previous work with Sheppard-Towner provided valuable experience. When the Social Security Act was passed in 1935, the Children's Bureau was entrusted with the task of administering federal-state services to mothers and children that involved annual federal appropriations to the states of some six million dollars. Titles V and VI of the Social Security Act provided federal government programs that the social workers would not have dared to dream of at the beginning of the century. "Of all the activities in which I have shared during more than forty years of striving," wrote Florence Kelley, "none is, I am convinced, of such fundamental importance as the Sheppard-Towner Act."[39]

In June 1934, Grace Abbott resigned her post with the Children's

38. K. Lenroot to Grace Abbott, June 19, 1928, Abbott Papers, Box 36, Folder #8; Grace Abbott to Arthur Kellogg, November 23, 1927, Folder #327, Survey Associates Papers, Social Welfare Archives. Florence Kelley, "Congress and the Children's Bureau," *The Survey*, Vol. 65, February 15, 1931, p. 544; Lillian D. Wald, "Federal Aid to Reduce Maternity Mortality," *Neighborhood* 4(September 1931): 231, and Lemons, "The Sheppard-Towner Act," 55(1968–69):785.

39. Goldmark, *Impatient Crusader*, p. 93.

Bureau to accept a teaching position at the University of Chicago School of Public Welfare. Katherine Lenroot was appointed as her successor as Bureau Chief.

The women who ran the Children's Bureau throughout the 1920s had worked hard to create a new perspective within state departments of public welfare; they attempted to convince state officials that they should be concerned not only with the custodial care and institutional training of children, but also with the prevention of social breakdown and the home care of those who previously would have been institutionalized. They helped to pave the way for the passage of the Social Security Act in 1935. Their position had consistently been that the state had a stake in protecting the family in every way possible, since a stable family and home situation rendered the best returns in terms of intelligent child welfare administration. In 1934 the President's Committee on Economic Security turned to the Children's Bureau for proposals for children's programs to be included under the Social Security Act. The roots of these proposals traced back to the beginnings of the Children's Bureau in 1912.

Women had played the central role in securing the enactment of measures designed to protect the interests of children. Julia Lathrop made the correlation more specific when she said "that the century of the woman has made possible the century of the child."[40] Although men such as Paul Kellogg, Owen Lovejoy, Homer Folks, and others had been involved, it was women who were the prime movers in the establishment of milk stations, child health centers, visiting nurse associations, juvenile courts, child labor legislation, and the Children's Bureau. When the Sheppard-Towner Act was in danger of lapsing, Grace Abbott confided to Lillian Wald that things were bad, but "perhaps we shall not have to bring up any heavy artillery just now." And when the Sheppard-Towner Act was finally on President Harding's desk, she wrote that "the women have done such a wonderful piece of lobbying that it is now almost a reality."[41] The General Federation of Women's Clubs had served as the nerve center for women's activities on behalf of children. When Julia Lathrop or Grace Abbott wanted to get letters to Congressmen, or use some other lobbying method, they usually asked Kelley and Wald to contact General Federation members. Katherine Lenroot observed that "the modern child welfare movement in the United States is due in part

40. Julia C. Lathrop, "Pass on the Torch," n.d., Hull House Papers.
41. Grace Abbott to L. D. Wald, November 25 (1929?), Folder #871, Survey Associates Papers, Social Welfare Archives, University of Minnesota Library. Grace Abbott to Dorothy R. Mendenhall, November 23, 1921, Abbott Papers, Box 36, Folder #1, University of Chicago Library.

to the public interest and support secured by the great non-professional women's organizations," and according to Jane Addams, one of the main services performed by Lathrop and Abbott was their effort "which made the women throughout the country—not alone those organized into federation of clubs and leagues of voters, but the immigrant women living on remote farms—realize that the Bureau belonged to them."[42]

The parents of Florence Kelley, Julia Lathrop, and Grace Abbott had encouraged their daughters to obtain the benefits of higher education, and some of them were sympathetic to the suffragist movement. It soon became evident that the backgrounds and interests of these three and Lillian Wald supported the claim that "feminism was no single strand of their being." In their long cooperative struggle to assert the rights of mothers and children to adequate health care services, they revealed the extent to which their feminism was involved with their total reform interests.

42. RG 102 Children's Bureau Central Classified Files, 1914–20, Box #146, Folder 8-4-1-1-6, Federation Women's Clubs, National Archives, Washington, D.C.; Katherine Lenroot, "Achievements of the Women of the U. S. in Promoting Child Welfare," August 1929, Abbott Papers, Box 51, Vol. 10, University of Chicago Library. National Conference of Social Work Dinner, 1932, *ibid.*

Index

Abbott, Edith, approves choice of Julia Lathrop as Chief of Children's Bureau, 186

Abbott, Grace, 126, 179, 196; assists with drafting of Social Security Act, 180; as Chief of Children's Bureau, 181, 188; lobbies for child labor amendment, 182; and Sheppard-Towner Act, 189, 192–93; resigns from Children's Bureau, 194–95

Adams, Abigail Smith, 1, 49; early life of, 50; marriage to John Adams, 51; views on education, 52, 54–55; views on slavery, 53–54; friendship with Thomas Jefferson, 54–55; views on 18th century European and English society, 56–57; and Shay's Rebellion, 58–60; political estrangement from Thomas Jefferson, 60–62; views on republican government, 61–62; and Revolutionary ideology, 63–64; views on Declaration of Independence, 63; views on Alien and Sedition Acts, 63–64; and Enlightenment ideas, 65

Adams, Mildred, comments on Flappers in New York Times, 159–60

Addams, Jane, supports creation of Children's Bureau, 185, 187; attacked for views on child welfare, 192

Adler, Felix, views on divorce, 134; as chairman of National Child Labor Committee, 184

Allen, Frederick Lewis, and Only Yesterday, 147

American Protective Association, 87; and "convent literature," 82–83; and Women's American Protective Association, 83

Antinomianism, 14, 17, 19, 22–23, 37

Ariés, Philip, and Centuries of Childhood, 130

Bard, Samuel, 93, 101

Battis, Emery, 14, 15

Beard, Mary, 3

Bedford, Gunning S., 95

Beecher, Catharine, as model for Japanese women educators, 162, 172, 174, 177

Birth control, 136; views of Condorcet on, 44; and efforts of Margaret Sanger, 125

Blake, Nelson M., and The Road to Reno, 127, 131

Bradford, Sarah, as biographer and friend of Harriet Tubman, 111–12

Carroll, Berenice A., 3

Chesterton, G. K., views on divorce and the family, 137

Children's Bureau, United States, founding of, 179–96; attacked by critics, 181–82; inspiration for, 183–84; Lobbyists for, 184–85; approved by President Taft, 186; research efforts of, 187–88; and Sheppard-Towner Act, 188–91; accused of bolshevism, 192–93

Child welfare, efforts to promote, 180, 182–83; need for, 187, 192–93; legislation attacked as socialistic, 193–94

Comparative historical method, as

197

"REMEMBER THE LADIES"

New Perspectives on Women in American History

was composed in 10-point Linotype Caledonia, leaded two points,
with display type handset in Bulmer
by Joe Mann Associates, York, Pennsylvania;
printed offset on Perkins and Squier 55-pound Litho
by Valley Offset, Deposit, New York;
Smyth-sewn and bound in Permalin' Black Crash Permacote over boards
by Vail-Ballou Press, Inc., Binghamton, New York;
and published by

SYRACUSE UNIVERSITY PRESS
Syracuse, New York 13210